WINNING POLITICAL CAMPAIGNS

A COMPREHENSIVE GUIDE
TO ELECTORAL SUCCESS

WINNING POLITICAL CAMPAIGNS

A COMPREHENSIVE GUIDE
TO ELECTORAL SUCCESS

WILLIAM S. BIKE

THE DENALI PRESS

Denali, derived from the Koyukon name *Deenaalee*, is the native name for Mount McKinley. Mount McKinley, the highest mountain on the North American continent, is located in Denali National Park and Preserve. The lowlands surrounding this majestic mountain provide a diverse wildlife habitat for a variety of animals, including grizzly bears, wolves, caribou and moose.

Copyright © 1998 by William S. Bike

Published by The Denali Press

Post Office Box 021535

Juneau, Alaska USA 99802-1535

Phone: (907) 586-6014   Fax: (907) 463-6780

E-mail: denalipr@alaska.net   http://www.alaska.net/~denalipr

LIBRARY OF CONGRESS CATALOGING-IN-PUBLICATION DATA

Bike, William S.
    Winning political campaigns : a comprehensive guide to electoral success / William S. Bike ; with a foreword by Fran Ulmer.
       p.   cm.
    Includes bibliographical references and index.
    ISBN 0-938737-35-X (pbk. : alk. paper) : $27.00
    1. Campaign management--United States--Handbooks, manuals, etc..
2. Electioneering--United States--Handbooks, manuals, etc.
I. Title.
JK2281.B55   1998
324.7'0973--dc21   97-52338
                                                CIP

∞ The paper used in this publication meets the minimum requirements of the American National Standard for Information Sciences—Permanence of Paper for Printed Library Materials, ANSI Z39.48. This book is printed on recycled paper, using soy based ink.

TO ANNE

Thanks to Margaret Bjerklie, Becky Carroll, James Lachowicz, Jean Lachowicz, and Anne Nordhaus-Bike whose editing sharpened both my grammar and my politics.

CONTENTS

FOREWORD

The motivation to run for office is a decision that comes from the heart—you want to make a difference, you want to contribute, you're convinced you can do a good job. More and more people are serving on school boards, city councils, state legislatures, and congress. Their involvement in public service directly benefits the well being of their families, their communities, and themselves. It takes an extraordinary amount of commitment.

But it takes more than heart and commitment to run a successful campaign. It takes organization, hard work, a lot of help, and a can-do attitude. Campaigns have become increasingly complex. For novices it can be quite intimidating. Unless you have a mentor, or can afford an experienced campaign manager, it's likely that a lot of mistakes will be made that could easily be avoided with some advice. In fact, I read the book with a little déjà vu! Some of the mistakes discussed were painfully real. On the other hand, I was delighted to find that many of the suggestions offered were part of the successes I've enjoyed. I found myself underlining passages to share with colleagues and to reflect upon for future campaigns.

Winning Political Campaigns gives you advice in an entertaining and well-organized manner. It's a worthwhile book for both experienced campaigners and newcomers alike. It provides essential tools, practical pointers, and valuable advice about running campaigns successfully. No matter how many campaigns you've been in or worked on, you'll benefit from *Winning Political Campaigns*. It will remind you of what you once knew and it will provide you with new insights and ideas.

The author has organized the material in a cookbook format, which allows the reader to easily return to a subject area for quick reference when needed. Voter registration questions? Time management ideas? Direct mail instructions? It's all here, presented in logical categories so that you can find it when you need it.

Many examples from dozens of campaigns are offered to bring the ideas and suggestions to life. Relevant anecdotes, memorable quotes, and amusing stories transform the training manual into an entertaining read. But its principal purpose is to explain, advise, and teach. The frequent checklists on what to remember are impressive and very helpful. Just a few examples of lists I found particularly useful:

- Organizing and planning the campaign
- Computer software needs
- Time management of the candidate and staff
- Crafting the campaign message

I particularly appreciated the sections on candidate conduct and family involvement. These should be read several times—before the decision to run, during the campaign, after the election, throughout one's term in office. Before I first ran for office I had a long conversation with my family because I knew that my success as a candidate and office holder was dependent on their comfort with the decision. Like the book says, running for and holding elected office "is not a job, it's a lifestyle." Finding the balance between family and the demands of being a public servant is crucial.

Winning Political Campaigns concentrates on the basics (your walkers will need easy to read, updated maps of the district), but also includes suggestions for the "extras" (one innovative use of the candidate's Web page is an issue survey of netizens). The author explains the obvious (the candidate and staff should make lists of all possible contacts for contributions; always deliver a yard sign to someone you promise it to; staff should be deputy registrars to make voter registration available). The author also offers unusual advice (how to scare off campaign spies and how to use brainstorming creativity to evolve proposals that will set your candidate apart from the pack).

Experienced candidates know that campaigns are not easy—there are many ups and downs and tremendous stress. But there are also wonderful opportunities and a deep-seated satisfaction that your contribution and service has made a difference. The book will give you the power and inspiration to go forward with confidence, and hopefully, help garner the votes you will need to win on election night!

Fran Ulmer
Lieutenant Governor
State of Alaska

PREFACE

"Most American political campaigns lurch along from one improvisation to another, from one immediate crisis to another. They are frequently underorganized, underplanned, and understaffed."
—Frank J. Sorauf, author, *Party Politics in America*[1]

Each year, thousands of candidates for elective office lose not because their opponents had better ideas, but because their rivals were better organized and prepared. The winners avoid the campaign mistakes that even experienced politicians make—and that send the losers home while their opponents' careers in government advance.

In more than fifteen years of covering political campaigns as a reporter for Chicago-area publications, I have witnessed candidates make mistakes that not only cost them elections, but their credibility as well. I now work for ANB Communications, a Chicago-based communication consulting firm for businesses and for candidates, taking rough ideas and shaping, smoothing, and polishing them for presentation to the public.

Whether you want to discover how to perform or oversee all the functions necessary to be a candidate, consultant, or aide in a successful campaign, or whether you are simply interested to learn how to hire or work with political professionals, *Winning Political Campaigns* provides the information you need. My experience is from both sides of the fence: as an outsider observing candidates and companies bring about their own success or failure, and as an insider helping to create public relations victories.

Much of what is contained in this book can, with a little creativity and a lot of hard work, be accomplished even on a modest budget. Of course, with more money you can increase your chances of victory, but regardless of funding you must be creative in any campaign. This book can help develop that creativity, whether you are running a well-funded or barebones campaign.

Although written from the perspective of attaining elected government office, much of the information also can be useful in academic, business, labor, professional, public interest, social, and other organizations.

Read the entire book for a broad overview, and then use it as a convenient reference guide for specific issues during the campaign. Your campaign does not have to accomplish everything in this book, and likely will not have the money nor the time to do so. Pick and choose what will work best for you; implementing these recommendations will put your campaign one step closer to victory.*

---

* Throughout the book I've used the term "progressive" for liberal, Democratic, or left-of-center references, and "conservative" for Republican or right-of-center references.

ADVERTISING

"You can fool all the people all the time if the advertising is right."
—Joseph E. Levine, business leader

There are five steps to the political advertising cycle.

- Learn about your audience.
- Create awareness of your electoral contest and candidate.
- Create familiarity with the candidate.
- Create a need or an urgency for the voter to cast a ballot
    for your candidate.
- Get an emotional commitment from the voter.

People's motivation is pretty basic: it usually comes down to economic security, personal safety, and the perception of like-mindedness between the people and the candidate. Your advertising should reflect this.

Before planning an advertisement, ask yourself the following:

- What is the purpose of the advertisement?
- Who is the audience?
- When is the advertisement needed?
- What is the budget?
- What will be the most effective medium?
- How will it be distributed?

When doing print, broadcast, billboard, or direct mail advertising, do not provide a litany of stances on arcane issues. It is much more important to make a lifestyle connection between the candidate and the citizen. Voters cast ballots for people they perceive to be like them and who appear to understand their lives. George Bush swept the South in 1988 because he successfully got voters to focus on the Texan aspects of his personality (such as an affinity for pork rinds), rather than on Bush's background as an East Coast blueblood.

People also vote for candidates who oppose the same things they oppose and who, once elected, will defend them against the opposition.

Learning all you can about the potential voters is vital (see also POLLING, page 158 and STRATEGY-TARGETING, page 178). If you do not know the people to whom you are sending your message, you are wasting your time.

Ads that entertain and are funny and clever are better than ones that are completely boring, but straightforward messages still do better than entertainment. They should not be preachy, academic, or condescending, however.

Most electoral contests have low profiles; if you are running for the local school board, the *New York Times* is not going to cover it. Therefore, your best media advertising buy is the small local outlet, such as the community newspaper.

Do not waste your scarce advertising resources on an outlet that does not reach your target audience. In 1991, a Chicago aldermanic candidate spent tens of thousands of dollars buying commercial time on Chicagoland's major television stations; about ninety-nine percent of the viewers lived in areas in which they could not vote for him. His opponent spent a few hundred dollars on a full-page ad in the monthly community newspaper, and won.

Advertising efforts should be integrated. Do all ads have a similar look and get similar messages across, or do the campaign's billboards look nothing like the direct mail, which looks nothing like the print ads? Also, remember to place the candidate's ballot-punch number (if appropriate) on all your advertising. In her successful run for mayor of Chicago in 1979, Jane Byrne's simple slogan of "Punch Ten" helped put her in office. It elected almost the entire Democratic ticket in Cook County in 1996.

Ideally, an advertising campaign should rely on multiple media. If you use only one form of advertising (television, print, "gimmes"), you miss all of the voters who do not see that particular medium.

The campaign should develop some short, snappy position statements, no longer than three sentences of five words each (you do not want your advertising to be too complicated). Put them in all your advertising efforts, and hit the voters with them over and over again.

If a print, broadcast, billboard, or other advertising outlet contacts the campaign to solicit advertising, make a decision in a few days and let the ad salesperson know the answer either way; do not string him or her along. Salespeople are used to being turned down. At a newspaper I worked for, whenever the ad salesman called a particular candidate, that candidate would tell the salesman to fax him information and then claim he never received it. He did not want to advertise, but was trying to spare the ad salesman's feelings by avoiding saying "no." The salesman shared with the editorial staff the opinion that the candidate was not too smart, and his opponent received the paper's endorsement.

Another candidate declined placing an ad in a publication I worked for and then called back a couple of times to apologize. This was odd enough, but then he had the gall to ask the ad salesman what he thought of a rival newspaper in which he was going to advertise. *Think of the impression you will create before you act.*

Think of the competition, too. Whatever the type of your advertisement, it is not just competing with your opponent's ad; it is competing with all the ads for toothpaste, dog food, financial services, and whatever else is fighting for a little piece of the voter's attention. So whether you want to or not, you have to make it look good.

DIRECT MAIL

Direct mail of campaign literature is one of the most important aspects of advertising. See CAMPAIGN LITERATURE, page 28, to learn the fundamentals of direct mail advertising.

Direct mail is employed both for solicitation of votes and solicitation of funds. For more about direct mail's ability to garner donations, see also FUNDRAISING, page 98.

A good rule is to devote about twenty percent of your direct mail efforts to where your candidate is strongest and/or weakest (and you may want to forget the area where your candidate is weakest altogether), and about eighty percent of your efforts to "swing" (persuadable) voters.

Direct mail is particularly effective at the very end of the campaign, because it can provide information that your candidate's opponent will find hard to refute. This is because it takes time to design, produce, and mail this type of advertising, and rivals probably will not be able to react to your piece quickly enough.

PRINT ADS

Keep the message simple. An ad salesperson I worked with once received from a candidate a fully filled, single-spaced 8-1/2-by-11-inch sheet, with instructions to fit everything into the ad. The ad was only a quarter of a page—a size smaller than the sheet of paper itself. The newspaper fit it in all right—in six-point type, (about the size of type in classified ads). It is a sure bet that no voters read through that massive, solid block of words. Keep your message short and readable.

Some candidates get too high-tech. One had all of his information (his ad, photo, and biography) available on computer disk, but not in any other form. The newspaper did not have a compatible computer system and had a very difficult time converting his information into a readable format. Having your information available electronically is great, but have it available the old-fashioned way, too: ads in "camera-ready" format, glossy print pictures, and sheets of paper with other information.

If the campaign is preparing a "camera-ready" ad, know the *exact* dimensions needed, as any two people will measure a page any number of different ways (do you include the outer border or not, how much space is between the ads, and do you include it or not?) Otherwise, your ad will be slightly the wrong size, the publication will have to resize it, and it may lose its sharp, clear quality. Extra production work also results in extra charges.

In most cases, publications do not even require camera-ready copy, and their production staffs will be happy to create ads based on your written instructions. Written instructions, faxed instead of mailed, are a good idea not only for advertising, but for virtually anything you will need in the campaign. A fax states your information clearly, gets it there fast, and leaves both parties with a written record.

You can produce ads or campaign literature on your personal computer, but test them by showing the results to friends and colleagues. Novice designers often over-design, rendering advertisements hard to follow or absolutely unreadable. Just because your printer can support seventy-two typefaces does not mean you should use them all in one ad. Use of a trained designer is best, however, and "trained" does not merely mean someone who has read the computer operating manual. If you cannot afford a professional designer, hire a design student from a local high school, college, or art school.

One old advertising tactic that still works: design your print ad to look like a newspaper opinion column, giving it a more credible journalistic, rather than advertising, appearance.

Print ads are emphasized because they still are often the campaigns' best buy. According to the Newspaper Association of America, "Study after study shows that newspaper readers are the highest turn-out voters."[2] Publications also offer zoned advertising opportunities, printing your ads only in copies that will be distributed in the district in which your candidate is running. In addition, publications often offer multi-publication buys in several allied publications at a discount.

Another source for discounted ad space is through CAPs (Campaign Advertising Plans). Twenty state press associations have created CAPs to offer discounts and multiple inserts for ads in publications that are press association members. Contact your state's press association for more information. In addition, many newspapers offer political rates for display ads, which are comparable to rates charged nonprofit organizations.

Since most elections are on Tuesdays, always advertise in the Sunday newspaper just before the election. It is widely read, and that's about the time in the campaign when voting decisions are made.

Broadcast Media: Television/Video & Radio/Audiocassette

You might think you cannot afford television advertising, but cable television can be inexpensive and effective. Cable television stations often have demographic, socioeconomic, and lifestyle data on their viewers, and cable television advertising sales reps are only too happy to place your ad.

Just as with newspaper ads, keep the message short and simple when doing television ads. It is tempting for the low-budget campaign to place numerous facts into its one broadcast shot, but that just serves to overtax and confuse the voters.

Time your television advertising for when it is most effective. The unknown candidate may want to place some ads early to increase recognition. Just as with print ads, however, the last days before the election are crucial for television.

The requirements of where to buy television time (all stations, only the biggest stations, cable, ethnic shows, daytime television to reach women, sports shows to reach men) are different in every campaign. Buying commercials during the news always is a good idea, though, because news-watchers also tend to be voters.

Most cable companies are required by law to broadcast public service announcements. Perhaps you can create a television spot that is not really an ad for your candidate but is instead ostensibly about an issue with which your candidate is familiar. The candidate, of course, should be prominently featured.

Television is not appropriate for all campaigns. If your candidate is running for subcircuit district judge, allocating money for television is a waste, as most of the viewers likely will not even live in your district. In a campaign in which television is being used, however, spending half of your budget on television commercials is not unrealistic.

A newer advertising medium is the videocassette. Campaigns have actually begun mailing videocassettes, some even made of cardboard, to voters. These often can be produced quite inexpensively. A campaign video production package should include videocassette duplication, a spine label, a printed sleeve, shrinkwrap, affixing of mailing labels and postage. A whole package like this can be obtained for as little as two dollars per name/address.

Be alert for overbooked video producers, who can cause disastrous delays. Obtain an estimate from the producer, and then plan on the project taking twice as long. A video ad campaign should therefore be planned and executed as early in the campaign as possible, or you might find the video still is not complete when the campaign is over.

Check references before contracting with a video producer. Some specialize in political television ad production, and the best way to locate them is through word of mouth. Talk to other political connections or representatives of previous campaigns that featured spots you found particularly effective.

Know in advance the cost of the following:

- Scripting.
- Duplicating.
- Editing.
- Filming/taping.
- Graphics.
- Location/studio rental.
- Makeup.
- Music.
- Production.
- Special effects.
- Voice-over.

To do television/video on a shoestring, see if you can utilize local college or high school video facilities, equipment, and students. Or, perhaps your political party can provide access to television facilities. With downsizing affecting the television/video industry, you can likely find some unemployed television production people who might be willing to work at a reasonable rate. Bear in mind, however, you do get only what you pay for.

Television production can be done inexpensively. A Sony digital camera can cost as little as $4,000. Material can be broadcast on satellite for as little as $350 per half-hour.

Television/video lets you communicate your message in the time you want to take to tell it—not in the few seconds news programs will provide. You can target your videos to particular groups at particular times.

Aside from prospecting for votes, television/video also can be used for fundraising and volunteer recruitment.

If you have a candidate who is comfortable in front of the camera, he or she should "carry the video." If you do not, using many still photos with voiceovers is the way to go.

While a video that comes by mail is still an unusual occurrence, its arrival alone may not be enough to induce the voter to play it. There should be an accompanying letter or ad that stresses the importance of viewing it.

Want to save on mailing costs? Have campaign footsoldiers deliver cassettes and collect them a week later. This gives them two opportunities to make a personal contact with the voter. Include information in the accompanying letter or ad that the campaign worker is returning to retrieve the cassette, or the voter is sure to toss it out. Do not just leave a campaign video for a voter; hand it to him or her personally. Do not leave it in the mailbox; that is illegal.

Just as the candidate should have more than one piece of campaign literature to target different audiences, so too should the campaign have more than one video advertisement. The homeowning families in one part of the district should not receive the same video as the young singles in another locale.

Another good medium for targeting is radio. It is cost-effective, allowing you to double or even triple your airplay compared to television advertising costs.

Like cable television outlets, radio stations have demographic, socioeconomic, and lifestyle data on their listeners. Often, this information is even better than that obtained by cable television stations, allowing your ads to be targeted even more accurately. Also, since voice ads are much easier and cheaper to produce than television ads, radio also allows you flexibility and immediacy when you need to change ads to avoid a dead issue or take advantage of a hot topic.

Generally, the same principles concerning timing, production, and other factors that apply to television advertising apply to radio advertising. Similarly, the principles of videocassette advertising apply to advertising by audiocassette. Audiocassette advertising can contain your radio commercials or longer, meatier, and targeted solicitations to voters.

Consider playing particularly effective soundbites from previous interviews with your candidate or from his or her speeches on radio or videocassette advertisements. Radio ads should not "sound" political, though. If it seems like a speech, it will turn people off.

A radio ad should include music (that is why people listen to the radio, anyway), and begin with a "grabber." Radio is a pop-culture medium, so references to pop culture are effective, as are humor and emotion. The simple message should be repeated frequently; with only their sense of hearing to rely on, people have to be hit with the information several times for the message to sink in.

Video or audiocassette distributions always are more effective if followed by a phone call or a mailing.

An inexpensive method of radio advertising is to forego producing an audiotape and just have the station's disk jockey read your ad script. While this can save money, you have less control over the delivery, particularly if he is one of the shock-jocks typically broadcasting in the morning.

Want to get free air play for your video or audio ad? See if you can get the media to bite on a pitch that the ad itself is a story. The Republicans did this in May 1996 when they screened a television ad for the media that criticized President Clinton's use of a military defense concerning sex scandal allegations.

ABC, CBS, CNN, NBC, and several radio stations ran the ad as news in their news broadcasts, and many publications covered the ad. It received so much play on the news that the G.O.P. never purchased any advertising airtime and never actually ran it as an ad, prompting speculation that they never intended to anyway. As presidential nominee Bob Dole said of Republican National Committee chair Haley Barbour, "Anybody who can get five million dollars worth of advertising without ever running a spot is the kind of guy we need."[3]

To counter this tactic if tried on your candidate, find out from the local broadcast media how much air time your opponent has bought. You are legally entitled to this information, so if the broadcast outlet balks, contact your attorney. If the media makes a big to-do about your opponent's ad but you can prove to them that they were merely being manipulated because there were no plans to actually run the spot, you can turn the tables.

When providing video or audio tapes to broadcast outlets for paid commercial time, include a label on the tape with the name of the spot and of the candidate or ad agency. Give your spot a name not related to an issue. If you call it "economic development," for example, someone at the station may tip your opponent in time for the opponent to produce a counter-spot. If providing a revised replacement tape for a spot, provide a new title. If you do not, the old one may be run mistakenly.

"GIMMES"

People love free stuff, so t-shirts, "gimme" hats, pens and pencils, post-it notes, magnets, hand fans, nail files, shopping bags, sponges, bumper stickers, posters and yard signs, and good old lapel buttons are good forms of advertising. See if you can persuade a friendly outfitter to donate the clothing and/or the silk-screening for the clothing as an in-kind contribution. Most "gimmes" can be obtained from one company, saving you work and assuring that they will be coordinated. If you can sell these items, that is even better. Never pass up any opportunity to fundraise, no matter how small it appears.

SIGNS AND LITERATURE

Campaign signs and posters still are effective, but you should not irritate voters by placing signs where they are not wanted. Also, make sure the signs are not an odd size or shape that renders them unreadable. A U.S. Senate candidate in Illinois in 1996 used signs in the shape of long, thin strips. They were hard to read and forced campaign workers to wrap them around posts so that the public could not view the entire sign from any angle, and their odd shapes also caused them to catch the wind and blow away. Traditional rectangular shapes are best.

Place signs where they are legal, and include in your campaign budget a line item for sign removal. If you place your signs in unlawful spots or abandon them after the votes are counted, the taxpayers will pay for their removal. This will not endear the candidate to the voters in future elections. Have your fieldworkers ask the voters if they will display signs on their own lawns.

Campaign literature is one of the oldest, but still most effective, forms of political advertising. (See also CAMPAIGN LITERATURE, page 28.) Direct mail is an example of a way to distribute campaign literature. A newer twist on campaign literature is the phone-mail combo, in which you conduct a phone survey to find out facts about potential voters, and then follow quickly with direct mail campaign literature targeted to their hot buttons—such as pro-choice oriented literature to choice supporters or gun-ownership oriented literature to right-to-bear-arms proponents.

TELEPHONE

Telephone can be an effective form of advertising, but the rules have changed somewhat in recent years. Since everyone from vinyl siding salespersons to the local art museum conducts telemarketing, people have come to resent these at-home intrusions.

As opposed to telephone polling, which should begin early and can be done any time during the campaign, telephone advertising, usually referred to as "phone banking," is done late.

The telephone also should be used to handle any late-breaking developments in the campaign when there is not time to change print or broadcast ads or to send direct mail.

Call your supporters and the undecideds close to the election and ask them to vote for your candidate. Request that they ask friends and family to vote for your candidate, too. Ask if you can answer any questions or provide information, and that is about it. Do not stay on the phone forever, alienating your candidate's potential voters. Always prepare a script for phone-bankers so they can be efficient and focused during telephone conversations.

The following is a schedule of calls the staff should make in the last few days before the Tuesday election:

- Sunday: Ask people to vote for your candidate and to tell their friends to do so as well.
- Monday night: Call people and ask them to vote early.
- Tuesday, election day: Contact people to determine if they need a ride to the polls, and remind those who have not voted to

go to the polls. Be prepared to provide addresses of their polling places.

The best times to call are between six and nine in the evening Monday through Thursday, and two to nine on Sunday. That early afternoon Sunday start may allow your callers to run through the cycle a couple of times to get back to those who were not home. People are most available at home on Sunday and Monday nights, and are not available on Friday and Saturday nights.

When your phonebanker makes contact with a supporter, ask if that supporter needs services ("Do you need an absentee ballot?") or if the supporter will help the candidate in some easy way ("May I send you a yard sign?" "Will you ask five of your friends to vote for Joe Candidate?"). Political consultant Nancy Todd from The Todd Company in Baton Rouge, Louisiana, says a surprisingly large percentage of people "will do something if you ask them to."[4]

THE LAST MINUTE

Timing is everything. While you must establish visibility for your candidate early, do not spend the entire advertising budget before your final big push the week before the election. Studies show that an estimated forty-four percent of voters make their decisions the week before the election.[5]

"You gang up the message right up to the event," according to Steve Laughlin of Milwaukee-based Laughlin Constable, which worked the 1988 Bush for President campaign. You target the undecided and the "soft" supporters of a candidate. "It is the last-minute swipe to get them off that fence....[t]hat support at the last minute can shift, especially if the issues between the two candidates are not highly divisive."[6]

TEST

Whatever kind of advertising you employ, test it with your staff at least, or with focus groups at best. This is necessary even for broadcast ads; you do not have to spend money to produce a broadcast ad before you test—just read people the script. How many ads make no sense? Make sure yours is not one of them.

Remember, your perspective may be skewed because you are in the inner circle of the campaign and are actually interested in the campaign and the issues. Voters may not be interested in either, so try to put yourself in their place.

Depending on local laws, the words "paid advertisement," "paid for by X," or another disclaimer may be required in print and/or broadcast advertisements and on other campaign literature, including sample ballots. Consult with your attorney to determine which advertising needs a disclaimer.

ALLIANCES

"All your strength is in union. All your danger is in discord."
—Hiawatha, legendary chief of the Onodaga tribe

Ron Faucheaux, editor of *Campaigns & Elections*, pegs coalition building as one of the three most important aspects of campaign strategizing.[7] (The others are the core message and communication of it.) Long before the election season, the candidate and campaign staff should identify community leaders and organizations with views similar to the candidate in an effort to gather support.

Each should be an opinion leader, according to Margaret Tutwiler, now head of Direct Impact Communications and formerly an official in the Reagan and Bush presidential campaigns, "whose voice counts because of either wealth or other influence, like an issue champion." [8]

They also should identify leaders of groups not in the candidate's "natural" base. If, after discussing the issues with them, the candidate can support their stands on those issues, he or she has forged a new, exciting coalition. In his last campaign for governor of Alabama, George Wallace actually came out in *favor* of opportunities for African-Americans, a position that coincided with his populist theme. The man who once stood in the schoolhouse door to block African-Americans even received an honorary degree from a traditionally Black college.

Do not, however, tell one group one thing and another the opposite. Let people know ahead of time what coalitions you are trying to build, but do it discreetly. What you *do not* want is for a local leader to give support, then rescind it when your other alliances conflict with his or her principles. The publicity resulting from a revocation of support could hurt your campaign more than not having the endorsement in the first place.

Determine who *really* speaks for the constituents. Is that ethnic organization active and capable of turning out votes, or is it simply resting on its reputation, with no clout?

Leaders and organizations from both your natural and coalition bases can help in a number of ways. They know the media, and more important, they know other community leaders who can provide advice and financing. If you can assemble an advisory panel of individuals unknown to each other, you are doing them as well as your campaign a service by providing a networking opportunity.

Do not be reluctant to approach the leaders in your community. Even if they indicate a lack of interest, you have not lost anything. Instead, they may welcome such lobbying on your part. If you inform them of a political or community issue of which they are unaware, they may even become an advocate of your position.

These community leaders also can form a citizens' committee, which lends a greater air of respectability and credibility when it chooses you or your candidate to run for office. It helps legitimize the candidate's status, and also can assist in finding candidates who share your views for other offices, increasing your roster of allies.

Such a recruitment committee can help you avoid what happened to Democrat Yolanda Castillo in running for mayor of Hartford, Connecticut. Needing to fill the Democratic slate for the lower offices, she recruited a man named Hector Santiago, whom she knew only from a three-minute conversation in a supermarket parking lot, to run for constable. Unfortunately, Santiago had a lengthy criminal record and was a street-gang leader. Both Castillo and Santiago were trounced on election day. A blue-ribbon citizens' committee would have done a better job in recruiting a running mate than the harried mayoral candidate.

Do not expect the committee to run the campaign. Its members may lend prestige and even some hard work. Certain members' "work" on the committee may merely be use of their high-profile names; the committee may seldom meet. Usually, in fact, the committee meets only to coordinate a fundraiser or a rally. Also, do not be cowed by the members' reputations into allowing them to take charge of the campaign.

As a manager who is not a strong supporter of meetings, I have chaired committees that have *never* actually met; I just parceled out work and coordinated it. You can establish the citizens' committee in this manner if you want greater control.

The candidate can gain the loyalty of community and political organizations long before the electoral contest begins by working for or with these organizations and their leaders. Richard Nixon spent the years between 1963 and 1967 traveling the country making appearances for Republican politicians; in return, he received their support for the presidency in 1968. More recently, Congressman Jesse Jackson Jr. of Illinois received support in his first congressional contest from sources whom experts predicted would back other candidates. According to Jackson in *Campaigns & Elections*, "I've helped them by registering their voters and campaigning for them. My father has helped them. They had no problems giving to me."[9]

Lay your groundwork early. Long before your candidate even announces, he or she should hit the local speaking circuit, seeking invitations from or offering to speak to local groups on issues of mutual interest.

When you cannot receive the endorsement or help of certain community leaders and organizations, the best you can work for is that they do not mobilize *against* your candidate. So even if support is denied, do not anger people of influence. If you cannot convince them to support your candidate, but you keep them from endorsing your opponent, you may have won a significant victory.

Once candidates have filed, visit the board of elections and request a list of candidates for non-competing offices on the ballot. Talk to other candidates about creating alliances. Legally, they must file their addresses (and often telephone numbers) with the board of elections.

The alliance option is a particularly good one for candidates for lower profile contests. If your candidate is running for water district commissioner, a congressional representative may not want to create an alliance with your campaign, but why not make an alliance with a candidate for judge or the state legislature? The candidates can attend each others' events, meet more people, and be listed on each others' campaign literature. Campaigns also can piggyback on each other by sharing headquarters, staff, volunteers, data, and purchases of services such as printing and computer software and hardware. They also can engage in joint advertising campaigns.

Political action committees and issue/interest groups also may be able to connect you or your candidate with hopefuls for non-competing offices who share your campaign's views, for the purpose of alliance.

The national Republican Party uses the "buddy system," pairing less experienced office-seekers "with senior incumbents who can introduce them to friendly political-action committees and other prospective donors," according to *U.S. News & World Report*.[10] If your local party organization does not have such a plan, do it on your own.

A number of underfunded and understaffed candidates may find that if they pool resources, they may all benefit. The Arkansas Republican Party has formed a "trust" to pay for research, mailings, and coordinated radio buys for state legislative candidates.[11] In Illinois, whether the Democratic Party is in the minority or majority in the state legislature, legislators share office space and some staffers and consultants through the office of House of Representatives Democratic leader Michael Madigan.

Visit your local party organization to determine if it has or is interested in starting a pool, but if not, approach some of the other lean-staffed candidates not competing with your campaign to discuss pooling resources. You can share fundraisers, data, and staff.

The candidate and his or her allies can produce a "slate mailer" or "slate ad." This is a direct mail piece or a print ad that lists the names of the offices on the ballot and the names of allied candidates. It is a convenient device that voters may take into the voting booth to assist with increasingly complex ballots.

Do not be afraid to boldly go where no one has gone before and forge alliances between strange bedfellows. Maine activist George Christie worked with groups "that haven't always gotten along, such as the Maine AFL-CIO and Common Cause," and successfully placed a campaign financing referendum on the ballot, collecting over 62,000 signatures in just fourteen hours. [12]

Consider allying with the private sector—"big business"—in your community. Usually seen as tradition-bound and wedded to the G.O.P., the private sector no longer is either and is open to alliance with both conservatives and progressives. Non-traditional policies like affirmative action have actually helped some sectors of business, and business also benefits from the status quo. This sometimes puts business at opposition with some of the modern anti-status quo G.O.P. constituencies of religious conservatives, anti-establishment entrepreneurs, militiamen, and Contract-With-America supporters. In the 1996 primary season, big business' donations and assistance went to Democrat Bill Clinton and not the G.O.P. candidates. So big business is fair game for candidates on all points of the political spectrum.

A candidate should not ally with another whose views are abhorrent to him or her. Senator John Warner (R-VA) was politically astute by refusing to back Republican senate candidate Ollie North for Virginia's other senate seat in 1994. An endorsement of an extreme candidate can come back to haunt a politician.

However, do not be so ideologically pure that you automatically refuse to ally with another candidate of your own party who does not agree with you on every position. Jesse Jackson put it best when he said that politics is the art of choosing from among live options, and it is better to win with someone you do not always agree with than to go down in flames with someone with whom the candidate is completely ideologically compatible. That only puts the opposition, whom you *completely* disagree with, into power. "We must all hang together or we'll all hang separately," said one of America's earliest politicians, Benjamin Franklin.

Unfortunately, not everyone heeds Franklin's words. Just because a powerful ally or party organization promises to support your candidate, that support may not stick. In 1980, Chicago Mayor Jane Byrne in a widely publicized dinner event endorsed incumbent Jimmy Carter for president—then betrayed him by switching her support to Carter's primary opponent, Ted Kennedy. If a power-broker has no fear about doing this to the president of the United States, he or she will have no qualms about doing it to your candidate.

On the other hand, investigate a candidate with whom your campaign is planning to ally. If you ally unwisely and a scandal breaks concerning the other office-seeker, your candidate could get burned.

Be careful of well-meaning allies who may turn voters off. While union support helped many Democratic candidates win congressional seats in 1996, it also harmed some Democrats in districts in which Republicans could whip up anti-union sentiment. You may have to encourage some supporters to keep a low profile.

If your candidate agrees to an alliance or to support another candidate, he or she should keep his word, short of revelations that the ally is a murderer, Ku Klux Klan member, or some similar horror. Voters do not like a turncoat. Chicagoans responded to Byrne's switch by booing Kennedy all along that year's St. Patrick's Day Parade route and by voting for Carter overwhelmingly in the Illinois Democratic primary. In a final demonstration of their opinion of Kennedy and Byrne, a few St. Patrick's Day revelers drove a '68 Chrysler into Lake Michigan to commemorate the senator's visit.

Alliances and coalitions are built not only with community leaders, organizations, and other office-seekers and office-holders; they are built with the voters, too. Even before declaring, examine the demographics of the district and determine what kind of coalitions are needed to squeeze out a victory. "We need eighty percent of African-Americans, fifty percent of Caucasian women, and thirty percent of Caucasian men to win," is the kind of analysis that is essential. This will help drive your strategies for achieving those numbers through alliance- and coalition-building.

PARTY BACKING

The best alliance is with your political party's regular organization. Although political "machines" and party "bosses" are pretty much a relic of the past, the endorsement of your party's regular organization still is the best ticket to electoral victory. The party has the money, footsoldiers, and other resources to get you the votes.

Parties choose their candidates in different ways, depending on local laws and customs. Party caucuses or nominating (slating) sessions bring local party officials (usually called committeemen), and sometimes rank-and-file voters, together to pick whom the party will endorse. Committeemen are chosen from local precincts, wards, or townships. With more than 100,000 precincts in the United States, many of these posts go unfilled, so becoming a committeeperson, either by election or party choice, is an excellent way both to get into regular politics and learn firsthand about the electoral process.

Party committees are formed from gatherings of committeepersons. Often, there are city, town, village, legislative, county, and congressional district committees. The county committee usually is the major one locally, but there also is the state central committee, as well as the party's national committee. Any of these committees can slate or endorse candidates (although if you are running for water commissioner, do not bother contacting your party's national committee). Contact your local party organizations to understand how they organize their slating sessions.

If the candidate just arrives at a slating session without having done any groundwork, he or she is going to lose. Before the candidate even announces for office, he or she should meet some commiteepersons and seek their support.

The candidate will do better if he or she has lined up some political allies in advance and comes in with a plan to promote the alliance and the party in the region. Such a plan might include:

- Ways to create a fun/positive image of the party.
- Promoting the concept of "when in doubt, vote for the X party."
- Courting and capturing undeclared voters.
- Money-raising ideas.

Sometimes, the best ticket to victory is to run away from the regular party's endorsement. For example, if you wanted to get elected in the "lakefront liberal" section of Chicago in the 1970s, you had to run against the Regular Democratic Organization.

Do not make the mistake of thinking that the people in the party with the formal power necessarily wield the *actual* power. (That can be true not only for political parties, but for any type of organization, such as a community group whose support you may want.) Lyndon Johnson lost the 1960 Democratic presidential nomination to John Kennedy partially because he thought that his fellow senators controlled their states' delegations in the nominating convention. They did not. Talk to journalists, community leaders, and party footsoldiers to see who wields the real power, and then work on alliance-building.

If the candidate receives the party's backing, he or she also should not assume the party will do all the work. These days, the party may do nothing more than endorse. Try to determine what resources the party will offer to your candidate and how much the party can be counted upon, but do not expect that it will be sufficient.

Parties may provide your campaign with advice on the following:

- Advertising.
- Campaigning.
- Candidate training.
- Communications.
- Computer systems.
- Database development.
- Fundraising.
- Insurance for events.

- Media.
- Operations plans.
- Phone banks.
- Policy.
- Polling.
- Publications.
- Television and radio production.
- Vendors.
- Voter contact, registration, and targeting.

Determine what services are offered before you re-invent the wheel or pay for something already available for free. See also APPENDIX TEN: DEMOCRATIC NATIONAL COMMITTEE, and APPENDIX ELEVEN: REPUBLICAN NATIONAL COMMITTEE.

The farther down on the ballot and the less visible the electoral contest is, the more people vote for the party instead of the individual. So for low-profile elections, party endorsement may be crucial.

ENDORSEMENTS

Two or three good endorsements may be worth a thousand campaign speeches. It is vital to get endorsements. "We are endorsed by the people" translates into "We are running such a lousy campaign nobody supports us."

Alliances with other candidates will at least give you their endorsements, which you can list in your campaign literature and distribute to the media.

The larger the organization the better the endorsement, but if you cannot receive the larger organization's blessing, a smaller section of it will do. While you may not be endorsed by the state Republican Party, perhaps you can be endorsed by the local ward's Republican Organization. Some endorsements worth seeking:

- Civic groups (chamber of commerce, Rotary, Lions, and similar).
- Interest groups (arts, business, civil rights, education, environmental, ethnic, gay/lesbian, good government organizations, pro- or anti-gun control, healthcare, seniors, tax reform, unions, veterans).
- Media (particularly the neighborhood or community newspaper for a race that is lower on the ballot).
- Political action committees (PACs).
- Political figures/elected officials.
- Political organizations (regular, insurgent, grassroots, independent).

- Political party committees (precinct, ward, city, town, legislative, county, congressional district, statewide, and national).
- Political party auxiliary groups (Young Republicans, Democratic Women's Caucus, other).
- Respected members of the community (military heroes, athletes, community activists, celebrities).
- Unions (including union locals).

Target the organizations from which you want to receive endorsements and learn their endorsement process. Do they have face-to-face endorsement sessions with all the candidates? With one candidate at a time? Do they base their endorsements on candidates' written responses to their questions? Do they just want to see your literature?

Give them whatever they want, and do not argue that they should run their endorsement process a different way—unless you want to make sure that your opponent gets their backing.

Endeavor to receive and play up endorsements from areas where you are weak. In Carol Moseley-Braun's successful run for the U.S. Senate in 1992, she was perceived as a Chicago candidate, so she highlighted endorsements from downstate media in her downstate advertisements. If you are perceived as "soft on crime" but strong on union issues, you may be able to get an endorsement from a police union, which you can tout among law-and-order voters.

Do not expect or ask for an endorsement from a media outlet just because you are an advertiser. It would be unethical for the media to provide an endorsement on that basis, and it makes you look unethical to ask. Rest assured, however, that your taking out an ad does not *hurt* your chances of being endorsed.

What happens if you get few or no endorsements? Position yourself as the underdog running against the entrenched, elite interests.

INTEREST GROUPS

There are literally thousands of interest groups to which the campaign can appeal for funds, volunteers, endorsements, support, research, or positions on issues. Whether they are established as for-profit or not-for-profit organizations, they are increasingly more politically active. Consult the telephone directory or the local library to identify them.

The following is a list of general interest group categories:

- Business.
- Citizens.
- Employee and labor.
- Farm.
- Foreign.
- Individuals and firms.
- Military and veterans.
- Political.
- Professional.

See also Appendix Three: Resources For Key Political Issues.

Not-For-Profits

As congress and state legislatures continue to reduce funding to not-for-profit and tax-exempt (501(c)(3)) organizations, these organizations have become increasingly politically savvy.

Not-for-profits are constrained by law as to the scope of their political work, but your campaign can still work with them. They can register voters and engage in nonpartisan "voter education" drives. They can host debates and organize accountability sessions between candidates and challengers.

While not-for-profits cannot work for or against particualar candidates, they can support or oppose ballot measures such as initiatives, referenda, constitutional amendments, and propositions. Therefore, while they cannot lobby for your candidate directly, they can lobby for or against a ballot measure that the candidate is closely identified with.

Local and federal laws and IRS regulations must be followed closely by a not-for-profit when it is involved with a political campaign. However, these organizations are very powerful—as proven by the 104th Congress' attempt to curtail their political activity, tax-exempt status, and free speech rights.

To make sure that a not-for-profit's tax-exempt status is not jeopardized by its intended political work, it should request the IRS to provide a private ruling as to the tax consequences of proposed action. Unfortunately, this can take up to nine months.

According to the publication *NFC Notable$*, the Nonprofit Financial Center in Chicago notes, "An IRS private ruling interprets and applies the tax laws to a specific set of facts," deciding "how a transaction or event would affect the agency's tax-exempt status." [13]

The IRS is required to follow its own ruling, and may even suggest how to restructure the proposal. For more information, contact the Internal Revenue Service, Assistant Commissioner (EP/EO), Attention: CP:EO:P:2, P.O. Box 120, Ben Franklin Station, Washington DC, 20044.

PACs (POLITICAL ACTION COMMITTEES)

Political action committees (PACs) can be a valuable source not only of funds but of information. Although "PAC" has become a bit of a dirty word in the media, if you already agree with a particular PAC's views, there is nothing wrong with benefiting from its resources.

Visit your local library or the Internet to locate lists of PACs that may benefit your campaign.

BUSINESS

"More people should learn to tell their dollars where to go instead of asking them where they went."

—Roger Babson, statistician

Conservatives and progressives may disagree on whether or not government should be run like a business, but they had better agree that campaigns should employ sound business practices. Those who do not may find that their campaigns are out of business.

BUDGET

Before the campaign even begins, develop a budget. You may not have to include all of the following, and the campaign staffers may be able to do many of these functions themselves or be able to secure donations, but this list should keep you from omitting anything:

Advertising.
- Broadcast (should be coordinated completely by the media consultant who produces the ads).
  - Writing.
  - Production.
    - Scripting.
    - Graphics.
    - Location/studio rental.
    - Music.
    - Makeup.

- Filming/taping.
- Special effects.
- Voice-over.
- Production.
- Editing.
- Duplicating.
- Air time.
- Mailing of videocassettes or audiocassettes.
- Print.
  - Writing.
  - Design and production.
  - Space in publication(s).
- Campaign literature (including media kits. Mailpieces and other campaign literature should be done by the media consultant working with a direct mail firm.).
  - Writing.
  - Design and production.
  - Photography (picture-taking and prints).
  - Printing.
  - List purchase/list creation (vital to this effort are fundraisers and outside organizations supporting the candidate).
  - Label creation (should be done in house).
  - Label affixing (can be done by volunteers to save money).
  - Postage.
  - House-to-house distribution (by volunteers).
- Billboards.
  - Design and production.
  - Printing.
  - Space purchase.
- "Gimmes": Window/lawn signs, bumper stickers, lapel buttons, hats, t-shirts, refrigerator magnets, pencils and pens, and similar items.
  - Design and production.
  - Printing/manufacture.
  - Sign removal.
- Telephone.
  - Basic phone company charges.
  - Expected monthly expenditures.
  - Phone bank/phone bank service.
  - Answering machine.
  - Phone system (such as call-waiting, rollover, other functions).
  - Cell phones for some staffers.
  - Phone conferencing (if the campaign includes consultants from out of state or in a different geographic area in-state).

Consultants.
- Accountant (try to get one for free).
- Attorney (try to get one for free).
- Media trainer.
- Other.

Election day expenses.
- Transportation.
- Attorney's fees, if required to deal with a last-minute legal issue.
- Other.

Events.
- Facilities rental.
- Food/refreshments (try to secure in-kind contributions).
- Invitations and tickets.
  - Writing.
  - Design and production.
  - Printing.
  - Label creation.
  - Label affixing.
  - Postage.

Fundraising.
- Telephone costs.
  - Phone bank/phone bank service (try to get free phone banking at the premises of supportive organizations, like law firms and labor organizations. Use a phone bank service only if you have money to spare.).
- Direct mail.
  - Writing.
  - Design and production.
  - Printing.
  - List purchase/list creation.
  - Label creation.
  - Label affixing.
  - Postage.
- Follow ups (thank-you notes, phone calls, other related actions).
  - Stationery.
  - Postage.
- Events (see above).

Get-out-the-vote.
- Registration programs.
- Absentee voting programs.
- Election day (calls, handing out literature, precinct work, checking who has not voted, driving voters, poll watching).

Grooming aids.
- New clothing for the candidate.
- Portable makeup/grooming kit.
- Image consultant.
- Speech coach.

Headquarters.
- Rent/lease.
- Electronic equipment (rental or purchase).
    - Computer(s).
        - Software.
        - Internet connection.
    - Fax.
    - Phones.
    - Audiovisual equipment.
    - Other (postage meters, additional machinery).
- Furniture (rental or purchase).
    - Chairs, tables, and desks.
    - Refrigerator.
- Alarm system (the building management should provide this for free, so shop around for space that includes this).
- Reference materials.
    - Dictionary.
    - Media guides.
    - Maps.
    - Newspaper subscription(s).
- Cleaning service (this should be provided by the building management).
- Refreshments (coffee, soft drinks, snacks).
- Utilities (gas, electric, water).

Miscellaneous.
- Insurance.
- Focus groups (to test ads, positions, other issues. These should be coordinated through a media consultant).
- Printing petitions to get on the ballot.
- Banking fees.
- Petty cash.
- Post office box.
- Filing fees.
- Membership fees.
- Gifts/donations.
- Messenger/postage.
- Unbudgeted expenses (add five percent to total).
- Pocket pagers/beepers for staff.

Office supplies.
- Letterhead (also can be used for direct mail).
    - Design.
    - Printing.
- Postage.
- Cassette tapes, desk supplies, easels, envelopes, paper, pens, phone message pads, tape, three-ring binders, videotapes, and more.

Polling (use of an outside polling firm is highly recommended).
- Phoning, mailing, or "person-on-the-street."
    - Benchmark poll.
    - Tracking poll.
    - Brushfire poll.
    - Push poll.

Research.
- Issues.
- Opposition.
- Voter identification.

Staff.
- Salaries.
- Benefits.
- Taxes.
- Volunteer solicitation and coordination.
- Expense reimbursement.

Transportation/travel (auto, air, train, public transportation, lodging).
- Candidate.
- Paid staff.
- Volunteers.
- Family.

Also, prepare a cash-flow timeline indicating when each expenditure is expected during the course of the campaign.

Part of the budgeting process includes listing all funding sources and creating columns for the minimum and maximum legal contribution. When you total the minimum figures, in reality you can expect to raise half of that. If the amount seems insufficient, remember that you will be adding more sources of income as the campaign advances through your fundraising efforts. Also, if your campaign catches fire, more money will be generated.

Decide at the beginning where you can cut the budget. Trim the fat early, and you will not be forced to trim the meat later.

Spending authority should be given to one person, who should have the final say on everything—including reimbursements to staff. Develop a spending reimbursement form (someone in the campaign probably works in an office that has a form you can copy), and do not provide reimbursements without one. Keep all receipts.

CREDIT

"It is difficult to begin without borrowing...," according to Henry David Thoreau. Unfortunately, it often is even more difficult for a political campaign to get credit than it is for the average business.

Unless you already have a superb business relationship with your supplier, do not expect to acquire everything in the campaign on credit. Every business knows that the campaign disappears once the election is over, and that losing candidates seldom pay their bills.

Whatever it is, if you need it, you may have to pay in advance.

Win or lose, whatever bills are owed after the campaign must be paid. Otherwise, the candidate is open to charges of being a deadbeat in future campaigns and can forget about any credit in the future.

While it is best to end the campaign with a zero deficit, a debt of up to twenty percent of the campaign budget probably can be wiped out fairly quickly. A debt larger than this is disastrous.

It even may be necessary to fundraise after the election to retire some old debt.

VENDORS

Follow standard business practices when dealing with vendors or potential vendors for printing, phone banking, consulting, giveaways, and other services. Solicit recommendations from others in the field about vendors to include in the bid process. If there is time, request competitive bids on projects—three is a good number. Ask for samples—do they pertain to your project? Ask for references, and verify them. Use the phone instead of a meeting whenever possible, but put every instruction in writing (faxes are great for this). Clearly outline what services you expect and make sure the vendor under-stands your request—and your deadlines.

Is there a positive chemistry between you and the vendor? If not, maybe you should find a different one. Is the vendor's focus low price, fast service, or quality work? If his or her focus is different than yours, you may have a problem.

Remember that suppliers' bids are estimates and only will be as accurate as the information you provide. When you present inaccurate or incomplete information, or when you change the specifications during the production process, costs increase.

Changes are expensive, and suppliers usually charge more for corrected work than for original work. Suppliers bill for services they provide, even if these were not specified in the original bid.

Ten percent overruns are standard for print jobs, so expect to receive and pay for more than you ordered. Cut your order by ten percent if budgets are really tight, or include in the contract that you will accept and pay for an overrun of no greater than two percent, five percent, or whatever you and the vendor will agree to.

Get the name of one contact person in the company, along with their home phone, cell phone, car phone, and pager number.

Make your supplier part of your team and ask for recommendations and advice before setting your specifications.

Determine if parts of the project will be farmed out to subcontractors, and if so, get the names and numbers of their service representatives, too. Do not use vendors who also are working for the opposing political party or worse, your candidate's rival.

CAMPAIGN LITERATURE

"Print is the sharpest and the strongest weapon of our party."
—Joseph Stalin

Whether it is created by the bad guys like Stalin or the good guys like your campaign staff, campaign literature distributed to voters is one of the oldest forms and most vital components of the marketing of a candidate.

The campaign should begin by printing letterhead, envelopes, stationery, and business cards. They are inexpensive, so there is no need to scrimp. Without them, the campaign looks unprofessional. Do not get embossed stationery and envelopes, though. When run through some laser printers, the varnish runs and stains.

The bulk of your campaign literature, however, will be advertising. Start early, because campaign literature production takes time, and you should start connecting with the voters as soon as possible. Too early always is better than too late. Too many campaigns have had to trash brochures because they came out too late—either because an issue was no longer relevant, or because it was simply too late to mail them before election day. And if you have to trash a whole press run, it is very likely the campaign will not have the money or the time to try again.

Do not expect delivery from the printer within a few days of project conception unless you are prepared to pay a premium. The amount of time varies depending upon the complexity of design and the printer's schedule.

When you miss deadlines, production time increases exponentially. For example, if you are two days late with a proof of your piece, your printing schedule will likely be delayed by *more* than two days, as you have now missed your scheduled press time and the printer has to fit your late project into a busy schedule. To get preferential treatment, you will have to pay a premium.

See also APPENDIX FIVE: MEDIA PUBLICATIONS AND SERVICES.

COLOR

Most campaign literature is in red, white, and blue for a good reason: studies have shown that those still are the most attractive colors to voters and the ones that cause the voters to trust the candidates. Some consultants would advise that you do not deviate from these colors just for the sake of being different, as your candidate may be considered just different enough not to be trusted. Others would advise that you need to do something to help your candidate stand out.

There often are good reasons for exceptions to the red, white, and blue motif. In a 1996 Illinois state senate contest, a candidate named Ken Dunkin produced literature in colors that mimicked those of the Dunkin' Donuts™ shops. Another exception is when a candidate is running in an area with a population dominated overwhelmingly by one ethnic group. A candidate running in a Mexican-American area may want to have literature in red, white, and green, for example. You also must think about the possibility of ethnic colors offending potential voters not of that group. However, if a certain college or high school is popular in your area, your literature may want to feature its colors. Beware of accidently using the favored colors of a local gang in your literature.

The fewer colors you use, the less costly your literature. Paper color does not count, so literature on, say, yellow paper with black ink is considered a one-color (black) job; literature on white paper with blue and red inks is a two-color job (blue and red).

Do not use more than four ink colors, because any color you desire can be created with four primary ink colors (red, blue, yellow, and black).

LAYOUT

A professional or competent student layout designer will produce the best look for your campaign literature. You can find designers in the telephone directory, or a local printer can recommend one. Low-budget campaigns can forego a designer and produce a decent design on a personal computer. Look for at least one campaign volunteer with design experience.

Whether you use a professional or not, however, keep the layout simple and clean. Here are a few other tips.

- Do not allow massive blocks of copy; people simply will not read them.
- Do not break the reader's eye flow with choppy, frenetic layout.
- Do not let the designer talk you into fancy, hard-to-read typefaces, too much decoration, inappropriate graphics, or odd color selections. Remember, your message—not the design—must take center stage.
- Do not use a lot of different typefaces: just because a printer has seventy-two typefaces available does not mean you should use them all.
- Do not let the unimportant overpower the important just because it is a good-looking graphic element.

MAILING

Have someone from the campaign talk directly to the post office you will be mailing from about regulations. Not only is there a dizzying array of conflicting postal rules, but interpretations of them vary from post office to post office. This conversation should happen early in the campaign, especially if you will conduct bulk mailings. Your request for a bulk-mail permit takes time to process.

The U.S. Postal Service has very detailed regulations on the size and weight of pieces, and how they must be labeled, sorted, bagged, and tied. There are basic bulk rates, carrier-route sorting, and a host of other factors to be taken into consideration. Some bulk mail is figured at a per-piece rate plus a per-pound rate. Again, talk to a specialist from your post office, or work with a representative from a direct mail consultant or fulfillment house (a firm that handles mailing chores such as label creation and affixing, sorting, bagging, and delivery to the post office). If you prepare it incorrectly, the Postal Service will return the whole job to you, undelivered—usually long after you wanted it in the voters' mailboxes.

I once had a direct-mail project that nearly drove me crazy. Bulk mail cannot be sent unless there are at least 200 pieces; if there are under 200 pieces, the order must weigh at least fifty pounds. Our project was 125 pieces, so first we considered trying to reach the fifty-lb. mark by including a useless piece of cardboard in some envelopes. But, we were told, each piece had to be identical. Then we considered mailing first class, which was incredibly expensive compared to bulk rate. Finally, we solved the problem by adding seventy-five names to the list. The piece did not need to be sent to those seventy-five people, but mailing 200 bulk rate was less expensive than sending 125 first class. These are the types of situations you will encounter time and again.

Postcards are an economical alternative to letters. For the Postal Service to process a postcard, it must be rectangular and a minimum of 3.5 inches by 5 inches, and a maximum of 4.5 inches by 6 inches, with a minimum thickness of .007 inches (a thicker stock holds up better when going through Postal Service machinery).

The postcard also must be the proper height-to-length ratio. To figure this, divide the length by the height. If the result is between 1.3 and 2.5, your piece is the proper size.

Do not design your piece first and try to calculate the postage later; comply with the rules from the beginning.

Try to barcode your mailing with five- or nine-digit zip codes (just above or below the address, or in a space in the lower right-hand corner measuring .62 inches high by 4.75 inches wide). This lowers costs while speeding delivery time. Computer software for creating barcoding is available.

Since 1996, the U.S. Postal Service has attempted to reduce "Non-Automation Compatible" direct mail in favor of "Automation Compatible," and the price differential is huge. Order Poster No. 97 as a reference guide.

The Postal Service uses electronic scanning equipment, so the address should be in a dark ink on a light background, and the paper stock should be matte (non-glossy) on the address side. Do not let your designer get too fancy. The address should be parallel with the long side of the piece, and the lines of the address should be flush left. Type of eight to fifteen points is acceptable for the address, with twelve being the preferred size. Sans-serif type (without curlicues) can be read better by equipment than serif type; humans, however can read serif type more easily.

If you print "address correction requested" on your mailings, misaddressed pieces will be returned, which is good if you want to update your mailing list but bad if you are trying to save money, because you will have to pay for the returns.

Also speak with a postal representative about the time it takes for pieces to arrive in the voters' hands from the time you deliver mail to the post office. It does your campaign no good if your literature arrives a month before people even know there is an election—or if it arrives a day after the election.

Ask specific questions. If the post office indicates your mail can take up to three weeks to arrive, does that mean three weeks from the moment you deliver it to the post office dock, or three weeks from when the post office begins to process it?

Individual campaigns do not qualify for bulk-mail discounts provided to not-for-profit organizations, but state and national parties and campaign committees may. You might want to work with or through your party organization on bulk mail.

Always "seed" the mailing list with the names of individuals, such as yourself, who will be able to report to the campaign when the pieces actually were received, if they were damaged, or if the labels were affixed sloppily. Such tests are a great spot-check for determining if something is going wrong.

Since there is so much that can go wrong with direct mail, use of a fulfillment house is strongly advised. Their people deal with mail all the time. Find one in the telephone directory under "direct mail" or "mail services."

TECHNOLOGY

With the advent of desktop publishing, even the most low-budget campaign can have good-looking literature. If you do not have access to a personal computer, your local printing firm, library, instant printing shop, college, or high school does. You can even do it at Kinko's™ copy shops with no training, as staff are happy to help. Scanners can turn photos into reproducible "halftones." (A halftone is a dot-patterned reproduction of a photo that allows it to be reproduced in printed materials.)

Most typesetters, designers, and printers want copy provided on a computer disk. Production from a disk is both cheaper and quicker than from traditional paper copy, known as "hard copy."

MESSAGE

Keep it simple and keep it clear. Your message should contain a call to action, and in this case the action is the recipient voting for your candidate.

Most readers are going to skim and not read the entire piece, so the most important information should jump out via larger or bolder type. Pay careful attention to headlines, as for a large number of readers, these will be the only copy they read. Do not boldface everything, though; all emphasis is no emphasis.

PRINTING

Shop around for printing. Obtain at least three competitive bids, as different printers have different specialties. The more comprehensive your specifications sheet, the more accurate the bid and there will be less chance for surprises. Specifications should include:

- Artwork (furnished by you, or will your designer/printer create?).
- Text format (hard copy or computer disk, with format/software indicated).
- Bleeds (artwork or printing that runs off the page).
- Binding (saddle-stitched [stapled] or glued).
- Colors, including number of colors.
- Delivery date.
- Delivery location and other instructions.
- Folds. (A three-panel piece, one with two folds to create three panels, is called a tri-fold, for example.)
- Name of job.
- Number of pages.
- Number of halftones (photos).
- Packing (do you want delivery in cartons or shrink-wrap?; are there other special instructions?).
- Paper stock.

- Quantity.
- Trim size (final size of the publication).

If you are unsure of specifications, your printer's representative can help. In addition, the printer can store some of your press run (at a fee) if you do not have the room. Standard acceptable overrun is ten percent, but you will have to pay for it, so you can request in advance a smaller overrun.

Use a union print shop; it may be slightly more expensive to print in a union shop, but it pleases labor without alienating anyone except the most rabid anti-unionists. Use the union symbol ("bug") on all your literature—but only if you are using a union printer.

TYPE

Make sure your typefaces on all materials are legible. If you have resources to hire a graphic designer, do not let him or her turn your literature into an arty showpiece that will win a graphics award but lose an election. If you do not like the design, chances are the voters will not either. If *you* cannot read the type, the *voters* will not even try.

Never handwrite any text that will be printed. Always type, even if it is just for a photo label or envelope. You may be able to read your handwriting, but there is a good chance someone else will not. Typing eliminates the opportunity for misunderstandings.

PHOTOS

I have never understood why so many candidates feel compelled to use childhood photos in their campaign literature. Everyone was a child once; is the voter more likely to vote for your candidate because he or she shows proof positive of childhood? Omit this type of photo in favor of one that actually has some relevance to the campaign and demonstrates the candidate's maturity and ability to do the job today.

Do not use bad photos on campaign literature. Nancy Kaszak, a 1996 Illinois congressional candidate, obviously spent a ton of money on one glossy, four-color direct-mail piece, which featured a fuzzy, blurry photo of her on the front. She lost.

Clearly label photos, but do not damage them by writing on them, even on the back. Instead, type pertinent information on an adhesive label and affix it to the back. Or use a grease pencil; its soft writing material does not harm the photo and can easily be removed. Do not put crop or sizing marks on the actual "live area" of the photo, but position them on the photo's white border instead, or indicate crop marks on a photocopy of the photograph.

See also MEDIA KIT-PHOTO, page 145.

COMMUNICATING WITH PRODUCTION PROFESSIONALS

When providing information for a printed piece to a designer, typesetter, or printer, the following tips will save you some headaches:

- The copy essentially should be in its final form. The first galley/proof is *not* an opportunity for rewrite. If you do major rewrites/reworks at later stages of the print process, the costs in dollars and time will be disastrous.
- Have your information on a 3-1/2" computer disk as well as in "hard copy" (printed) format.
- Delete any other files from the disk.
- Label the disk clearly with the program in which the file was created, file name(s), and a name and phone number for a campaign contact. Label the hard copy with the file name.
- Put directions on the hard copy only, not the computer file.
- When supplying a photo, put identifying information (name, page number it will be going on in the printed piece, photo number, anything else required) on the back of a photo. Ideally, place that information on a label first and then stick the label on the back of the photo. If you write on the back of the photo, the indentations will show through. You may wish to include a photocopy of the original photo to clearly illustrate positioning of the photo.
- Never write on the front of a photo.
- Never paper-clip a photo.

DIRECT MAIL LETTERS

Direct mail letters can be used not only for fundraising but to garner votes as well. For information on creating an effective direct mail letter, see FUNDRAISING-DIRECT MAIL, page 103. These principles generally are applicable to the vote-raising direct mail letter as well.

In vote raising, the one thing direct mail letters do better than anything else is to get voters who are not your candidate's natural constituents to vote for him or her—if the letters compellingly state the case why the voter's fundamental, personal interests are at stake and will be protected by your candidate. A well-crafted direct mail vote solicitation can get a Republican to vote for a Democrat, and vice versa.

But do not spend too much time on voters who oppose or strongly support your candidate. Target the majority of your efforts to the "swing" voters. See also STRATEGY-TARGETING, page 178.

SAMPLE BALLOTS

You may live and breathe politics, but to most people it is a difficult, confusing, and bothersome process. The sample ballot makes things easier for the voter because it shows him or her exactly where and how your candidate's name will appear on the ballot. The sample ballot should look exactly like the regular ballot; inclusion of your candidate's punch number (if appropriate) is crucial.

Sample ballots should be mailed, distributed door-to-door, or handed to people on their way to vote as close to the precinct door as legally possible.

Local laws may require that the words "sample ballot" or another disclaimer be included or that the sample ballot be of a different color than the actual ballot.

CAMPAIGNING

"Political campaigns are designedly made into emotional orgies...."
—James Harvey Robinson, *The Human Comedy*

The campaign will take an enormous amount of time from the candidate, the staff, and the candidate's family.

With time and money limited, concentrate your efforts on where they will do the most good. See also STRATEGY-TARGETING, page 178.

For your base, which already supports your candidate, minimal effort is necessary. Just letting the voters know you are out there may be sufficient. For example, if your candidate is a Democrat, the party faithful and Democratic straight-ticket voters may need only to know his or her name, party affiliation, and office, and you will receive their support. Do not ignore them, but do not waste a lot of time campaigning where you are strong, either. Do not preach to the choir. (Mine strong supporters for funds and volunteers, however.)

Concerning the base that is opposed to your candidate: forget them. This is hard for politicians who want everyone to love them. Even Ronald Reagan campaigned in Minnesota the weekend before the 1984 election—despite the certainty that Minnesota would go for

Walter Mondale. If the candidate is a liberal feminist, it is pointless to try to convert staunch conservatives—they are not going to change their minds, so do not squander precious resources.

The only effort you should make to reach the opposition's support is to create enough doubt in their minds about their candidate that they will not vote for him or her. See also CAMPAIGNING-NEGATIVE CAMPAIGNING, page 40. They are not going to vote for your candidate, but their sitting home or voting for a third-party candidate might help your candidate win. In 1992, both Bill Clinton and George Bush were successful in planting doubts among their opponent's traditional supporters. Bush-doubters were not going to vote for Clinton, but many of them did vote for Ross Perot, and that helped Clinton win.

You have to walk a fine line, however. If you get too negative, they will make a special effort to vote for their candidate despite their doubts. Harold Washington, as a South Sider, was initially not very popular with Chicago's West Side African-Americans, but virulent negative attacks on Washington by the opposition in his 1983 contest for mayor energized the West Siders' support for him.

The undecided and the ticket-splitters are your real battleground. They are the people on whom the campaign must focus at least eighty percent of its efforts. According to Dan N. Hazelwood, president of Targeted Creative Communications of Alexandria, Virginia, they fall into three categories: those who should be with you, but need a little encouragement (people who share your views but are slightly disenchanted); those who could be with you, if you work hard to get their votes (Reagan Democrats, for example); and those who could be with you only under unusual circumstances (such as suburban Republicans who voted for Illinois Democratic senate candidate Carol Moseley-Braun in 1992 because of the virulent attacks directed against her). [14]

Do not assume that voters will behave as they always have. Most Democrats did that in 1994, and most of them lost. An exception was Ted Kennedy, who ran a tough, hard Senate campaign that took pains to explain in detail what Democrats had done for the voters in the past. He won because he knew the voters had changed and he did not expect that they would continue to vote for him automatically.

Do not extrapolate the wrong data. In a typical election voters may behave in predictable ways, but wild-card factors unique to a particular election will skew that behavior. For instance, since Bill Clinton had no opposition in presidential primaries in 1996, some

Democratic voters took Republican ballots in primaries either to cast a vote with some meaning or to sabotage electable Republican candidates. This helped insurgent Republicans and hurt Republican regulars, while having the opposite effect on the Democrats.

Campaign efforts should focus on the candidate's strengths and away from weaknesses. John Kennedy and Ronald Reagan were born to be on television, but Richard Nixon should have avoided it. Both JFK and FDR were quick wits, capable of making incredibly funny, off-the-cuff comments at press conferences. If your campaign's candidate is like them, offer numerous interviews to the media. If the candidate is more plodding, he or she should appear in more controlled situations. If the candidate is energized by large audiences, more speeches are called for. If the candidate is awkward in large groups but is relaxed in small ones, hold more neighborhood coffees.

Do not criticize the voters. It was almost unbelievable, and after forty years in politics he should have known better, but Bob Dole when running for president in 1996 essentially told the voters they were stupid if they did not vote for him. While campaigning using this tactic, his poll numbers actually dipped below thirty percent, showing the utter lack of effectiveness of this unusual strategy.

Despite what the polls and your instincts indicate, always run a campaign as if you are five points behind and need to close the gap. Many campaigns have been lost by complacent favorites who thought they had the election wrapped up and relaxed. The *Chicago Tribune* notwithstanding, Thomas Dewey was unable to loaf his way into the White House.

Political consultant James Carville recommends a twenty-four hour schedule for the candidate on the final day. "You fill the entire last day with events," he said in *Campaigns & Elections*. "It tells voters that you really want the job. It captures all the media reports. Everybody loves it."[15] Such a schedule for Bob Dole at the end of the 1996 presidential campaign did not garner him the presidency, but it did galvanize Republican voters to re-elect a Republican congress.

Do not magnify the importance of your own electoral contest in the eyes of the voters. If your candidate is a Democrat running for dog-catcher in a Republican presidential election-year landslide, do not think that people will split their ticket. Facing such a situation, your candidate may find it more prudent to run in an off-year election or in one that holds more promise for your allies at the top of the ticket.

LAUNCHING THE CAMPAIGN

The announcement that your candidate is running for office is your first chance to make a splash and gain some publicity, so do not waste it by failing to host an event or by making that event boring.

Make sure the event is creative and fun. Invite the media and make sure friends and family attend to swell the size of the audience. Hand out press packets containing the candidate's biography, news releases on various subjects related to the campaign, and a "gimme" (a button or bumper sticker).

It is helpful to launch a campaign around something that will reinforce ideas about your candidate and the campaign itself—something that will play into a "theme" of the campaign. For example, if your candidate will be stressing ethics and honesty, you can launch the campaign against a backdrop of a statue of Abraham Lincoln.

On the platform, the candidate should be surrounded by a large group of heterogeneous supporters: men and women who are community group leaders, other poltical figures, local heroes, and area residents of various ethnic backgrounds and constituencies.

Your candidate should humanize the reasons he or she is running. Instead of dwelling on dry statistics, the candidate should highlight how his or her election will make the lives of real people better.

Do something that creates a photo opportunity. Is your candidate opposed to cuts in school-lunch funding? Have a group of youngsters at the campaign write letters on paper plates and send them to legislators, as one Illinois group did! Take an issue dear to your candidate and develop an interesting activity.

COFFEES

Coffees are small social gatherings in the homes of "regular people." Although they are small, coffees can have a significant impact. Ask as many supporters as you can to host a coffee.

These "regular people" supporters or volunteers invite friends and neighbors to their homes via a mailed invitation to meet the candidate, and then follow-up with a phone call. It is best to provide those invitations to the host, rather than taking the chance that the host will remember to buy invitations. The invitations should of course include the name, address, and phone number of the host, and time and date of the event. A map to the person's home is also useful.

Also, provide a checklist to the host of what he or she needs to do, with guidelines for hosting the event, including: "send invitations, follow up by phone, buy food and refreshments, clean the house," and other suggestions to make the event successful.

A member of the campaign should call the host a couple of days before the event as a reminder and to encourage the host to make those follow-up phone calls.

On the day of the event, a campaign representative must arrive before the scheduled time to help set-up and to place sign-in sheets or cards and campaign literature.

The candidate need not be there at the scheduled starting time; guests are going to trickle in late anyway. The campaign rep can talk to them until the candidate arrives. When the candidate arrives, the host should introduce each individual to the main attraction.

A key to coffee success is for the candidate to leave after:

- Explaining why he or she is running.
- Asking for the attendees to vote for him or her.
- Asking about issues in which the guests are interested.
- Taking a few questions.

Not only can the candidate visit several coffees or other events in an evening or on a weekend day by getting in and out fairly quickly, but he or she leaves the job of asking for money and volunteers to the host. In this way, the guest's friend is the "bad guy," not the candidate, and it is tough to say no to a friend.

The campaign must send a thank-you note to the coffee host afterward, and ideally to everyone who attended as well.

NEGATIVE CAMPAIGNING

"Going negative" is not a step to be taken lightly, although today more campaigns go negative more quickly than ever before.

Janice M. King, president of Janice King Communications, when discussing negative advertising in general, said that negative messages about competitors create FUD: fear, uncertainty, and doubt.[16] You have to consider seriously the implications of your candidate causing FUD and its resulting stresses on the political system.

Campaigns & Elections reported that Cathy Allen, president of Campaign Connection of Seattle, indicated that going negative might be the proper course when taking on an incumbent, when the opponent is outspending the candidate by large margins, when there is irrefutable information that the opponent has done something wrong, and when the candidate has little name recognition.[17]

For better or worse, negative campaigning works. According to Dean Michael Mezey of De Paul University,

> ...what negative advertising does is get your supporters committed and excited. Those who are indifferent are so turned off that they are less likely to vote, as are people who are for the other candidate—so not only does it help you, but it depresses turnout. The ideal, rational goal is to turn out your most committed supporters and make sure nobody else turns up. [18]

If you are making an outrageous charge against an opponent, document it. U.S. Senate candidate Al Salvi in 1996 insulted Jim Brady, President Reagan's former press secretary, a gunshot victim, and a national hero, by calling him a former machine-gun dealer. (Brady had endorsed Salvi's opponent, Richard Durbin.) The charge had not been verified and was completely unsubstantiated and, coming the last weekend of the campaign, was a gaffe from which Salvi could not recover.

Double-check everything. In a 1992 California state assembly race, a campaign released to the media information that its opponent was a pornographer—but the pornographer was actually a different man with the same name. Oops! In 1996 a Quebec legislator, in claiming vote fraud, gave an example of allegedly fraudulent names registered in his district: "Omar Sharif" living with "Martina Navratilova." Oops again. Turns out that Sharif is the son of the actor, and his wife is a stockbroker whose name really is Martina Navratilova.[19]

If you discover something damaging about your opponent, do not send it to the media anonymously. You can come right out and make charges, or you can request that the media print or broadcast the information without attribution to you or the campaign. The media generally will honor that request. If they receive it from an unknown source, however, they will either figure it is a trap or have no way to follow-up and learn more, so their only alternative is to ignore it.

Likewise, if your campaign receives unsolicited material about an opponent, it could be a set-up. Do not use it without independent verification.

What if the particular media source you release it to will not use it? Generally, there are others. If the newspaper is not interested, go to a radio station.

You also will have to do most of the research to convince the media to bite. "If you get seventy percent of the work done, that's about enough for reporters to follow it up," one Republican opposition-researcher told *U.S. News & World Report.* "If you give them thirty percent, most won't do the story."[20]

If the media will not cover the negative information on their own and the campaign has to promote it, the candidate generally has to be the one responsible for releasing the negative information, rather than a member of the campaign team. If the campaign is going to launch an attack, the candidate cannot expect to take refuge behind a staff member when the inevitable return-shelling commences.

If you are campaigning negatively via mailed or distributed campaign literature, however, the candidate should be kept out of the piece, with nothing more than a "Paid for by Citizens for Joe Goodguy" disclaimer. You do not want Joe Goodguy's picture on the piece so that the voters will actually think the negative information is about *him* instead of his opponent.

Negative literature should not be sent to your strong favorables or strong unfavorables. Send it to the swing voters.

Negative information has the most credibility if it comes from an outside source. If you can convince one of your supporting organizations to release it, so much the better. A Sierra Club rep saying your opponent is a polluter has more credibility than if you say it.

Do not bombard the public with reams of negative information; instead focus on potential hot buttons that are easy for voters to understand. The governor's mansion's massive food budget was always an issue when James Thompson was Illinois' chief executive in the 1970s and 1980s. People understood that what the state was spending on the governor's groceries was far out of whack compared to what they were spending at the supermarket.

Set the stage. Start making noises that the opponent is a big spender or a hypocrite before dropping the big bomb. Set that bomb off early. The closer to election day a negative attack is made, the less credibility it has.

Humor can be an effective form of negative campaigning. Although he did not win, Illinois Lieutenant Governor Bob Kustra gained some points in his 1996 U.S. Senate primary against state Senator Al Salvi by depicting Salvi, a personal-injury attorney, in humorous commercials showing a lawyer literally chasing an ambulance.

Do not make the attack too mean. In the 1993 Canadian national election, conservatives attacked the physical handicaps of the liberals' candidate for prime minister. Not only did the liberal win, but voters were so appalled at the conservatives' behavior that only two Tories were elected to Parliament from the whole country (the conservatives had previously held 154 seats)—effectively wiping out the entire party for one election cycle.

When the candidate is running against a member of another religion, he or she can attack the opponent's political positions on the issues, but not his or her religiosity. The candidate also must not act as if he or she is religiously superior to the opponent. These tactics have always backfired whether the opponent was John Kennedy or a member of the Christian right.

Negative campaigning can backfire in many other ways. It turns off voters and causes opponents to respond in kind. It can cause voters to wonder if your candidate has some of the same negatives his or her opponent does and can create a negative campaign opening for your candidate's opponent.

In a 1992 West Virginia Democratic congressional primary, Harley Staggers responded to a negative attack by an opponent by bragging that he never voted for a congressional pay raise. This gave opponent Allan Mollerhan an opening to point out that Staggers actually accepted the pay raises, which cost Staggers the election.

It is amazing how often campaigns make an attack on the basis of something on which their own candidate's record is less than stellar. In 1995 and 1996, supporters of the multi-married Bob Dole, Newt Gingrich, Phil Gramm, and Pete Wilson loved to tout how these—supposedly unlike Democrats—were "family values" candidates.

If you are the victim of a negative attack, come clean; do not lie or fudge. Admit "error" (rather than "guilt") if there was one. You *must* respond—and quickly. If you do not, the attack becomes the truth in the voters' minds. Mike Dukakis was incredibly slow to respond to attacks in the 1988 presidential campaign and has an early retirement to show for it. Bill Clinton, on the other hand, usually was the master of rapid response, and that skill brought him to the White House.

The campaign and the candidate should have discussed fully any negatives in the candidate's background before the attack, so the defense is prepared and waiting. When the attack comes, only the candidate and a few of the senior advisors should respond and should do so quietly. You do not want your attack-deflection strategy itself to become a story in the media. Unfortunately for the senator, press coverage of how Ted Kennedy's advisors were strategizing about Chappaquiddick brought increased media scrutiny of the incident.

The following are several methods and tactics of negative campaigning that may be used against your candidate:

- *Guilt by association*. An attempt to call into question the character, competency, honesty, or policies of a candidate because of asssociations with individuals with whom the candidate may be only peripherally involved. An example is the Democrats' effective use of Bob Dole's political association with House Speaker Gingrich against Dole in the 1996 presidential derby. A form of this is *vote pairing*, comparing the voting records of a candidate to that of an unpopular elected official. Democrats used this tactic against several members of congress in 1996 by comparing their votes to Gingrich's positions.
- *Gutter flyer*. Political literature circulated late in the campaign, attributable to no source, that offers vicious charges against a candidate. An example is the crude, racist literature circulated against Harold Washington in his 1983 race for Chicago mayor.
- *Red herring*. Use of a side issue totally unrelated to the campaign to make voters fear your candidate. North Carolina Senator Jesse Helms' 1990 campaign, in which his staff created an anti-affirmative action television commercial, helped make voters fearful of Helms' opponent, African-American Harvey Gantt, and Helms won.

The following are a few traditional strategies for dealing with a negative attack:

Admit it before the attack even comes. Jerry Ford was candid about the fact that he had started dating wife Betty before her divorce from her first husband was final, and Jimmy Carter's campaign could not make an issue of it in the 1976 presidential race.

Attack the attack, criticizing your opponent for negative campaigning, or you can respond with negative information about the opponent or the attack tactics as well—what lawyers call discrediting the witness. This is what the 1992 Clinton presidential campaign did with Gennifer Flowers. If possible, get a blue-ribbon source to refute the attack. [21]

Turn the attack into a positive. President Truman's Secretary of State Dean Acheson had once been dumped from an economic advisory post by President Roosevelt. That could have been considered a negative among FDR supporters, but Acheson's disagreement with Roosevelt had been over devaluation of the dollar, which could have been played as a positive to sound-money advocates. It is all in the spin.

Deflect it with humor. In 1988, Illinois Cook County board president George Dunne was tainted by scandal when two women he had sexual relationships with were later hired for county jobs. Supporters defended him by arguing he was a widower and therefore single, stressing the jobs were extremely low paying and not political plums, and marveling that a man in his seventies could be involved with two women. Amazingly, this worked, as most of the media comments were jocular ones on the "wow, what a man" defense. Everyone had a good chuckle and the scandal disappeared.

The humor strategy can backfire, however. If the charge is serious and the candidate is making jokes, that can alienate and anger even more voters.

Deflect it with sorrow. This is effective when the story is instinctively something that the public knows should have remained private, like the fact that the candidate's wife was pregnant when the couple married. Express your sorrow that the media or the opposition would bring up something so personal that is irrelevant to the campaign.

Stonewall by saying there is no story. This *never* works. Richard Nixon's resignation as president is the ultimate proof.

Stonewall citing higher motives. This seldom works because it makes the candidate look falsely pious. One situation in which it did work is when opponents accused 1990 Texas gubernatorial candidate Ann Richards of having smoked marijuana in the 1960s. She refused to answer the charges on principle, stating that for her to do so would encourage people not to give up drug or alcohol use because no matter how long they had been clean they would have to face those allegations. Believe it or not, it worked—in Texas yet. Richards not only won in 1990, but the issue did not arise during her reelection campaign in 1994.

Admit the indiscretion and ask for forgiveness. Ask people to make their decision on more important issues. This is the strategy actor Hugh Grant employed to return to the public's good graces after he was caught with a prostitute. Another lesson is to know when to remain silent. Grant took it too far by appearing on almost every talk show, and the public began to tire of his apologizing.

Neither admit nor deny the allegation. Instead, release reams of pertinent information, financial documents, and other related items that are so difficult for the media and the public to wade through that they will forget the whole thing.

Deny the charge and demand proof. This works only if the charges actually are not true. Spiro Agnew did this and discovered that the media had rock-solid proof of his crimes.

Deny the charge and demand an apology. This also does not work if the charges are true.

Blame the media and demand they reveal the unidentified source. This seldom works, unless the voters in your district generally hate the media. Plus, it angers the media so that they go after your candidate with an even greater vigor. Agnew loved to blame the media and ended up resigning the vice presidency.

Ignore it. If the charge is small or little-publicized, sometimes it will go away. Mayor Richard J. Daley of Chicago did this with the only allegation of financial impropriety that had ever been made against him: a charge in the 1970s that he and his wife had secretly established a real estate firm that did business with the city. The firm was small, the business was petty, nobody cared, he ignored the criticism, and the charges disappeared.

Whatever your initial strategy is to counter the attack, stick with it. If the campaign fumbles around changing from strategy to strategy, that in itself becomes a story in the media.

Once the campaign has responded, move on. It is tough for talky candidates to be quiet about the subject, but if they are, coverage of the scandal usually diminishes.

If the charge is sexual impropriety, it is imperative for the candidate's spouse to publicly stick by him or her.

The setting for denial may be important. Your candidate sitting on a living room couch with a spouse is more effective than appearing alone at a podium.

If you cannot do the time, do not do the crime. Scandal usually results from sexual or financial indiscretion or lying. If the candidate avoids these traps, they cannot come back to haunt him or her.

Low-Profile Campaigns

The smart candidate "plays possum" strategically in a low-profile contest because the contests far down on the ballot are where the old-fashioned political rules still apply. There will not be much media coverage, so the campaign has to concentrate on increasing the candidate's name recognition through flyers; newspaper and (if affordable) broadcast advertising; billboards and yard and window signs; and giveaways such as hats, buttons, bumper stickers, and t-shirts. Party backing and/or alliances become all the more important.

Keep the message simple. No one wants a thirty-point plan from a candidate for dog-catcher.

If you can focus on some oddity in the candidate's low-profile run, so much the better. While a race for congress is not low-profile, Illinois congressional candidate Rod Blagojevich used an interesting tactic in the 1996 primary. He ran broadcast commercials with people mangling the pronunciation of his name and ads and billboards with the syllables and accent marks highlighted, thereby creating name recognition—and a victory.

Write-in Campaigns

In 1996 in Chicago's Twenty-Fifth Ward, Ambrosio Medrano was the only candidate on the ballot for ward committeeman. Then he was convicted of bribery and sentenced to prison. He refused to remove his name from the ballot, even going so far as to admit that he was remaining so that after he won he could resign and the party bosses, instead of the voters, could pick his successor. Cook County Commissioner Joseph Mario Moreno, an elected official with a blue-ribbon track record and well-financed campaign coffers, decided to run a write-in campaign against Medrano. It was not even close: Medrano, the candidate on his way to the federal pen, won easily. It may not take a Harvard degree to write-in a candidate's name, but it might as well.

If you are considering a write-in campaign, I have two words for you: forget it.

Relaxation

Both the candidate and the staff should build in some time away from campaigning to relax. That is easier said than done, but a tired candidate and staff make mistakes that often are fatal to a campaign. A candidate and staff who have spent some time with family, friends, and hobbies become recharged, reenergized, and can think more clearly.

Ronald Reagan, when running for president in 1976 and 1980, tried to take a nap every day. Despite his advanced age, he looked fresh and could think fast enough to make the jokes that put people at ease. Bob Dole in the 1996 presidential campaign was obviously an individual who did not nap—and should have.

CANDIDATE

"One must have the friendliness of a child, the enthusiasm of a teenager, the assurance of a college boy, the diplomacy of a wayward husband, the curiosity of a cat, and the good humor of an idiot."
—Emmanuel Celler, former New York congressman

The potential candidate and staff must inventory their strengths and weaknesses and compare those to other candidates' strengths and weaknesses. As part of that inventory, candidates must ask themselves the following questions:

- Do I really want the political office?
- Do I know what I want to do with the office? ("The vision thing," as George Bush said.)
- Do I have the time to take away from my job to campaign and the time to serve in the office?
- Can I gather a staff who also can afford to take time off from work?
- Is this the right time?
- Can I and my family take the inevitable criticism?
- Can I win?
- In terms of my reputation and bank account, can I afford to lose?
- Can I raise the money?
- Can I afford a loan if I need more money than I can raise?
- Can I pay off the debt that may be left at the end of the campaign?
- Can I muster the other resources of other individuals? (Endorsers, consultants, specialists, volunteers.)

If the balance is positive and the candidate has good credentials, it may be the time to enter the contest.

Columnists Jack Germond and Jules Witcover report a joke campaign managers tell. A dog food manager complains to a staffer about poor product sales, saying "We use the best ingredients; we have the best packages and the lowest price. We have the most salesmen. What's wrong?" "Dogs won't eat it," the staffer replies.[22]

The candidate with the best credentials in the world cannot win without at least some likability and some ability to connect with the voters. Sometimes it does not take much; the electoral success of Lyndon Johnson, Richard Nixon, and Phil Gramm is proof of that. Before entering the race, however, take a serious, sober assessment of the candidate's likability and humanity. The candidate must show some warmth with people and must appear tolerant, concerned, and caring even when asked ridiculous questions. If there just is not any humanity at all, or if it cannot be credibly cultivated, the race may not be worth running.

The race also is not worth running if the candidate does not particularly know why he or she is in it. A Roger Mudd interview with Ted Kennedy in 1980 sunk the senator's presidential bid when it revealed Kennedy did not have a clue why he was running. If the candidate and the campaign do not know, the voters will not either.

It also is seldom productive to make a kamikaze run for an office the candidate is guaranteed to lose just to get his or her name known. While that is a strategy that worked in the days of Abraham Lincoln, in today's winner-take-all society, a defeat gives the candidate the image of "loser" that is a serious handicap in the next electoral contest.

The candidate must seriously consider whether the campaign will bankrupt his or her family. Although not running for office, Bill Veeck, when he fulfilled his dream of buying the Chicago White Sox in 1975, mortgaged his home to do so; he and his wife never lived there again. Some politicians have done the same in an attempt to fulfill their dreams, but that is a very serious gamble in which *all* family members should be in *complete* agreement. George Washington and Thomas Jefferson died in debt. Jimmy Carter discovered he was over one million dollars in arrears when he left the White House, and as of this writing, Bill Clinton's personal deficit is even larger.

Potential candidates also should take a long, hard look at their pasts to determine if there are some sexual, financial, or family indiscretions that could become public knowledge—or even some innocent action that can be twisted into something sordid. Rest assured, the information *will* become known. One Chicago political activist jokes that if he ever runs for office, he is sure someone will find a photo of him taken in the 1970s with the Village People.

It is unfortunate, but even as we approach the millenium a candidate still will do better if he or she is married or engaged. Opponents have been known to run whisper campaigns about the sexual orientation of candidates who are single.

Candidates should be themselves to the greatest extent possible, though. Remember how President Ronald Reagan's people kept saying "let Reagan be Reagan"? They realized that when they let the Gipper be his whimsical self, people liked him, but when they tried to force speeches on him that did not suit his personality, the results were disastrous. It was painful for all to watch Reagan criticize the Democrats during the 1992 presidential campaign for consistently nominating governors for the presidency (when everyone knew that having been a governor had essentially been Reagan's only qualification for the office of chief executive). Who stuck that speech in front of him?

On the other hand, the campaign should try to mute the candidate's more oddball behaviors for the duration of the race. If a candidate is fond of flashy or out-of-date clothing, raunchy jokes, conspiracy theories, lewd gestures, or diatribes against certain sexual, ethnic, or racial groups, he or she should forego indulging in these charming personal idiosyncrasies until after the election. Although he won, Congressman Martin Hoke of Ohio was not helped in his 1994 campaign by his on-air comments about a woman's "beeeg breasts." [23]

If the candidate has a hot temper or appears too loud and boisterous, here is a tip: drill the candidate again and again with questions that normally elicit an angry or loud response. Drill to the point of boredom. The candidate will begin to sound boring giving the answer, too, which is exactly what you want. Better boring than bizarre. Boring candidates win more often than bizarre ones.

Laughingstocks never win. Dan Quayle may still emerge victorious in some election, but having been the butt of jokes nationally for four years, that is unlikely.

The candidate should never make a comment in public that he or she does not want to be known to everyone. Do not feel it is safe to joke about a certain ethnic group when you think none of its members is present, or to make an anti-female comment to an all-male group. Republican Clayton Williams was sailing along toward becoming governor of Texas in 1990, until he made a joke about rape to an all-male audience. Female voters found out about the remark and turned against him in droves. Ann Richards was elected to the post Williams had sewn up until he opened his mouth.

As Richard Nixon proved, not every successful candidate instinctively is comfortable with handshaking and meeting people. These are necessary, so work on them if the candidate is not a natural. Handshakes should be firm but not wimpy, nor too strong. Do not give a woman a wimpy handshake either—use the same shake for everyone.

Above all, the candidate should believe in what he or she is advocating. It was clear to the voters in 1984 that Illinois Senator Charles Percy, after having been the quintessential progressive Rockefeller Republican all his life, did not really agree with the right-wing opinions he was espousing to curry favor with Illinois' Reaganites. His phoniness turned off supporters and opponents alike, and the three-term senator lost—to a liberal Democrat, Paul Simon.

Thomas Boswell in his book *Why Time Begins on Opening Day* described the five types of major league baseball managers.[24] With the addition of one, Boswell's definitions correspond quite nicely to the different types of political candidates.

Boswell's categories are:

- The Little Napoleon.
- The Peerless Leader.
- The Tall Tactician.
- The Uncle Robbie.
- The Immortal.

My addition is:
- The Bureaucrat.

"The Little Napoleon" was the nickname for John McGraw, a baseball manager from the 1890s through the 1930s, primarily for the New York Giants. Little Napoleons are scrappy, intense, emotional—and usually are in hot water for one reason or another. "A person of passion," Boswell wrote. A person who had to fight for everything he got.

A more modern-day baseball counterpart would be Billy Martin, a successful but often-fired manager during the 1970s and 1980s. A political counterpart would be Harry S. Truman.

"The Peerless Leader" was the nickname for Frank Chance, boss of the Chicago Cubs from 1905 to 1912. A Peerless Leader usually was a

player who was very good but not a superstar, "a man of discipline, honesty, courage, and dignity...a person of character," Boswell wrote. A modern Peerless Leader would be Joe Torre of the New York Yankees. A political Peerless Leader would be Adlai Stevenson.

"*The Tall Tactician*" was Connie Mack, manager of the Philadelphia Athletics for fifty years. Tall Tacticians are strategic and intelligent, even cunning. Interestingly though, despite their brainpower, they often fail as managers.

Gene Mauch, who twice brought the California Angels to the last game of the playoffs only to blow the pennant, is an heir to the Tall Tactician title. Lyndon Johnson and Richard Nixon, two crafty politicians who ultimately failed, were Tall Tacticians.

"*Uncle Robbie*" was Wilbert Robinson, the Brooklyn Dodgers' skipper from 1914 to 1931. Uncle Robbies are compassionate, humorous people-pleasers who, despite sometimes appearing to be not too smart, often are incredibly successful.

Tommy Lasorda of the Los Angeles Dodgers was an Uncle Robbie, as are Gerald Ford and Bill Clinton.

"*The Immortal*" is the superstar who becomes boss as an accolade for playing accomplishments that have nothing to do with management ability. Ty Cobb and Frank Robinson were immortals.

In the political arena, Ulysses S. Grant, Dwight Eisenhower, and Ronald Reagan were Immortals, honored with the presidency because of their successes in completely different venues. It never seems to matter whether or not Immortals are successes as managers or elected officials. The public continues to love them anyway.

Boswell wrote his book in 1984, before the sixth type of baseball manager became prevalent. *The Bureaucrat* is unfortunately exemplified by most of today's major league managers—bland, faceless entities, more interested in policy than people, promoted from somewhere in the organization to toe the company line while ostensibly appearing to be in charge.

In the political arena, these types get elected and defeated with depressing regularity without the public feeling very strongly about them one way or another. George Bush and Michael Dukakis fit into this category.

How do these categories affect your campaign? First, you need to determine into which category your candidate naturally fits so he or she can run on the strengths inherent in it. If the candidate is a

Bureaucrat, that is fine; bureaucrats get elected. He or she should focus on policies and reliability, rather than look phony pretending to exhibit the passion of a Little Napoleon.

They also let you define your candidate's opponent. Once you categorize the opponent, you can play on the weaknesses endemic among his or her type.

They also let the campaign fine-tune the candidate's behavior. If the candidate is an Uncle Robbie, considered friendly but a lightweight, perhaps he or she should take steps to exhibit more of the characteristics of the Peerless Leader.

Baseball managers seldom move between categories, but politicians often do. Bob Dole has unfortunately gone from being a Peerless Leader to a Bureaucrat. Ronald Reagan was an Immortal, but worked on displaying the attributes of the Peerless Leader and could easily have been described as an Uncle Robbie.

If your candidate is an Immortal—a football star, entertainer, or well-known military hero—you have nothing to worry about.

Play ball!

RESIDENCY

Very often it is legal for a candidate to run in a district in which he or she does not live. Legal yes, smart no, as the candidate's opponent is guaranteed to make this an issue. It is not enough, and is insulting to the residents, for the candidate to say, "I'll move if I win." The candidate has to demonstrate some commitment to the district by moving prior to the election—even if it is just by renting an inexpensive apartment. Doing so just for the duration of the campaign can be made into an issue too, however, so rent the apartment—and move into it—well before the beginning of the campaign.

NICKNAMES

Nicknames are best to be avoided on the ballot. Friends may know the candidate as "Sugar" or "Slugger," but it is best to use his or her given name on the ballot. Most of the voters do not know the candidate by the nickname, and it usually makes the candidate seem to be not very serious.

An exception is a nickname by which the candidate made his or her claim to fame. The musician known as "Iceman" ran for Cook

County commissioner, and his name on the ballot was Jerry "Iceman" Butler so his fans could know who he was. He won.

Particularly to be avoided are nicknames based on an issue, like Joe "Non-Incumbent" Smith and Richard "Save-a-Baby" Roe. These make the candidate seem a bit far out.

They also can get a candidate removed from the ballot. In 1996 in Illinois' Seventh Congressional District's Republican primary, a judge voided Les "Cut-the-Taxes" Golden's candidacy, ruling that not only was "Cut-the-Taxes" not allowable, but that Golden due to his use of it could not appear on the ballot at all—even without his slogan.

COMPORTMENT

"Don't apologize. Lose it your way or win it your way."
—Whitey Herzog, baseball manager [25]

"In politics it's better to be setting the pace than reacting to other people," said political consultant David Axelrod of Axelrod & Associates. "Campaigns are about defining the issues upon which the election is going to be decided, and making sure those issues are your issues and not your opponent's issues."[26]

Campaign staff always should give the appearance of being in control. Always enter a room confidently, comfortably, and self-possessed. Take the initiative. It is human nature to react to a crisis by hoping it will go away. Be the one putting the opposition into that reactive mode by taking the initiative; conversely, you should never think that a crisis is going to go away by itself, although sometimes you get lucky.

As in football, the best defense is a good offense. Whether in a debate, interview, or speech, the candidate should take charge and get his or her points across without waiting to be asked a specific question that may never come.

Be surprising. Ronald Reagan rattled Jimmy Carter by giving the Georgian a robust handshake before their 1980 presidential debate, and Carter was off-balance the rest of the evening. In a 1996 debate, President Clinton shook up Bob Dole by furiously writing notes in plain sight on the platform before the debate began, giving Dole the impression that Clinton was suddenly thinking of all these great points to make and forcing Dole to loose his concentration.

Self-confidence inspires trust; fear and evasiveness create bad feelings among members of the media and voters alike. Arrogance, particularly a tone of moral superiority, creates resentment and should be avoided. That is why arguments should be framed as how voting for the candidate will improve the everyday lives of the public, rather than as great ideological issues that people neither understand nor care about. That is the mistake that both the extreme left and the extreme right make, and that is why their condescending attitudes of moral superiority turn people off. Liberals stumbled in the 1980s because they were perceived as caring more about process than people, and conservatives sometimes lose because they are perceived as caring more about ideology than people.

Self-awareness is important too, because it allows the candidate to confront an issue instead of being engulfed by it. Mayor Richard M. Daley of Chicago has never been particularly articulate, but he knows it. In a television commercial in his 1989 campaign, he said "I may not be the best speaker in town, but I know how to bring people together and run a government." He diffused the issue before it became one.

Be disciplined; do what you know has to be done, and do it with focus—rather than going off in several different directions.

While smoothing the rough edges and suppressing unusual personality quirks, the candidate should essentially be himself or herself. Who can forget how ridiculous Mike Dukakis looked in 1988 riding in an Army tank? It just was not who he was.

Ideally, the candidate will look like an underdog. Americans love a long-shot, but demand the long-shot look like a winner, too. You want to give the impression that your candidate is fighting hard to prevail over tough odds, but not that he or she is a loser.

The candidate may want to select a role model to emulate. Bill Clinton did that, emulating John Kennedy, and it worked. But as James Coppersmith of WCVB-TV Boston says, "Don't just be a style thief. Discard what's bad about them and improve what is good. Then mix these elements into *your* style—without trying to *become* the person you are emulating."[27]

Encourage criticism and ideas. It is easy to be removed from real public opinion in a sea of supporters and admirers. Criticism and suggestions allow the campaign not only to follow public opinion, but to understand how to shape it as well.

The candidate and senior staff never should express any doubt that the candidate is going to win. If they do, morale will plummet—and contributions will cease. Instead, they should publicly express confidence that the candidate is going to win, period.

Take some risks, and never second-guess yourself. Do not let what went wrong yesterday put a damper on today and tomorrow. Learn from your mistakes.

ALCOHOL/DRUGS

"Providence looks after fools, drunkards, and the United States," according to the old saying. However, it is best not to tempt Providence too much. A candidate may want to abandon alcohol consumption (at least in public) during the course of the campaign. In the atmosphere of the 1990s, few people are going to pressure an individual who declines a drink. If that happens, the candidate should indicate he or she is driving or taking medication.

It is a bad idea to drink alcohol before a speaking engagement as, depending on the individual, it may dry the speaker's mouth or throat and change the timbre of his or her voice. Alcohol obviously also can make a person less sharp or alert.

On the other hand, it may be desirable to take a drink or two for fellowship. Former Congressman Dan Rostenkowski once told a class at DePaul University that Jimmy Carter would have been a much more successful president had he merely had a few drinks with congressmen. Much of President Truman's achievements were created with the help of bourbon, while Lyndon Johnson's were lubricated with Cutty Sark. Jim Thompson, a high-priced attorney, served four terms as governor of Illinois. Occasionally he would have a few beers in public with college students to show he was a regular guy.

Obviously, drinking has to be a personal decision by the candidate and each member of the staff, but it is obviously much better to err on the conservative side. No one from the campaign, particularly the candidate, should ever drive after having had even one drink. The first scandal that plagued Rostenkowski was when his car was stopped by a police officer after he had a couple of beers at his high school reunion. No big deal for most of us, but disastrous for a politician. If the candidate has had even one drink, a staffer should drive or the candidate should take a cab. It is a good idea to choose one aide as the designated driver for any event serving alcohol.

No one has developed a simple answer for dealing with past use of illegal drugs. There is the "I didn't inhale" approach of Bill Clinton, which leads to ridicule. There is the "I only tried it once" approach of many politicians, which sounds phony. There is the full-disclosure approach of Congressman Patrick Kennedy of Rhode Island, and there is the no-comment approach of former Texas Governor Ann Richards. The campaign must examine the unique circumstances of the candidate and the constituency to determine which approach is best. See also CAMPAIGNING-NEGATIVE CAMPAIGNING, page 40.

If a candidate is taking a prescribed medication that also is frequently abused by drug addicts, he or she may want to obtain a prescription to a less notorious drug. President George Bush came under fire for his use of a legal and prescribed air-sickness medication.

GROOMING

The candidate's grooming and clothing deliver the first message about him or her to the voters, who make a decision about the trustworthiness, education, sophistication, viability, and other attributes of the candidate based on that message. The cliché is true: you never get a second chance to make a first impression.

Candidates should dress for where they are going, not where they are. Since the candidate's goal is government service, most of the time he or she should dress as if going to an interview for an office job. Any other mode of dress—such as Lamar Alexander's flannel shirts — opens the candidate to ridicule.

It is a mistake to dress down to suit the crowd. An audience of truck drivers or waitresses is not going to vote for someone just because he or she dresses like they do. But everybody wants to vote for someone who looks like a winner. If the candidate is attending a more casual event, he or she should dress in appropriate sportswear and should not look like Richard Nixon walking on the beach in a business suit and wing-tip shoes. Even sportswear should be tasteful and of high quality, however.

Candidates' clothes should be fashionable but not faddish, and slightly on the conservative side, even if the candidate and constituents are members of ethnic groups who favor more trendy clothing. One of the first things campaign spokesperson John Jenkins told me when I interviewed him about African-American Chicago Alderman Ed Smith's 1996 candidacy for congress in a predominantly African-

American district was that Smith was "a hard worker, not flashy or fly."

Wearing darker-colored clothing results in your candidate being taken more seriously than if he or she were in lighter-colored apparel. Although women can be more colorful than men, they should avoid bold stripes, polka dots, and flowery or large patterns and frills, which draw attention, but not to the candidate's message. Solid colors look better than patterns, and some patterns do particularly strange things in television or newspaper pictures, as do shiny fabrics.

Blazers are generally great for women, with either pants or skirts. Dresses are great if they are fashionable—they should not make the candidate look like Granny on the *Beverly Hillbillies*, however. Skirt lengths should be around the knee, with stockings flesh-colored or off-black. The skirts Cybill Shepherd and Christine Baranski wear on *Cybill* are fine for Beverly Hills divas, but are a little too short for candidates who may wish to emulate their glamorous look—and who want to sit comfortably in front of people. Yet, women have to be careful about looking too masculine or severe.

Women generally should not wear hats, which create odd shadows on the face, particularly under bright lights. The hats also become objects of attention and sometimes ridicule, and you do not want the focus to be on the candidate's chapeau instead of on her message.

Men should not wear short-sleeved business shirts. The candidate is running for elected office, not math teacher. A stationery store's worth of pens in the breast pocket is not a great fashion accessory either.

Men should wear polished shoes with laces—they do not call the other kind "loafers" for nothing. Socks should be dark and over the calf. Nothing looks worse than six inches of a man's hairy leg showing between a pants cuff and a sock when he is on a dais—or on television—with his legs crossed. Pants cuffs should rest slightly on the shoe when a man is standing—otherwise, he looks like he is waiting for a flood.

Bow-ties are out. They convey the message that the wearer is a bit of an oddball, and they flutter like a butterfly when the wearer speaks. Senator Paul Simon was an exception; he made the bowtie his trademark and wore it well, but his neckwear got him some ribbing on *Saturday Night Live,* and jokes may not be the type of attention your candidate needs.

The candidate should buy clothes that actually fit, not the size that fit ten years ago or the size that he or she would like to be. Stocky celebrities Orson Welles and Jackie Gleason always looked great in real life, but when Gleason was playing a character who was a loser, he wore clothes that were too small. A candidate who is skinny but who is wearing clothes that are too big looks either like a little kid or a victim of a fatal disease.

For a man, a wristwatch, wedding band or one other ring, cufflinks, and a tieclip are about the maximum in jewelry that can be worn. ID bracelets, earrings, and medallions and chains around necks and over suits and ties all give impressions of shiftiness or extremism. In a casual situation, one neck chain with a religious or other appropriate symbol revealed by a partially open shirt is acceptable.

Women can of course wear more jewelry, but it should not be excessive, large, or tasteless. Madonna, so far, has not achieved elected office. Avoid necklaces or bracelets that might bang into a microphone. One pierced earring in each ear is stylish, but more than one or body piercings elsewhere make the woman who wears them appear as if she wants to be a rock star.

When choosing a hairstyle, women should think about how it will look in a photograph and particularly how it will look when the newspaper inevitably uses it five years down the road. More mainstream styles are therefore preferable over something trendy.

Choose one that is easy to maintain, unlike Nancy Reagan, so you will not need the constant companionship of a hairdresser. Also, the hairstyle should be able to bounce back and look fine on a windy day. It also should not cover the candidate's eyes.

Men, being bald is okay. If Captain Jean-Luc Picard of *Star Trek: The Next Generation* were running for office, no one would hesitate to vote for him. People love to play "spot the toupee," however, and tend to laugh at the man wearing one. Transplants usually can be spotted, too. Never comb remaining hair in an odd way to cover a bald spot. Rudolph Giuliani's comb-over has actually become an issue in his mayoral campaigns, and one would think New Yorkers might have more important things to worry about.

Men also should avoid excessively long hair and ponytails. If the candidate colors his or her hair, frequent touch-ups are a must during the campaign. Hairspray should be kept off the skin, because it adds an extra shine.

For men, I think beards and mustaches are acceptable, but some political consultants are dead-set against them. If you wear a beard or a mustache, keep it well-trimmed and even. Grizzly Adams, like Madonna, has not yet been elected to office.

Overhead lighting deepens the shade of dark circles under the eyes, so keep your head up. They also can be eliminated with a concealer makeup.

Women should avoid the Tammy Faye Bakker look. Eye shadows should be natural, never bright. Keep eyeliners and shadows away from below the eye. Lipsticks should be somewhat natural as well; avoid the Joan Crawford 1940s cherry Life-Saver look. Fingernails also should be well-groomed. Avoid odd designs or long spikes.

Carry your own makeup for touchups or a complete redo for television. Men's campaigns should not be afraid to carry makeup for television appearances, either. Richard Nixon, after his five o'clock shadow helped him lose the 1960 presidential race, would have been the first to agree. As late as the 1980 presidential contest, candidates made an issue of makeup. Now, they all wear it.

Outerwear is just as important as inside attire. In 1992, George Bush kept campaigning in a raincoat that looked like something Columbo had discarded, and this did not help the perception of the president's "transcendent dorkiness" (columnist Molly Ivins' phrase).

Glasses are acceptable, but have them coated in a glare-dulling material. Otherwise, bright lights reflecting off the lenses could give the candidate an odd look. Large, dark-colored frames or tinted lenses send the wrong messages, so stick with thin frames and clear glass.

Before going out, stand in front of a mirror and squint. If something is particularly noticeable even through blurred vision, take it off or change it.

Posture is important, so stand up straight like your mother told you. Tall women and extremely tall men tend to hunch over to deal with the rest of humanity—do not do it. Standing up straight makes you look more confident and in charge, and studies have shown that the taller candidate usually wins the election.

The candidate should bathe. I have met enough candidates to know this is not something that can go unsaid. Use deodorant and cologne or perfume, but nothing too heavy. You do not want the voters to smell the candidate before they see him or her.

Give your fieldworkers a tactful lecture about grooming. You do not want them turning off more voters than they recruit because they look scary. Remember the "clean for Gene" tactics Senator Eugene McCarthy's fieldworkers used when he sought the 1968 presidential nomination? His hippie supporters got haircuts, shaved, bathed, and put on ties or dresses when they went in the field to promote their candidate. Something else that unfortunately cannot go without saying: your fieldworkers should not smell like liquor, either.

IMPROPRIETY

"Caesar's wife must be above suspicion," according to the traditional saying. Like Caesar's wife, the candidate, family members, and top staff must be above suspicion as well. Time was when a candidate could engage in conflict of interest or infidelity and, if it was not on a grandiose scale, get a pass from the media and the public. No more.

If you can not do the time, do not do the crime. Before the campaign even begins, the candidate should sell or place in a blind trust financial interests that may cause conflicts. For example, the candidate for city council needs to divest of stock in a company that the council will consider as a vendor.

As Chicago's appointed consumer services commissioner, Jane Byrne was famous for racking up parking tickets. When she decided to run for mayor, she paid all the tickets long before she declared or filed. End of issue.

QUESTIONS

The candidate should answer questions calmly. When the audience or reporters keep asking the same question over and over again to get a rise out of the candidate, he or she should coolly repeat the answer with slightly different wording. The questioner will eventually give up.

The candidate also may be asked the same question more than once at different times. He or she should be on guard for this and give the same answer as the previous time.

Sometimes in an attempt to befuddle the candidate, a questioner will ask a confusing package of questions. The candidate should simply pick the question he or she can answer best, respond to it, and ask the questioner to repeat the others. Chances are, he or she will not bother. Once when asked a particularly complex series of questions by a reporter, President Lyndon Johnson retorted, "I'll answer that if you can repeat it." He could not.

When an audience is present, if a question comes from someone without a microphone it should be repeated by the candidate as a service to all those present. It also gives the candidate a chance to pause and think about the answer, and to blunt a sharp question, if necessary.

When an audience member asks a strange or belligerent question, the candidate can reframe it in a more advantageous manner. For instance, if the questioner asks, "Why are you a flag-burner?," the candidate can respond, "What I believe the gentleman is asking is why am I opposed to a constitutional amendment that would specifically prohibit flag desecration. While I abhor flag desecration, I believe the fundamental right to free speech must be protected...."

The candidate never should ridicule the questioner, no matter how tempted. It makes the candidate, not the questioner, look bad.

HUMOR

The ability to be humorous is a great asset, as Franklin Roosevelt, John Kennedy, and Ronald Reagan proved. Humor can relieve pressure, diffuse difficult situations, and be used to avoid answering tough questions. When humor falls flat, however, it can be a disaster.

If the candidate does not have a natural, sophisticated ability to pull off humor like FDR, JFK, or Reagan, or if his or her sense of humor tends to the bizarre, crude, or cruel, keep it under wraps. Better boring than bizarre, and better serious than losing all credibility by looking like the village idiot.

FUN

"The day most wholly lost is the one on which one does not laugh," said the French author Nicolas Chamfort. In the heat of battle, it is easy to take things too seriously. Try to have some fun in the campaign. It is fun to meet new people, to have an effect on others, and to work together for a good cause.

John Kennedy was startled by a senior advisor's counsel to have fun in the president's first meeting with Soviet Premier Nikita Khrushchev, but after a rocky start the two used their personal relationship to diffuse the Cuban missile crisis and create the Nuclear Test Ban Treaty.

The candidate's having fun has a good effect on the voters. Franklin Roosevelt and Ronald Reagan clearly enjoyed campaigning and governing, and the voters responded positively.

CONSTITUENCY

"There is very little difference between one man and another; but what little there is, is very important."
    —Words of a carpenter, quoted in *The Importance of Individuals*

Learn something about the electorate. If the candidate's top issue is opposition to immigration and he lives in a predominantly Hispanic district, there is no reason to waste time and money running. Talk to people in the district, journalists, and party officials to find out about the constituency before making the run.

When making a campaign appearance, the candidate or campaigners should address issues important to the particular audience. The host group or organization is your best source on those issues. By your boning up on the issues, not only can the audience's needs be addressed, but the campaign can become prepared for the tough questions that the audience will likely ask.

VOTER PROFILES

It is imperative to know the demographics of the district in which the candidate is running. I have worked for a community newspaper in Chicago (*Near West Gazette*) with a distribution that comprises African-American, Hispanic-American, Italian-American, and yuppie areas. It amazes me how often African-American candidates endeavor to appeal only to the African-American community, Italian-Americans to the Italian-American community, and others to only their perceived base constituencies.

They lose, while the winners know what makes all of those communities tick. While it is true that the campaign should essentially ignore people dead-set against the candidate, it should definitely not ignore voters outside its core base who may be persuadable. In 1996, *National Review* reported, Bill Clinton's presidential campaign actually ran ads on Christian radio stations, indicating that Clinton's views were in sync with Christians on such issues as curfews and school uniforms. The Clinton campaign was going after every vote.[28]

Learn about voters from the county clerk or board of elections, census data, property tax records, and the demographic research performed by the local college or university. You also can speak with members of the media. You want to know about:

- Age.
- Ethnicity.
- Family patterns (marrieds, singles, children, gays/lesbians).
- Gender.
- Hot issues.
- Income.
- Party affiliation.
- Population.
- Voting habits (high turnout/low turnout, frequency of absentee voting, related issues).
- Typical political leanings of area residents.

Michael Barone, in an article in *U.S. News & World Report,* categorized the seven species of voters, even giving examples from television shows. The magazine's "field guide" of voters can be used as a tool to categorize your district's voters in order to run a more effective campaign:.

- *Populist traditionalists.* Exemplified by the father on *Roseanne,* Dan Connor, populist traditionalists are blue-collar conservative, anti-corporation, and distrustful of institutions. They tend to be male, working class, married, under forty-five, and television watchers, and comprise fifteen percent of the electorate. They are Republican on values issues but Democratic on economic issues.
- *Stewards.* Exemplified by millionaire Thurston Howell on *Gilligan's Island,* they are pro-management, affluent, older, and college educated. They also comprise fifteen percent of the population. Traditionally Eisenhower Republicans, they have a tough time with modern G.O.P. stands on social issues.
- *Dowagers.* Exemplified by the women on *The Golden Girls,* they are older, middle-class, and do not have a higher education. They make up six percent of voters. They are "Clinton voters still voting for FDR," *U.S. News* wrote. But they also may vote for a trustworthy Republican, such as Ronald Reagan.
- *Liberal activists.* Exemplified by Murphy Brown, they are educated, young to middle-aged, include working women and African-American males, urban, and Democratic. Their fervor can turn off more mainstream voters. Twenty percent of the electorate can be placed in this category.

- *Conservative activists.* Exemplified by Alex Keaton on *Family Ties.* Reagan conservatives, they are young, advocate family values, "tend to think most Americans are like them," and Republican. They can be either yuppies or members of the Christian right, but in either case, their fervor is a turnoff as well. This group makes up another twenty percent.
- *Ethnic conservatives.* Exemplified by Louise Jefferson and Edith Bunker on *All in the Family.* Religious, older, and having grown more conservative, they also are the remnants of the New Deal coalition and are not hostile to government if it is doing the "right" things. They comprise thirteen percent of the electorate. Classic swing voters, they are Democratic or Republican on an issue-by-issue basis.
- *Agnostics.* Exemplified by Frasier Crane on *Frasier,* agnostics are tolerant culturally but conservative on economic issues. They oppose the religious right, are educated, and live in upscale suburbs. They make up twelve percent of the voting population and are slightly more Democratic than Republican—but do not hit them in the pocketbook.[29]

In the mid 1980s, Paul Whitehead, a University of Massachusetts journalism professor, defined a "new" type of voter that did not fit into the traditional "blue collar" or "white collar" categories. He called this voter "new collar."[30]

The new collar voter falls somewhere in between the definitions of the old categories. New collar voters' jobs are not labor or management; they may work in service professions. They may have some college, but they do not always use it on the job. They are socially liberal on issues like abortion and sex, but economically conservative.

Politicians make a serious mistake when they try to place these people in the old "blue" and "white" collar categories. Liberals lose when they think that just because these voters are lefty on social issues, they are lefty on everything. Conservatives lose when they try to sell social agendas along with economic protections.

Conservatives often believe that economics is the issue most dear to people, and if you deliver financially, you can take more extreme positions on social issues and and still get the votes. That does not always work, as many Americans, not only those who fall in the new collar category, still favor the social progress made in the 1960s and 1970s. Sometimes, issues such as fairness and civility become even more important than the pocketbook. Many suburban Republicans supported African-American Democrat Carol Moseley-Braun in the 1992 Illinois U.S. Senate contest because of attacks on her that went far beyond acceptable on matters of race and gender. Civility, believe it or not, actually was more important to them than economics.

Some psychologists categorize people into four basic personality types. Determining how many of each are in your district and tailoring messages to each of them will also benefit the campaign.

- *The parent.* Exemplified by Ward Cleaver on television's *Leave it to Beaver.* Follows rules, respects authority, loyal, dependable, stable. If you are in a district with homeowners with families, you have "parents."
- *The wild child.* Exemplified by Maryann on *Cybill.* Witty, spontaneous, impulsive, easily bored, energetic, hates routine, creative. If the district has twentysomethings, artsy types, 1960s-style activists, gays and lesbians, and other "Bohemians," you will be dealing with the "wild child."
- *The computer programmer.* Exemplified by Mr. Spock on *Star Trek.* Wants explanations and answers, analytical, intelligent, unemotional, loves work. Running in a suburban community full of engineers working in high-tech? You have "computer programmers."
- *The counselors.* Exemplified by Counselor Deanna Troi on *Star Trek: The Next Generation.* Sympathetic, compassionate, idealistic, spiritual, romantic, looks for meaning in life and wants to help others. If you have "new age" types in your district, social workers, people in helping professions, and nurses, you will be dealing with "counselors."

Do not automatically write-off non-voters in your district. If you know who they are, you may be able to develop a way to motivate them.

Northwestern University's Medill School of Journalism and Chicago television station WTTW conducted a study of nonvoters in July 1996, and grouped them into five categories:

- *Doers.* Under age forty-five and making over $30,000 annually, they follow current events but feel too busy to register to vote.
- *The unplugged.* Under thirty and making less than $30,000, they feel alienated.
- *Irritables.* Middle-aged and earning more than $30,000, they are skeptical of government.
- *The don't knows.* Over forty-five but making under $30,000, they are generally uneducated.

• *The alienated.* Over forty-five but earning more than $30,000, they often do not pay attention to the news.

Lyndon Johnson won his first campaign for congress by targeting nonvoters. He campaigned heavily in the most rural areas, and managed to persuade the people living there to vote for him.

ETHNIC/RACIAL APPEALS

Ethnic and racial appeals are fine if they are positive instead of negative. Mark Hornung in *Crain's Chicago Business* formulated four excellent rules for ethnic and racial appeals.[31]

• Appealing to ethnic pride is okay, provided it is not based on exclusion of other groups.
• Chastising individuals for forming unconventional trans-racial political alliances is out of bounds.
• Candidates should not advocate positions that reinforce an unjust racial status quo.
• When making light of ethnic divisions, poke fun only at the group to which you belong.

It is not easy, but it is possible to win in a district with a racial or ethnic majority different from the candidate's own heritage. In 1995, overwhelmingly African-American Gary, Indiana, elected a white mayor for the first time since the early 1960s. Candidates should not make the mistake of writing-off a block of voters just because of their ethnic heritage—*if* (and this is a *big* if) the candidate actually offers something that can benefit these voters.

If you are backing the gay/lesbian candidate in a district that is partially gay/lesbian and partially comprises African-American Christian homeowning families, you might be tempted to write-off the African-American voters. Yet if your candidate can deliver municipal services, or jobs to the community better than the opponent, play on these strengths to the candidate's non-traditional base.

Some candidates do not campaign in certain areas, particularly African-American areas, because they are scared. "Nobody gives Black coffees," said one Chicago pol in the *Chicago Reader*, "but Black people [are] important too."[32] The petite Jane Byrne was not afraid to venture into any of Chicago's toughest neighborhoods in her 1979 run for mayor. Voters in those neighborhoods made a tremendous effort to defy the Chicago Democratic machine to cast their ballots for her. She won, becoming Chicago's first "reform" mayor in fifty years.

If the candidate has nothing to offer a certain ethnic/racial bloc, however, it is best to target precious resources elsewhere. There is no need to try to get every vote. All it takes is fifty percent plus one.

CONTACT

"Speaking or writing without thinking is like shooting without aiming."
—Arnold Glasow

In the nineteenth century, candidates ran what were known as "front-porch" campaigns. They would sit on their front porches and invite anyone interested to hear their positions on the issues.

Today, campaigning is a full-time commitment, and campaigning contact requires thoughtful planning. Sometimes candidates even quit their jobs to devote full time to campaigning. (Actually, I recommend against that because being unemployed harms your credibility, but I use it as an example to show how committed a candidate must be).

One thing that has not changed in politics is the importance of the "footsoldier" or "fieldworker." Muster as many troops as possible to go door-to-door to deliver your literature and work your phone banks to create as much one-on-one voter contact as possible.

The candidate should not feel that an army of footsoldiers can take the place of candidate contact, however. Nothing is as important as the candidate personally meeting as many voters as possible. When my wife and I moved into a new area right before an election, we put a poster in our window for one of the candidates. Her opponent came to our house himself and sat in our living room for a half-hour trying to persuade us to vote for him instead. It worked.

While I do not recommend the candidate visit every home, he or she should go to malls, supermarkets, houses of worship, post offices, transit stops, community meetings, bingo games, public fairs, colleges, meetings of influential local organizations within the district (business, fraternal, military/veterans, union, environmental, interest-based, other), and more to meet as many people as possible.

A member of the campaign should identify the names of the leaders of influential organizations, the issues important to them, and try to get on their agenda. If possible, send someone from the campaign to the organization's meeting that precedes the one during which the candidate will speak, just to get the "lay of the land."

Those organizations, as well as local newspapers and the broadcast media, have information about upcoming events—a perfect opportunity for the candidate to meet voters. Such events include parades, picnics, festivals, art openings, and much more.

Candidates should always appear accompanied by at least one aide, and more if possible. The image of the lone wolf may work for Arnold Schwarzenegger, but it creates an image of "lonely loser" for most candidates.

Whether the candidate is appearing publicly or attending a private meeting, he or she should never be alone. One never knows what kind of nefarious charges or claims someone may make about a one-on-one situation, so it helps to have a witness.

Aides can take notes and keep track of promised actions on the part of the candidate. Also, the assistants can keep the candidate moving when voters want to bog him or her down.

On the other hand, a huge army of flunkies pushing people out of the way and fawning over the candidate creates the image of a strong-arm dictator and turns people off, so try to strike the right balance.

To create even more excitement, University of Illinois at Chicago political science Professor Dick Simpson in his book *Winning Elections* recommends having an assistant with a video camera on hand at times, since cameras always attract attention (and the tape also can be used for commercials and campaign videos).[33] If you do not have a video camera, a large tape recorder with an obvious microphone may attract some attention, as well as garner you a soundbite from the candidate or from an exchange between the candidate and a voter that you can use in a commercial.

Simpson also recommends staking campaign workers at various locations around a site to cover more voters, and instructing those workers to ask voters if they want to meet the candidate.[34]

Yet, the campaign's contacts also must be targeted, which is sometimes hard for gregarious candidates to understand. "Do not contact everyone," said political consultant Nancy Todd, who is "adamantly opposed" to scattershot contacts. "Identify your voters," she said. "It is more important to [contact] *your* voters three times than all voters once."[35] As stated before, it is even more crucial to contact the swing voters with even greater frequency.

Contact is a dialogue. The candidate and campaigners provide information, get information back, and utilize that feedback.

There are three steps to the dialogue process. They can take the form of door-to-door, telephone, or mail contact.

- *The sensitizing contact.* This is the contact that informs voters that your candidate is running, is a good person, and shares their interests.
- *The identification contact.* This contact is to discover how the voters feel about the candidate. By phone or in person, this contact asks if the person is going to vote for the candidate. Forget about the strong supporters and the strong contrarians; this contact finds out who the maybes are. These are the people you target.
- *The persuasion contact.* This one talks about what is important to potential voters to try to get them in the candidate's camp.

HELP

Every contact with a voter should include a request for help. Of course you cannot be obnoxious and turn people off, but you will be surprised at what you receive if only you ask.

When you discover, via door-to-door campaigning or telephone polling, voters who support your candidate, ask if they want a window or yard sign. Then return with it later for a second contact.

If you find someone particularly enthusiastic about your candidate, give their name to the campaign's fundraiser for a follow-up contact. At a speech or event, ask for volunteers. When you have volunteers, ask if they will do more. If they currently are phonebank callers, ask if they will host a coffee.

You must strike a balance between asking for too much and not asking for enough, but surprisingly, most campaigns err on the latter.

COMMUNICATION/CORRESPONDENCE

Every correspondence, whether a letter, press release, or other form of contact, must have a name and phone number for response. The person named should be *available*. It renders your correspondence useless if the potential donor or member of the media cannot reach anyone when they telephone; they will not continue calling for long.

The campaign should have an address, even if it is a post-office box; a *listed* phone number; a fax; and at least one pager. A cell phone and an e-mail address are becoming necessities as well.

Return telephone calls and answer mail and other communications as quickly as possible—always within twenty-four hours. Also, make sure whoever answers your phone knows how to place callers on hold or transfer them without cutting-off the call. There should be paper and pencil handy at every phone, too.

Concerning any correspondence or message: if you do not want the media to see it, do not put it in writing (or on tape).

On the other hand, commitments should be put in writing. Verbal communication can be misunderstood or forgotten.

VOTER GUIDES

The Christian right has done a very effective job with voter guides that discuss their candidates' and their opponents' stands on issues. Consider publishing your own guide or, better yet, work with some political allies or a political activist or party organization to create one. Disseminate them wherever the campaign makes voter contact.

DISABILITIES

In the course of the campaign, the candidate will likely have contact with and speak about people with disabilities. The following are a few tips.

- Put the person first—define people by their humanity first, and their disability second. "People with disabilities" is a better phrase than "the disabled;" "man who is blind" is preferable to "blind man" or "the blind."
- Avoid well-intentioned but patronizing language. A person with a disability is not necessarily inspirational, courageous, or nice just because he or she has that disability.
- Use better alternatives to old buzzwords:

Old	Better
Afflicted with, suffers from, victim of	Has
Birth defect, deformed	Born with
Blind person	Person who is blind
Confined to a wheelchair, wheelchair-bound	Uses a wheelchair
Dwarf, midget	Short-statured

Crippled, lame	Uses crutches, uses a cane
Deaf and dumb	Hearing- and speech-impaired
Hunchback	Person with a spinal curvature
Insane, crazy	Mentally impaired
Mongoloid	Down Syndrome
Spastic	Person who has muscular dystrophy, seizures, multiple sclerosis, or Hodgkin's Disease

- When dealing with a person who is vision-impaired, identify yourself and introduce others present.
- When dealing with a person who is hearing-impaired, lightly touch his or her arm to get the person's attention. Speak directly to the person, slowly and clearly, to allow lip-reading.
- When dealing with a person who has a speech impediment, make statements or ask questions that can be responded to with a few words. Do not interrupt, especially a person who stutters.
- When dealing with a person who uses a wheelchair, sit down at his or her eye level.
- When dealing with any person with a disability, talk directly to him or her instead of his or her assistant, and do not talk to the person as if he or she were a child. Do not raise your voice or talk particularly slowly, as if the person had a hearing or cognitive problem. Offer to assist the person, but wait until he or she accepts the offer before helping.
- Use sign-language communicators only when people with hearing impairments are likely to be present, not just for show.

If all this smacks of political correctness to you, it really is just good manners—something of which most Americans agree we desperately need more.

CREATIVITY

"If the only tool you have is a hammer, then it's not long before every problem begins to look like a nail."

—Abraham Maslow, psychologist

Sometimes, you just need a whole new approach or solution to a problem. That is where creativity comes in.

Studies have shown that the worst places to be creative are at your desk or in a meeting. The best creative ideas come to people when they seemingly are not thinking about them, like in the shower or driving in the car. (In reality, the subconscious has been working on the situation all along.)

There are a few exercises you can engage in to foster creativity:

• Think of what the consequences might be if you solved the problem by performing the solution that appears to be *least* likely to work—the thing that you would *never* do. It just might be the answer.

AIDS researchers engaged in this exercise in creativity a few years ago. Instead of working on how to *cure* AIDS, which was the obvious solution but which was going nowhere, they asked themselves what they should do if they decided people could just *live with* AIDS, which initially seemed to be a ridiculous premise. But this "ridiculous" premise allowed them to develop better recommendations on nutrition, better advice on exercise and lifestyle, and drugs and alternative modalities such as acupuncture and homeopathic medicine to control symptoms and ancillary diseases. As a result, people with AIDS are living far longer.

At a Council for Advancement and Support of Education conference a few years ago, creativity expert Chic Thompson of Creative Management Group of Charlottesville, Virginia, told the story of Thompson and his brother deciding what would be the least appropriate gift for their elderly parents: a personal computer. They bought it, and their parents thought it was the stupidest gift they ever received. But a neighbor's grandchild taught them how to use it, and soon they were on the Internet, performing tasks as simple as their grocery shopping and as significant as communicating with people. [36]

• Think about what the consequences would be if no one said "you can't do that" or "we have never done that before." This is particularly hard for political types; one study showed that more than ninety-one percent of letters from the federal government start with a variation of the phrase "you can't do that." [37]

• Do an "association tree." Write a word or phrase in the middle of a piece of paper and think of anything related to it. Write those down, too. Think of words related to the related words and branch off. Write down opposites, too. The solution may be in there somewhere.

• Do a "benefit tree." As with an association tree, you start with a word or phrase and think of all the benefits that can result from it. Then you think of the benefits that can result from those benefits. That may give you a way to "sell" your candidate or his or her ideas.

Debates

"Honest differences of views and honest debate...are the vital process of policy-making among free men."

—President Herbert Hoover

Debates can take place with other candidates or with groups or media personalities opposed to your candidate's views. Often, they are held at "meet the candidates" sessions sponsored by various organizations for the benefit of the community.

The campaign does not have to wait for invitations to debate. Suggest to local community groups that they host some debates; they will probably welcome the opportunity to liven up their otherwise mundane meetings. If the candidate's opponent(s) fail to appear, you have the positive image of the candidate, who cares about the organization that issued the invitation, debating the "empty chair" of an opponent who does not.

Generally, challengers want debates because it provides an opportunity for publicity. Incumbents want to avoid them to escape face-to-face criticism (and required defense) of their records, and particularly to avert a fatal utterance such as President Gerald Ford's comment in a 1976 debate with Jimmy Carter that there was no Soviet dominance of Eastern Europe. The lack of understanding of foreign politics that comment revealed cost Ford the support of Eastern European ethnics and of people who expected him to have a better grip on reality.

If the candidate is an incumbent, he or she should never appear to be ducking a debate—it makes the candidate look scared. If the candidate is a challenger, ducking a debate is simply not an alternative—it makes the candidate look either arrogant or inept.

Make sure the audience at the meet-the-candidates session or debate includes some of your supporters. The candidate should not be alone with no one cheering while the supporters of the other candidates go wild every time the opponent utters a coherent sentence.

In preparing not only for debate but for the campaign in general, staff should be familiar with opponents' positions and arguments—and how to counter and topple them. Become familiar with the pros and cons and with the emotional issues connected with the central issues. Elections can be won or lost on emotion-tugging side issues that serve as red herrings. Or did you think Michael Dukakis actually advocated flag burning?

It will not be very hard to predict most of the questions that will be asked and the issues that will be raised, so prepare for them.

Learn the format for the particular debate and prepare accordingly. In a 1955 Chicago Democratic Party municipal office slating session, incumbent Mayor Martin Kennelly did not prepare much of an opening statement, because he knew he was particularly good at answering questions. Unfortunately, there would be no Q&A session. The party slated Richard J. Daley instead, and Kennelly was soon an ex-mayor.

Will the candidates be permitted to address each other or to address the audience, or make remarks only in response to moderator questions? How much time will be allotted to opening and closing statements? Are visuals or other props allowed? How many supporters can the candidate bring? Will admission tickets be required? Request a change in format if it suits you.

Become familiar with the debate setting. If someone from Richard Nixon's 1960 presidential campaign had checked in advance, they would have discovered that the background for the first Nixon-Kennedy debate was light gray and could have advised him not to wear the light gray suit that made him virtually fade away.

Find out if there will be a lectern or a table, and again, do not hesitate to ask for changes if they are not too difficult to accommodate. In 1976, since Jimmy Carter was shorter than Gerald Ford, Carter's people demanded that the floor behind Carter's lectern in the Carter-Ford debates be built-up, and they got their wish. However, do not press your demands too much. George Bush looked like he was attempting to avoid the 1992 presidential debates by insisting on too many conditions, resulting in ridicule when a demonstrator dressed like a rooster to indicate that the president was "chicken."

Make sure there will be time cards indicating how much time remains and ensure they will be displayed where your candidate can see them. If there will be television or videotaping, the cards should be displayed near the camera.

Get all the details in writing, and ask that representatives of all the campaigns agree to them and sign the document.

The candidate should have a light schedule or some relaxation time before the debate. This is not an occasion on which he or she can afford to appear tired, distracted, or harried.

The candidate should address the audience, not the opponents. The voters are the ones who really matter. As a corollary, the candidate should avoid fighting with the opponents or the moderators, and if two opponents are arguing with each other, the candidate should stay out of it. It is better to be above the fray than "in a pissing match," as Lyndon Johnson used to say. It may be necessary for the candidate to stand up for his or her rights, however, but avoid acting childish. Bob Dole's sharp, short admonition to George Bush in the 1988 Republican presidential debates to "quit lying about my record" was forceful without being whiny.

It also was a good soundbite, and it is vital to toss out a few of these during the debate. Debates generally are not well-attended, and more people will read in the newspaper about what your candidate said, see it on television, or hear it on the radio than will actually attend the debate.

In a multi-candidate debate, the candidate should look for an opening to stand-out in the crowd. Ronald Reagan clearly broke out of the pack in a 1980 Republican presidential debate when the moderator tried to cut off a speaker. Reagan asserted, "I *paid* for this microphone," and never looked back on his way to the nomination.

If one of the minor opponents draws the candidate into a one-on-one argument, he or she should attack one of the major candidates' positions to refocus the attention. But the candidate should not make an unsupported attack, forcing him or her to explain and fudge. You do not want your candidate to sound like 1968 Republican presidential candidate George Romney: "I didn't say that I didn't say it. I said that I didn't say that I said it. I want to make that very clear."[38]

The candidate should not interrupt his or her opponent, unless the opponent makes a particularly scurrilous attack that requires an immediate response. The candidate should not let the opponent interrupt, either. Also, the candidate should not exceed the allotted time.

The candidate should never look at his or her wristwatch during a debate, as George Bush did during a debate with Bill Clinton in 1992. This indicates to the audience either that the candidate would rather be someplace else, or that he or she cannot wait for the debate ordeal to end.

Work on the closing ahead of time. The candidate should be ready to change it in response to what was said during the debate, particularly to rebut any damage inflicted by opponents, but should definitely not plan on winging the entire closing.

Have your spin doctors seek out and provide information to reporters afterwards. Their articles or broadcasts will reach more people than the debate ever did.

ELECTIONS

"Just because you have elections, that doesn't mean you have democracy. The local people here don't know what they want."
—Gloria Chen of Taiwan's New Party[39]

The election cycle starts fifteen to eighteen months before the election, so you have time to help the people "know what they want." That persuasion effort, as well as the decision to run, research concerning the issues, building an organization, and fundraising, all take time.

Usually, the candidate has to run twice to get elected to office—once in the primary, which is where voters choose among candidates in the same party to determine who will run against other parties' candidates in the general election. Then second, of course, the candidate must run in the general election.

In some locations, a caucus takes the place of a primary or precedes a primary. In a caucus, party members who attend a meeting get to select the candidates. Caucuses afford a marvelous opportunity for an organized campaign to get its candidate on the ballot, because not as many people attend caucuses as vote in primaries. If you can get your troops out to the caucuses, you win. For example, in Minnesota in 1994 Evangelical Christians got their troops out to Republican caucuses, and they nominated one of their own for governor *over an incumbent Republican governor.*

ELECTION DAY

"...Thou knowest not what a day may bring forth," says Proverbs 27:1; the *Bible* could have been talking about election day.

Election day is not a day to sit back and relax, because even if your candidate is ahead in the polls, you never can predict what surprises will occur on the last day. You can prevent some unpleasant ones by being proactive.

Election day actually starts the day before, with footsoldiers/ fieldworkers visiting, or other campaign volunteers and workers calling, all the voters who have indicated (through your earlier phone polls and fieldwork) that they are supporters, and reminding them to vote the next day. Voters whom the fieldworkers see in person should be given campaign literature, particularly sample ballots or palm cards, to take into the voting booth. Fieldworkers should leave campaign literature under the door for voters who are not home. Never put literature in a mailbox—that is a violation of federal law.

Campaign posters should be placed along the routes to the polling places in the district.

On election day, campaign staff, volunteers, and perhaps even the candidate should go around the district and get the voters to the polls—remind them to go, and drive them there if necessary.

Have fieldworkers distribute campaign literature—most important, sample ballots—to people on their way to vote. Fieldworkers should stand as close to the polling place as legally possible. Often, particularly if your candidate's contest is far down on the ballot, people will skip it unless they have a piece of literature with your candidate's name. Legally, people can take any literature with them into the voting booth.

To make sure your votes are not stolen on election day, some of your staff and volunteers should register to be election judges and poll watchers. Generally, not enough people volunteer to do either. Be sure the judges attend the election judge training session and that they closely follow the guidelines and rules in the judging guide. They should understand the laws and aggressively protest or stop any illegal behavior they observe.

Often, fortunately, your campaign's mere presence is enough to reduce cheating. Have your people arrive well-dressed; one poll watcher told me that because he wears a suit and tie when he visits a polling place, people often automatically assume he is from the state's attorney's office and cease whatever shenanigans they were performing.

Most problems in the polling place can be dealt with by a quick discussion with the election judges; very likely, they are errors rather than deliberate attempts at sabotage. Each election judge and poll watcher should have a manual outlining election day procedures, and you can indicate what they are doing wrong. Or, you may want to suggest to them that they call the board of elections' special election-day number for election judges.

If, however, you get strong opposition, your people should have the phone numbers of the candidate's campaign office, the police, the state's attorney, the board of elections, the U.S. Department of Justice, and other applicable agencies.

It is a good idea to have someone in the campaign office all day to help poll watchers or fieldworkers with any problems.

If you do not succeed at first when you call one of the official law enforcement or election governance agencies (because you reached a worker who could not or would not deal with your problem), just call again. Be persistent. At worst, they will keep transferring you until you finally reach someone who will help. Also, on election day, these agencies are usually more responsive. But if an official protest fails, as a last resort, contact the media.

Be on the watch for voting machines with totals that do not read zero at the beginning of the day and for election judges who want to open precincts late or close precincts early.

Have your people visit various precincts to observe if they have the right ballots with your candidate's name. In the 1996 primary for congress, Bobby Rush of Illinois discovered several precincts that did not have his name on the ballot—and he was not only the incumbent congressional representative but the ward committeeperson too! So if the bad guys felt comfortable pulling a dirty trick on someone like him, they will not hesitate to do it to your candidate.

Make sure the ballot box slot for accepting completed ballots is open. Activist Dave Dowling tells the story of voting and being told to hand the ballot to an election judge who wanted to hold onto it and *not* put it in the ballot box, because the slot was locked and the judges could not open it. Dowling replied, "The secret ballot is my constitutional right and I'm not leaving my ballot with someone who's going to change it and throw it out. *Get the [expletive deleted] slot open now.*"

They did.

Be on the lookout for voting booths facing the wrong way (if the judges or workers can see the voters, some individuals feel intimidated). The rule is one person per voting booth, and only under rare circumstances can people receive assistance voting, so watch for attempted fraud here, too. Look for campaign literature or campaign workers too close to the polling place.

Assign someone to the board of elections' official returns drop-off point once the polls close so you can receive up-to-the-minute returns, and to let you know if some polling places are taking too long to come in (a possible indication of fraud—get poll watchers over there right away).

EVENTS

"Much of politics is really theatre."
—Brian McPartlin, advisor to President Bill Clinton [40]

A campaign event is a theatrical production, so start your planning early. One of the first things to do is to verify that there is not a conflict with another event. If your candidate is running for dog-catcher and the mayor is holding an event that night, or if the seventh game of the World Series is scheduled, forget it. Do not even hold an event if there are fewer than six weeks to sell tickets.

Create a schedule of planning functions that clearly delineates what everyone is supposed to do as well as a projected budget that includes invitation printing and mailing, food, location rental, decorations, entertainment, and other costs. Update the budget once the work actually starts. See what you can get supporters to donate: food, mailing, the location itself, or more. Perhaps a lobbyist or interest group can assist. Some supporters are willing to donate items instead of money; accept these donations and hold an auction or raffle at your fundraising event to convert the items to cash.

Fundraising events should feature food and liquid refreshments—away from the front door so attendees will move into the room. Entertainment and cheap giveaways also are good. Sign a contract with the entertainers specifying when they will arrive and how long they will remain. Also, make sure that bartenders are *real* bartenders—you do not want people grousing about long lines because the college kid at the bar does not know how to make a Manhattan.

Decide early whether the event features a sit-down meal, a stand-up buffet, or just drinks and snacks. If it is not a sit-down event, make sure the plates are big enough to hold a drink while attendees are shaking hands.

Find an accessible location—with parking. If there is valet parking, the valets should hustle and not keep guests waiting.

Fundraising events can be sponsored by the candidate/campaign or by friends (individuals or organizations). People will come to the "friends" events because they have a relationship with the host, not the candidate. "Friends" events can be somewhat aggravating for the campaign, so put together a letter or a document for the host that details the guidelines for hosting an event.

Create a host committee from the candidate's list of donors and supporters with the clear understanding that these hosts are to sell (or purchase) a preset number of tickets. Send them a letter from the candidate and then have the candidate (ideally) or a high-level staffer contact them by telephone. Once the hosts agree, someone from the campaign should check with all ticket sellers in the weeks before the event to see if they are meeting their quotas.

Solicit advice from the hosts. Do not assume that you know best. Besides being able to give you good advice, the hosts also need to feel it is their event—it is *they* who made it happen.

When organizing a fundraising event, it is best to request a higher donation than a lower one and to organize a larger event than a smaller one. A low-priced, small event takes as much time and effort as a higher-priced smaller one, so you might as well realize a greater return for your effort. In fact, studies have shown it is actually easier to sell entire tables than single tickets for a sit-down event.

Nothing draws a better crowd than a VIP, and the bigger the VIP, the more you can charge. The fundraiser that garnered the most money ever for a candidate in one day in Illinois was a stand-up buffet that raised $600,000 for U.S. Senate candidate Dick Durbin in 1996. The VIP he convinced to be the keynote speaker? The president of the United States. While you will not be able to get the president, a sports or war hero or entertainment celebrity might be available and will guarantee a great crowd.

When holding an event, confirm with the hosting venue regarding liability insurance. If needed, perhaps the political party organization or another supporter can cover it under an existing policy.

Invitations should be tasteful and ideally should arrive three to four weeks prior to the event. Mail them to the host committee and other prominent individuals earlier to allow them to start selling tickets. Invitations must be followed with phone calls—ideally to every person who was invited. Such phone banking is another task suitable for volunteers.

Include the date, time, and location on all printed materials. Also provide as many details as possible: a map, address, room location, phone number, parking location, and times, including when the reception is, when the actual event will begin, and when it is expected to end. Include a list of the host committee members. Be sure to proofread all the copy.

Schedule the event to receive maximum public and media attendance, and get your publicity out early. It is a good idea to offer the media free meals even if other attendees are expected to pay. The media will never pay to cover your event.

The speakers, including your candidate, should be informed in advance the ideal length of their speech (never more than a half hour), the size and composition of the group expected, whether there will be a question-and-answer session, and the exact time they are needed and how long they must remain. You may have to allow some speakers to skip the reception or the post-speech part of the program. Make sure arrangements are made for parking the candidate's or speakers' cars. Let them know where the restrooms are.

You should obtain information on the speakers' or candidate's special needs, such as dietary restrictions, a lectern, whether they will be bringing guests, whether they need audiovisual equipment (and make sure it is working), and emergency phone numbers to reach speakers in case they are late, including the phone number of where each speaker is scheduled to be immediately before your event and their cell or car phone numbers.

Coordinate the topic of the speech with all speakers so they do not address a topic completely different from what the audience was expecting. Also, do not ever expect speakers to conduct a drawing or present an award, without coordinating with them first.

Have someone in charge of seating. If it is assigned, have people at the front of the venue who can quickly and efficiently direct people. These people should be pre-advised about guests with special needs, such as an escort from the campaign or disabled accessibility. There also should be an easy-to-read diagram of the room at the front, both for guests and those in charge of seating. The front staffers also should be prepared to assist with walk-ins with cash in hand.

Prepare a detailed itinerary and timeline for everyone on the dais. See *Appendix One: Sample Itinerary for Speakers at a Political Dinner*.

Keep the event moving. People would much rather it move a little too fast than drag on. However, if it does go off schedule, have a contingency plan. For example, at the Durbin fundraiser mentioned above, the president arrived later than expected because of a photo session with donors. Event planners should leave sufficient time for such occurrences, knowing that candidates often are late. Speakers should have some additional remarks prepared, so it does not *appear* to the audience like the speakers are padding.

An event with a sit-down meal should begin with a reception, generally a half-hour in duration before lunch, an hour-long before dinner, or two hours-long if there is entertainment, such as music.

Coordinate with the hosting venues or caterers to determine that your desired serving schedule is acceptable. Work with the supervisor of the actual serving staff, not just top management.

Designate someone to shepherd the speakers to where they should be at all times. If possible, assign one staff person to each speaker and/or VIP to accompany them throughout the event. Give each speaker a five-minute warning before he or she is scheduled to be introduced.

Have a written, prepared introduction for each speaker that lasts no longer than one minute. If the speaker is famous, disregard obvious or outdated information in favor of current and less-well-known accomplishments.

Always have cards or sign-in sheets, and try to get all who attend to leave their names, addresses, phone numbers, fax numbers, and e-mail addresses. The card should offer several types of volunteer options (organize a precinct, host a coffee, work a phone bank, other). You will be surprised at how many people will check one or more. Make sure you contact them (phone is best, but mail is acceptable) within two weeks to fulfill their commitment.

All this applies to events that someone else is hosting as well, except in that case someone from the campaign should coordinate the schedule and logistics with the host ahead of time.

The operative phrase is: *no surprises.*

Events do not always need to be huge productions, especially if a smaller one will resonate better with your constituency. How about a bake sale? Events do not always have to be meal-and-speeches events, either. Perhaps a golf outing; a trip to a sporting event, play, or museum; a wine or gourmet coffee tasting; a pancake breakfast; a cookout in the park; or a booksigning (if the candidate has written one)?

See also APPENDIX TWO: EVENT PLANNING CHECKLIST.

ADVANCE

The person in charge of advance is the eyes and ears of the candidate, and his or her principal job is to make everything run smoothly. The advance head or team has succeeded if the story in the media after the event is the candidate's message—instead of the event itself.

Advance functions are:

- Lead advance (sets things up).
- Site advance (checks out the site of an event and deals with on site problems).
- Press advance (advance person or team works with media relations person or team on this).
- "Motorcade" (transportation) advance.
- Hotel advance (if the candidate has to stay overnight).

See also FUNCTIONS, page 95.

The person in charge of lead advance should prepare a detailed itinerary for everyone involved in the event. This itinerary should include as much information as possible concerning when to do what and where to go. This may seem like a lot of detail work, but if you do not do it, somebody will make an error and look foolish. You do not want anyone from the campaign to fumble, but you particularly do not want the candidate to do so. See also APPENDIX ONE: SAMPLE ITINERARY FOR SPEAKERS AT A POLITICAL DINNER.

In performing site advance, visit the facility before you book it. Also, re-visit the site early the day of the event to deal with last-minute problems. Is the microphone there? Is it working? (This should be determined in advance because you do not want the candidate speaking into a dead mike or tapping it to see if it is working.) If there is a slide or video presentation, is that equipment working? Are there enough electrical outlets and cords for the media, and where are they located?

Staff should be stationed at the door to smoothly guide media and the voters into the event. The last thing you want is your supporters and the media looking and feeling uneasy because they do not know where to go and what to do.

Press advance includes news releases and phone calls to the media, arranging "exclusive" interviews with certain members of the media if necessary, determining any special media needs, and much more. See MEDIA, page 129.

"Motorcade" advance can be as simple as having someone drive the candidate's route in advance to note if it presents problems such as road construction, bumper-to-bumper traffic during rush hour, or other unforseen circumstances, and to find potential solutions.

Hotel advance includes making a reservation for a candidate so that he or she is not booked at an inferior or difficult-to-access location, insuring that the hotel can accommodate any special candidate needs (such as special diet, exercise equipment, or quick checkout), learning of any special transportation problems (are cabs unavailable near that hotel during rush hour?), discussions with security, and evaluating the candidate's route and access to exits inside the hotel.

FAMILY

"Without Hillary, [Bill] Clinton would have wound up as merely the most popular law professor at the University of Arkansas."
—Paul Begala, political strategist

No matter how qualified a candidate is or how much he or she desires elective office, the candidate's family is a major consideration in determining whether to run.

How does the candidate's spouse feel about it? Being the spouse of the candidate is a full-time job, requiring campaign appearances and a public presence. If the spouse does not want to do it, or if the spouse is against the candidate running, he or she likely should forego the campaign. Even someone as powerful as Newt Gingrich decided not to run for president in 1996 because his wife was against the idea. Colin Powell withdrew from the campaign for the same reason.

Get the family to buy in. If the candidate wants to run but the family is dead-set against it, you can guarantee this will cause a problem later. A separation or divorce in the middle of a campaign is not a vote-getter.

At best, consult with the family on major decisions. At worst, inform them, but do not ever ignore them. Campaign staff should bend over backwards not to alienate them (and not to alienate the candidate's close friends and associates as well). They will be talking to the candidate over the breakfast table, in bed, at the club, and at work, and the staff cannot hope to compete with that kind of access.

Every aspect of the candidate's family's life (and not just the immediate family) will be examined by the media and the opposition. Can the family stand the scrutiny? Not too long ago there was a prominent Democratic senator from a midwestern state who was slightly on the conservative side. He appeared to have great presidential possibilities yet never even considered a run. I asked one of his staffers why and was told off the record that the senator's brother's business affairs would give the media a field day.

Does one of the candidate's children have a drug problem? Did the candidate and his or her spouse start dating before one of the party's first marriages was over? Was one of the candidate's children born fewer than nine months after the candidate was married? Does the candidate really want the whole world to know about these things?

Are the kids just too young for mom and dad to be out campaigning all day and night, neglecting the car pools, sporting events, social obligations, and thousands of crises that come with rearing grade-schoolers?

Remember Geraldine Ferraro's husband's business dealings? Marilyn Quayle's religious beliefs? Billy Carter? The Reagan offspring? Does your family have characters like these?

Even if each of the candidate's family members is like James Madison, with "a soul so pure if you turned it inside out there would not be a spot on it," can the candidate's family life stand the upheaval that the campaign and holding elected office will cause?

The candidate will never be home, and neither will his or her spouse. One former Chicago alderman reports that in the four years he was in office, he managed to visit his family's summer home for only two weekends. The demands of the campaign and the job will always take precedence. The campaign and public will make demands on the candidate's spouse and children, as well.

"It's not a job, it's a lifestyle," said political consultant Mary Matalin in *Campaigns & Elections*. "And your mate has to get it, because it's all you've got and all you care about."[41]

Are there potential conflicts of interest in the family? Your candidate may not have talked to his brother in ten years, but if he is running for an office that will affect zoning and the brother is a real-estate developer, you can bet someone will make this connection. Check it out.

Are there any family members dead-set against your candidate? I consulted for a progressive Democrat who wanted to run for congress in a Republican district, and as a former military man he actually had a chance. However, some members of his family were Republican Evangelicals and could be counted on to do whatever it took to sink his campaign. He decided that the effort, and the inevitable permanent breach with those family members, would not be acceptable.

Is there something else going on in the family that precludes a campaign? One potential candidate I know had the opportunity in 1993-94 to do one of two things she always wanted: buy her dream house, or run for congress. She chose the house, and decided to forego the election. She could not have it all, and wisely avoided the family stress that would have been caused by trying to do both.

On the other hand, the candidate's family can be his or her greatest asset. Lady Bird Johnson hated public speaking but learned to do it for Lyndon Johnson. She also became like the daughter he never had to House Speaker Sam Rayburn, always inviting him over to the Johnsons' for dinner and other social occasions, thereby smoothing LBJ's way into the corridors of power.

Betty Ford was more popular than her husband and got him more votes than he would have garnered on his own, and the Kennedy and Bush children not only were assets to their fathers' campaigns, but made politics the family business.

As with volunteers and paid staff, find the right role for family members. If the spouse hates speaking to large gatherings but loves talking to people one-on-one, have him or her go door-to-door instead of making speeches. Maybe one family member hates anything to do with campaigning but is willing to watch the kids and pick up the laundry to free other family members to work on the voters.

Fieldwork

"Get there first with the most men."
— Nathan Bedford Forrest, Confederate General

Fieldwork is the precinct-by-precinct, door-to-door grunt work by volunteer and staff footsoldiers. It is run by a field director or coordinator who creates the organization of footsoldiers, trains them, coordinates them, issues orders, communicates information from senior campaign officials to them, and relays reports from them to those top officials. Below the coordinator are additional coordinators assigned to sub-areas of the district such as wards, precincts, or even blocks. Reporting to them are precinct captains, who in turn coordinate workers and volunteers.

Coordinators recruit workers, disseminate strategy to them, and communicate what is happening in the field back to the campaign higher-ups. The captains, workers, and volunteers are the ones who have face-to-face contact with the voters.

The middle managers should be part of the campaign's decision-making process. Decisions made in a vacuum should not be imposed upon them. They also should have some contact with the candidate so they do not feel they are busting their tails with none of the upper echelon even aware of their accomplishments.

Recruiting fieldworkers is tough. Lists of them from previous campaigns and from political and community organizations are a great source. Colleges and universities are good, too. If you receive the endorsement of a political association, such as a ward or township organization, you will get their fieldworkers, too.

You may not have sufficient fieldworkers to cover your whole district. Then the campaign has some logistical choices to make: spread people out thinly throughout the area, or concentrate them on areas with the largest potential for votes.

Fieldwork lets the voters know there is an election. It runs the petition drive that gets the candidate on the ballot, which also lets the voters know that your candidate is running. It informs the voters why they should cast their ballots for your candidate. It also lets the campaign know what issues are on the minds of the voters and where support is particularly strong or weak—and why. It canvasses voters, identifying those who need to be registered and registering them. It also can run a petition drive on a particular issue that can serve to galvanize voters and get them interested in your candidate's key issue. Fieldworkers also identify and assist absentee voters.

Start early in gathering information about key districts or precincts, and decide what you should do to get their support. For example, if there are many single family homes in a changing neighborhood, inform those voters that your candidate is the one supporting home-equity protection.

Create maps and lists of voters for each footsoldier and a standardized information form for reporting to the campaign. Reverse phone directories that list people by street address rather than name may be useful.

Decide the best way to contact the voters. Campaign tactics should be determined by what different constituencies prefer. Busy, well-to-do professionals want print advertisements and direct mail; they do not want to deal with a person. On the other hand, in Chicago's traditionally blue-collar Taylor Street, people have always welcomed a visit from a campaign worker. According to the late, great Democratic precinct captain Donny Piemonte, neighborhood residents would greet him with open arms and say, "Donny, who should we vote for?"

Political consultant James Carville believes African-American voters respond best to "person-to-person testimonial campaigning ... almost door-to-door," and, he added, "Black people believe Black leaders; they distrust white ones."[42]

One candidate for alderman in Chicago's old First Ward discovered that poor people living in housing projects just would not let him in—they distrusted authority figures and thought he might be a government representative there to make trouble. So he hit upon the strategy of bringing a little gift for the kids, like candy. The kids would let him in, and the adults warmed up to him.

Another tip from the field: if there's a bowl of water or dogfood around, be *very* careful. The owner's pet might love to take a nip at a campaign worker's leg. A simple umbrella often can be an effective weapon against a dog attack. Open it, use it as a shield, and retreat.

Fieldworkers should ask people if they would like a window poster (or bumper sticker, button, or other "gimme"), but *not* give the person the item at that time. This not only prevents squandering items on people who only say they want them to be "polite," but it gives the fieldworker an excuse to make another contact when delivering the item.

And do come back with the item. I once received a phone call at home from a campaign staffer who asked if I would take a yard sign promoting her candidate. I agreed, and she indicated she would send it immediately. Nobody ever came.

While almost nobody likes to do door-to-door work, almost nothing you can do is more important. In the 1996 primary for congress in Illinois' Fifth District, Nancy Kaszak raised more money, but Rod Blagojevich had the campaign workers. By the last weekend of the campaign, Blagojevich's troops were visiting some voters more than once a day. Blagojevich won.

Have your young or first-time campaign workers accompanied by a veteran doorbell ringer for the first few forays until the rookies are comfortable. Female campaign workers should never travel alone, and today that holds true even in the most upscale areas.

Never argue with the voters in the field (or on the phone, for that matter). Belligerence will not change their minds, but your courtesy might if they are actually not strong supporters of the opponent. Besides, arguing is a waste of time; move along to more fertile fields.

In fact, politeness makes a big difference. Besides his obvious capabilities, Congressman Jesse Jackson Jr. is popular with his constituents because he addresses indviduals older than himself as "ma'am" and "sir."

Do not underestimate the voters' intelligence. In Chicago's Northwest Side Thirtieth Ward, longtime Committeeman Ted Lechowicz's troops in 1995 and 1996 started providing blatantly spun, disingenuous information to voters. Even though they had been winning elections in the district for years, Lechowicz's candidate for alderman lost in 1995, and Lechowicz himself lost his committeeman's post in 1996.

Campaigns should familiarize fieldworkers with local nuances, such as terms for familiar parts of the community and quaint traditions. If everyone in the area calls Lincoln Township High School "LT," that is what the fieldworkers should call it, too. I once worked a precinct for a candidate, and a fellow volunteer asked a voter why his house was covered with toilet paper. He replied, "You're not from around here, are you?", and explained that the local cheerleaders before a big game "TP" the houses where the best student-athletes live. Let your fieldworkers know about such oddities ahead of time, so they do not get branded as "not from around here."

Modern lifestyles have created new challenges for fieldworkers, who sometimes have a difficult time getting into security-restricted buildings. Former Chicago Alderman Dick Simpson offers some advice in his book *Winning Elections*. According to Simpson, the best way to gain entry is to find a supporter who resides there and have them let you in; if no one involved with the campaign lives there, call residents until you find one who will admit you to "talk about the election." After speaking with them, visit other areas of the facility to contact as many voters as possible. Bring several fieldworkers, so once you are in you all can canvass the building. Another way to gain access is simply to follow a resident in to the building. [43]

The candidate certainly can do some door-to-door fieldwork. The campaign should place signs or do a mailing a few days ahead of time to let the locals know the candidate is coming around. That way, they can make sure that they are home (or *not* home).

The candidate should not only go door-to-door, but visit where people gather, like a local diner. Bars are best to be avoided; you do not want some drunk to spout insults or take a poke at the candidate.

It helps the candidate on door-to-door rounds if someone from the neighborhood accompanies him or her. Not only will the neighbor assist in persuading people to open their doors, but he or she also can keep the candidate from getting lost.

Create a calendar of local events for your candidate and footsoldiers to attend: fairs, meetings, sporting events—and opponents' events, if your candidate has the guts. Do not send your footsoldiers to an opponent's event, however, unless you can keep tight control over them and you know they will behave appropriately. One of the largest vote-getters for Democratic candidate Harold Washington in Chicago's 1983 mayoral contest was a filmclip he used in his commercials of supporters of his opponent screaming in hatred at Washington—at a church, yet.

See also FUNCTIONS, page 95 and ORGANIZATION, page 147.

VOTER REGISTRATION

The campaign must take an active role in voter registration. Harold Washington never would have won the 1993 Chicago mayoral election if his campaign had not registered tens of thousands of new voters. Even in a electoral contest that's not as high-profile or emotional as Washington's, it is an axiom in politics that an overwhelming majority of new voters are going to vote for the candidate of the campaign that registered them.

Washington's voter registration drive is an interesting case study. Activists targeted October 5, 1982, as the big voter registration day. They developed a slogan, "Come Alive October Five," and received progressive and African-American support for advertising. They advertised in the African-American media and in African-American neighborhoods, so the entrenched power structure, which never reads or listens to those media and never visits those neighborhoods, was unaware. The Come Alive October Five campaign was therefore, paradoxically, massively advertised, yet a "stealth" registration campaign at the same time. Before the traditional power structure could react (or even know that it had to), tens of thousands of new opponents had been registered.

Some of your staff and volunteers should be certified as deputy registrars. They can either go door-to-door or stake out posts in highly traveled public areas (like malls and stores) to register new voters.

The footsoliders/fieldworkers are responsible for the voter registration drive. Their jobs are to discover who has moved from their areas and remove their names from your (and the Board of Elections') voter lists; re-register voters who have moved into the district by having them complete change-of-address cards; and register new voters. If the fieldworkers are not deputy registrars, they will likely have to direct these new voters where to register.

Examine the demographics before you decide where to mine for new voters. If you are a progressive running in a district that is half poor inner-city and half well-to-do suburban conservatives, stay within the city limits.

Be aware of the last day people can legally register to vote. There is no need to continue the drive if they cannot vote in your election.

CANVASS

An early canvass consists of footsoldiers/fieldworkers walking the precinct to discover who is not registered to vote and then seeing to it that they become registered.

Another canvass essentially "polls" the voters to discover who is favorable, lukewarm, unfavorable, or undecided. Performed either by footsoliders/fieldworkers or by phone, it lets you know on whom the campaign must concentrate its resources. "Polling" canvasses can be done early to provide information on whom to target, or three or four weeks before the election to help you determine what to do in the home stretch, or both.

Canvasses are conducted with lists of voters. Have one mark for those who intend to vote for the candidate, another for voters on the fence, another for those opposed, and a fourth for people who were not home or did not answer the phone so you know to contact them again. Staff must focus on the undecideds in the final weeks. (Those who indicate they have decided to vote for the candidate can be mined later for financial or volunteer support.)

Another type of "canvass" is the local board of elections' count of the ballots after election day. (Depending on the locale, the ballots are counted initially by the election judges on election day, but the board of election's canvas results in the final, official count.) This is the canvass in which any legal objections to the election are made.

GET OUT THE VOTE

In the end, if you cannot deliver your voters to the polls, you have lost.

Have your troops working the district, meeting people and providing services. If a voter needs a new garbage can or a street paved, have your footsoldiers note the information and provide it to the campaign. Then do your best to deliver. Lyndon Johnson, first as a young congressional aide and then as a congressman, sometimes paid for services out of his own pocket, even during the Great Depression, just to maintain his reputation as someone who could get things done.

Keep your word. If you say you are going to give the voter a sample ballot, a new trash can, a repair crew to fix a pothole, or whatever, then do it. If you do not, the voter will remember on election day.

A tricky tactic sometimes used to reduce the vote totals is moving the polling place to a different location from that of the last election. Voters do not know where the new one is, go to the old one, and end up not voting at all. A few days before the election, verify from the board of elections where the polling places are in your district. If any of them have moved since the last election, get footsoldiers into those precincts pronto to let the voters know. Print or photocopy maps for distribution.

On election day, call or visit the voters one more time to remind them to vote.

Much of what campaigns do can be described cynically as voter manipulation. So it is good to keep in mind that the voters often are much smarter than they are given credit for.

Despite increasing cynicism about government, the public still cares about the country and wants to see it improve. That is why despite the media's and the politicians' sometimes scornful view of the electorate, the people continue to rise to the occasion—and the media and the pols often miss that reality.

As proof, look at the race-baiting, Confederate-flag and *Dixie*-singing 1996 presidential campaign of Pat Buchanan. Where did he meet his defeat? In the Southern primaries that he and the media assumed would be his for the taking. They completely misunderstood the Southern voters who, rather than the moonshine swillin' barefoot "peasants with pitchforks" the media and the pols thought they were, voted for the much more moderate Bob Dole. You would think the "experts" would have learned after Pat Robertson's 1988 presidential campaign similarly went down in flames in "his" South to the more moderate George Bush. They keep ignoring reality in favor of stereotypes.

Do not make this mistake by underestimating the voters or assuming that outdated clichés still hold true. Learn who the voters are and what they really think and base your campaign on that. You may have to educate voters, and it may be more tempting to try to package the candidate like a new dog food in the short run, but the effort will pay off in the long run.

Whether in speechmaking, fundraising, or any other aspect of human contact, treat the voters as intelligent equals. A condescending, patronizing attitude or out-and-out lies drive the voters into the arms of the opposition every time.

After your candidate wins a stunning upset, let the media scramble to try to explain it.

FUNCTIONS

"In [Ronald] Reagan's army, Reagan was the general, but there were also a lot of captains, majors, and colonels. With [1996 presidential candidate Phil] Gramm, he's the general and everyone else is a private."
—An anonymous Phil Gramm advisor [44]

No candidate can do everything alone. A campaign team can consist of everyone from the candidate, family and friends, to an extensive network of volunteers and paid staff. Team members should be trusted and given responsibilities. Abraham Lincoln, Dwight Eisenhower, and Ronald Reagan achieved tremendous success by delegating. Delegating authority is not *surrendering* authority, however.

No matter what the size of the candidate's staff, the following functions have to be assigned and performed:

- *Advance.* An advance person or team chooses sites for events and makes sure the event is set-up, the food and beverages are there, there is a comfortable place for the media, and the candidate knows how to get there and will be on time. In short, the advance person or staff attempts to plan for every thing that can go wrong. See also EVENTS-ADVANCE, page 84.
- *Advertising.* That is paid campaign coverage.
- *Campaign management/coordination.* The campaign manager reports directly to the candidate and has ultimate responsibility for everything, so he or she picks and manages the staff. While the campaign manager consults with the candidate, like the managers in Reagan's army and unlike the ones in Gramm's, he or she has the responsibility to make actual decisions. The campaign manager has ultimate spending authority.
- *Candidate.* Do not laugh; often groups would like to elect someone to represent their views, but cannot find anybody willing to spend the time and money to seek office.
- *Computer management.* Someone has to be on hand who understands computers.
- *Fundraising.* The finance director oversees the fundraising, treasurer's, and accounting functions. Sometimes, the head fundraiser is designated as the campaign chair.
- *Grassroots organizing.* The person in charge often is called a field director or coordinator or sometimes a precinct coordinator. Handles the development/recruitment of volunteers and management of precinct operations. Also is in charge of social events ("coffees") and of making sure fieldworkers

have posters, yard signs, bumper stickers, buttons, videos, and other "gimmes" See also FIELDWORK, page 88 and CAMPAIGNING-COFFEES, page 39.
- *Issue/message development and strategy.*
- *Media relations.* Develops free publicity opportunities. Works with issue/message development and strategy team. Helps set schedule. Assists with development and placement of paid media ads
- *Office management.* Includes maintaining schedules on computer.
- *Scheduling.* Includes coordinating with other top campaign officials to decide what information should be placed in the candidate's daily schedule folder. Also, the scheduler is in charge of travel arrangements.
- *Volunteer coordination.*

You will probably have to pay the campaign manager, head fundraiser, office manager, and media relations coordinator, although they certainly may be able to work part-time. If you get people willing to do this work for free, make sure you can trust them to deliver. The adage "you get what you pay for" should guide your decision on how to handle these most important duties.

Sometimes, people do not understand how the role of candidate, campaign chair, and campaign manager differ. They are not one and the same. The candidate's job is to campaign; he or she cannot be everywhere and do everything. Therefore, the campaign chair often acts as a surrogate candidate, meeting with people, raising funds, and otherwise troubleshooting in place of the candidate.

The campaign *manager,* on the other hand, takes care of the day-to-day operations of the campaign—something that the candidate *will not* have time to do. Candidates should not act as their own campaign managers.

If you have the luxury of time, staff, or money, assign an individual to the following functions:

- *Campaign chair* (different from the campaign manager, the chair is a community leader who lends prestige to the campaign and attempts to raise money from among his or her influential friends. The campaign chair is much like the chairperson of the board).
- *"Coffee" coordinator.* See also CAMPAIGNING-COFFEES, page 39.
- *Election judging.*
- *Opposition research.*

- *Poll watching.*
- *Voter registration.*

While it is natural and desirable to assign people to their areas of expertise, the better campaigns make sure every member of the core team has some familiarity with the other functions. This is particularly important for the smaller campaign. An advantage of this is an ability to deploy a number of people to handle a particular function when a crisis develops. In addition, if someone leaves in the middle of the campaign, others are trained to take over.

Avoid overlapping and unclear lines of responsibilities, however. This leads to turf wars, bad feelings, and confusion. When staffers are feuding, the campaign manager or candidate should remind them of the campaign's higher purpose. To avoid this problem, organize the staff along lines that promote unity instead of friction.

You do not necessarily need people with prior campaign experience to run a campaign. Good leaders in business or community affairs often have transferable skills. Organization, inspiration, and perspiration go a long way.

The campaign staff must work like a team, not as a bunch of individuals. Make sure they focus on outcomes, instead of methodologies and tasks, which often can be mundane. Remember the big picture.

Does the campaign staff know what they are supposed to be doing, and why? Do they have a role in the decisionmaking process? If they do, the candidate and campaign manager have done their jobs.

Lastly, the candidate is the coach, quarterback, general, president, and CEO. He or she should be prepared to do or guide any function (including the unpleasant ones) when necessary and not delegate tasks that really do come under the jurisdiction of the boss. Get it done and move on. The staff will respect the candidate all the more and work even harder.

Fundraising

"I am deeply touched—[but] not as deeply touched as you have been coming to this dinner."

— President John F. Kennedy [45]

It is unfortunate, but money is the most important resource in politics.

People donate to causes, but they more readily give to people. Fundraising should demonstrate a personal reason to contribute: either because they like the candidate or because election of the opponent will have a devastating effect on the donor's personal life.

I have worked in fundraising for several universities and have learned that all fundraising is based on five steps.

- Identification.
- Qualification.
- Cultivation.
- Solicitation.
- Stewardship.

Identification consists of deciding whom the candidate or staff feel is *able* to make a contribution. Prospects are not always obvious, so ask yourself who, if properly motivated, can be cultivated? Make the prospect list a broad one, have many people involved in the brainstorming, and become creative.

Qualification is determining whether the individual or organization has an interest in giving. In the case of a campaign, does the potential donor have views similar to the candidate's? Have he, she, or the organization's representatives come to the candidate's events? Has the potential donor given to similar candidates in the past? If so, that donor is qualified.

Cultivation consists of everything from talking to potential donors, bringing them to events, writing thank-you notes, and delivering services—anything that meets the potential donors' needs. It is amazing how often fundraisers hear "No one has ever invited us to lunch" or "No one has ever thanked us." Focus more on the *donor's* needs, wants, and desires, than on the candidate's.

How do you do that?

- *Listen* to the donor.
- Respond to the donor's agenda.
- Determine how to match the candidate's agenda to the donor's.
- Help the donor with his or her problem(s).

Solicitation means asking for money—the toughest part and the most vital. If you have properly qualified and cultivated your potential donors, though, this is the natural next step. If they are as qualified as you think, most will expect and even welcome a solicitation.

Stewardship simply is cultivation that occurs after the donation is received. Your best donors are the ones who have given before, so if you handle stewardship correctly, these donors will *never* stop giving through the course of your candidate's career.

The fundraiser has to do three things:

- Ask for money.
- Say what the campaign intends to do with the money.
- Explain the dire consequences that will result if the donor does not provide support.

Request a contribution for something exciting and emotional: "I need funds to keep Joe Opponent from silencing our voices in the state legislature," but also be specific on *how* the campaign will do that—via a mailing, ad, or other venue. Do not ask for money to pay for mundane items such as campaign rent and expenses, even though you will need to use some of the funds for those purposes.

As in most situations, do not clutter your fundraising with too many messages. Keep it simple.

Donors

There are three kinds of donors. Some people want to donate money, but do not want to do anything else. Some people do not have the money to donate, but want to become involved and spend time working for your candidate phone banking, going door to door, writing on issues, or in other ways. Some prestigious people do not want to donate money *or* time, but will lend their reputation to your campaign. If the local military or football hero endorses your candidate and does nothing else, you have really received something worthwhile.

To engage these types of donors, you must begin by asking them.

And before you buy or rent *anything*—printing, headquarters space, entertainment for an event—determine if you can get it donated instead. First contact family, friends, and business associates.

SOURCES

The campaign, particularly for the less visible office, must contact the following potential sources of money:

- Candidate's or spouse's business associates.
- Candidate's fellow congregants in his or her house of worship.
- Candidate's or spouse's community organizations.
- Candidate's family.
- Candidate's friends.
- Donors to previous campaigns (of the candidate or other candidates with similar views).
- Groups/organizations that have endorsed the candidate. Interest/advocacy groups with the same positions on issues as the candidate, or with a stake in the election outcome.
- Profession-based advocacy organizations.
- Ethnic organizations.
- Other organizations to which the candidate or his or her spouse belongs (community groups, social clubs, P.T.A., candidate's alumni associations).
- Political contacts.
- Political action committees (the Federal Election Commission has a list of PACs or check your local library).
- Political party organizations, including state and local campaign committees.
- Political organizations not affiliated with a party (EMILY's List, WISH List, similar groups).
- The public.

Federal election laws prohibit candidates for federal office from accepting contributions from corporations. If the candidate is not running for federal office, check state laws regarding corporate contributions.

VEHICLES

Fundraising vehicles include telephoning, face-to-face, direct mail, and newsletters. Whichever strategies are used, if you fundraise from a large database try a test first. Do not spend $10,000 on a mailing that turned everyone off; spend $500 on a small sample. For a small list (five-hundred or under), do not bother testing. That list *is* the test.

Newsletters have been time-tested as fundraisers, but are surprisingly underutilized in the politcal world. The alumni magazine from your high school or college is not sent just because the dean is a nice person. It is a fundraising cultivation tool. The idea is if readers learn about initiatives that strike a particular chord of interest, they will donate money. This works for other fundraising vehicles as well.

Incumbents sometimes do newsletters, but with the proliferation of desktop publishing, you are likely to see challengers publish them, too. Newsletters are a lot of work, but if you have staff proficient with computers, you might consider publishing one.

The newsletter should obviously include news about the great work of the candidate, with the objective to get people who agree with his or her actions to donate. Like college magazines, candidate newsletters can include profiles of donors. This not only makes the donors happy, but inspires others who also might like to be profiled. Honor roll lists of donors are good, too, because they alert colleagues or competitors that they perhaps ought to give as well. Newsletters also can communicate information about upcoming events.

See also APPENDIX FIVE: MEDIA PUBLICATIONS AND SERVICES.

SELLING POINTS

Whether the pitch is being made by the candidate or a fundraiser or in person, on the phone, or by direct mail, there have to be *reasons* to make people want to contribute. The following are a few selling points:

- Danger of the opponent winning.
- Economic benefits to the donor of the candidate winning.
- Ideology/philosophy is compatible with the potential donor's.
- Opportunity to become part of an important movement.
- Opportunity to create a better future.
- Other donors (peer pressure).
- Quality of the candidate.
- Record of accomplishments by the candidate.
- Social benefits to the donor of the candidate winning.

TELEPHONE FUNDRAISING

Most fundraising is performed by phone, and whether a small campaign or a large campaign, the candidate is the key fundraiser. The candidate has to review his or her phone book and holiday card list and brainstorm with associates and family members. The person assigned to fundraising then prioritizes the candidate's contacts and includes high and low dollar amounts after each name. (Be realistic; do not kid yourself that the candidate's grandmother is going to give $10,000 when she is living on Social Security.) Overall fundraising goals and timeframes are established. Then, a phone script for the candidate or other callers is prepared.

The candidate or fundraiser must be specific about the amount he or she is requesting: do not ask "can you help me," but instead ask for "$250, $500," or another designated amount. Also, be specific about what the money will be used for, such as a mailing or an ad.

The candidate not only has to be involved in the initial fundraising planning, but must be an active part of the ongoing fundraising effort. It is no fun for the candidate, who would much rather be doing just about anything else, but such involvement is crucial. It is tough for the candidate to ask friends and associates for money, but it is equally difficult for the person being asked to decline. If the candidate does not work at raising money, it means that he or she is not taking the election seriously. It also means the candidate is going to lose.

A staff member should sit with the candidate during fundraising calls to keep the candidate on track. Otherwise, gregarious person that he or she likely is, the candidate will chat with friends and never progress through the list. Do not let the candidate be interrupted during fundraising time, because he or she will likely grasp any excuse not to do it.

Candidates should not hesitate to call particular individuals because they do not "know them well;" during the solicitation candidates should *act* as if they know them well.

Keep a sheet for each person contacted that includes the person's name, address, phone number, date contacted, amount pledged, attendance at campaign events, willingness to help in ways other than money (such as hosting a coffee, stuffing envelopes, or performing other functions), and any other petinent information. Keep the sheets in alphabetical order in a three-ring binder for easy access during follow-ups—including future campaigns.

The candidate should plan to dedicate two to four hours daily to fundraising. While this may seem excessive, remember that other demands for the candidate's time will invariably occur every day, so this amount should be allocated knowing that it most likely will be reduced.

Funds also can be raised through phonebanking—having a group of workers phone an organized list of potential donors. A phonebanking effort can be as small as a few of the candidate's friends and family making some solicitation calls, to as large as one that involves hiring a telemarketing firm.

Some campaigns have started using "900" or "976" numbers to fundraise. With these numbers a set fee is automatically charged to the respondent's phone bill. Jerry Brown used his 900 number quite successfully in his 1992 presidential campaign. Establish the number in advance to avoid any glitches with your local phone company. Ask for a number that spells something (976-VOTE, for example), and publicize the number.

FACE-TO-FACE

The campaign should establish a minimum dollar figure for which the candidate will have a one-on-one meeting with a potential donor. The candidate should not waste valuable time doing face-to-faces for donations under that figure, unless that donor has a large circle of friends or unless he or she is attending a specific fundraising event where the candidate can see many people at the same time.

If the candidate's spouse does not feel comfortable campaigning in front of large audiences, he or she can host small fundraising events. John Kennedy's opponent after one of JFK's successful runs for the Senate credited his victory to "those damned tea parties" hosted by the Kennedy women.

The best nights for fundraising events are Tuesday, Wednesday, and Thursday. The worst are Friday and Saturday.

See also *EVENTS*, page 80.

DIRECT MAIL

"Direct mail is a political alchemy by which even obscure candidates can transform lists into gold," writes John F. Persinos in *Campaigns & Elections*.[46] Formerly used only by national candidates, direct mail fundraising, thanks to modern technology that has made mailing lists available by subject, is increasingly important in local campaigns. See also *RESOURCES-LISTS*, page 167.

Customize fundraising letters for each group or list based on issues important to the targeted group. You do not have to start from scratch, though; each letter will contain many similar elements.

People get so much "junk mail" today that the envelope itself has to be a grabber—otherwise it will go straight into the recycling bin unopened. The envelope should include an action alert on the outside that hooks people into opening the envelope. Something like "Open immediately to learn how you can stop polluters from dumping raw sewage in your drinking water!" An odd size helps, too, because it makes the piece stand out from other mail.

Direct mail fund solicitations should be on letterhead—something clean and professional, nothing too fancy or cluttered, but nothing *too* slick, either. You do not want to give potential donors the impression that the campaign is *not* desperate for their money.

The lead should be a grabber. Indicate the danger to the reader if the opposition wins. Direct mail is particularly effective in making the opponent look like a bad guy, and this tactic is especially important for unknown candidates who need to provide the electorate a reason to contribute and vote for them.

Contrast that danger with your candidate's positive stand on a particular issue and state why it is imperative that he or she is elected. The first few paragraphs must appeal to the emotions, otherwise the reader will just toss the piece. These paragraphs must relate to the readers and their concerns, rather than focusing on the candidate.

Point out the importance of money, why it is needed *now,* and the tremendous obstacles the campaign is trying to overcome from malevolent outside forces. (Ever notice how the direct mail solicitations from religious organizations always indicate that churches are particularly prone to natural disasters, and how the forces of darkness will be marching down main street unless you send that check *today?*)

Then ask for money, and do not beat around the bush. Request a specific range of donation early in the letter. Later, reinforce how it is vital for your candidate to be elected, and restate the request.

Almost nobody believes this, but a longer fundraising letter often does better than a shorter one. Do not go above six pages, however, and double space between paragraphs with key words in each paragraph underlined, bolded, or italicized to break up the gray blocks of copy. While the letter can be long, paragraphs should be short, however—no more than six lines. The opening sentence should be fifteen words maximum, and no sentence should be more than twenty-one.

Try to strike a balance between regular type and emphasized type, because all emphasis is no emphasis. Consider using type slightly larger than normal typewriter type. This makes it easier for older people, who tend to be larger donors, to read.

In almost all instances, the letter should be signed by the candidate (a mechanical reproduction of the signature is fine). An exception might be a fundraising letter by a local celebrity or hero asking for support for his or her friend, candidate X. The letter should *never* be signed by a staffer; the donor should be aware that the candidate has actually seen the letter.

Always include a P.S. with something new that is *not* a restatement of an earlier section of the letter. If the rest of the letter did not grab them, the P.S. often does. P.S.s, along with headlines and their own name at the top, are the parts of the letter everyone reads.

Use proper grammar in direct mail, but keep in mind there are some other rules you can break. Remember that hatchet-faced old English teacher who taught you a paragraph must have at least two sentences? In direct mail, a paragraph can consist of only one *word,* if need be, according to direct mail writer and guru Herschell Gordon Lewis, president of Communicomp in Plantation, Florida.[47] Lewis writes you can start a paragraph with a conjunction or ellipsis, but do not confuse "its" and "it's," and make sure the numbers (plural vs. singular) of the subject and verb agree. Also, Lewis recommends using a typewriter typeface ("Courier") and a ragged right column instead of a justified right column to give the letter a personalized feel.

Direct mail should be as personal as possible. Does the main letter look like it is on the candidate's personal or office stationery? It should. Can you convince the candidate to scribble a personal handwritten note on each one (or at least electronically reproduce a personal note that *looks* handwritten)? In one university I worked for, the dean would cross out the typed salutation "Dear Dr. Jones" and scribble in "Dear Sam"; get a staffer to replicate the candidate's handwriting.

Include reply devices such as an insert card that offers specific amounts to be checked off (make them high, but include an "other" line or box as well) and a return envelope.

Do not be afraid to "clutter" your piece with a lot of inserts; the potential donor is bound to read one of them. Among these can be interactive devices, such as a petition or response card on a hot issue that donors can sign and return. Try including a membership card that makes the donor a member of the candidate's "inner circle."

need cash quickly, however, direct mail is not the best People set the solicitation aside or place it in their bill pile.

...ail also is not designed to secure large checks; responses to ...rect mail usually are low-dollar amounts. Direct mail is effective over the long term, though; it is the "steady Eddie" of fundraising. See also *APPENDIX FIFTEEN: SAMPLE DIRECT MAIL PIECE*.

CLOSING THE SALE AND TAKING CARE OF THE DETAILS

Fundraising should be coordinated. The direct mail, phone calls, and events should all offer the same message and have the same look and feel. In addition, one reinforces the other. If you receive a commitment or a "maybe" on the phone, you can follow with a direct mail piece. If you get a "hit" through direct mail, you can follow with a phone call later in the campaign as part of your last-minute fundraising or get-out-the-vote strategy. The better-funded campaign can follow direct mail by sending a videocassette.

When a potential donor makes a commitment, immediately send a confirmation letter. Do not delay more than two days. If you do not receive the money in a week, make a follow-up call. Do not hesitate to ask if someone can come by and pick up the check.

Some people are not going to contribute even if they indicated they would. Do not rely on a contribution until it is actually received.

Once you receive a donation, send a thank-you note immediately. This is a task the campaign can assign to a volunteer. More importantly, any "hit" is a name that goes on your permanent list for future mailings, phone calls, or requests for volunteer activities.

Do not assume that certain individuals or organizations will not contribute. Ken Dunkin, an Illinois state senate candidate in 1996, reported that he received a donation from a social service organization that was in the midst of its own fundraising efforts by articulately explaining his support for its goals.

Every solicitation should include a request for other action: ask donors to consider hosting an event, volunteering for the campaign, organizing friends and neighbors, and more.

When possible, every solicitation should offer something to donors. For example, offer to place their names on a petition the campaign is sending to an elected official concerning action on a favorite cause.

Also, ask your donors to write letters to or otherwise solicit their friends and colleagues; the thank-you note is one place to request this.

You even can include a sample solicitation letter that donors can either photocopy or retype to be sent over their own signatures. Ask donors to provide the names of friends to whom they send these letters, which will build your donor list. You will find all this activity really makes donors feel like a part of the campaign.

In addition, create a finance committee of interested friends of the candidate. Then you can go through their lists of associates to broaden your fundraising base.

The campaign must become familiar with campaign finance laws. Some financial information that may be governed by law:

- Campaign loans and collateral required.
- Cash.
- Deadlines.
- Disclosure.
- Donations from the candidate and his or her family or from government contractors.
- In-kind gifts (office equipment, other needed items).
- Out-of-state contributions.
- Party contributions and activities.
- Spending limits.

Bad bookkeeping can sink the campaign and even send people to jail, so follow standard accounting and legal practices.

Solicitation also means resolicitation of donors. You need not discuss why the donor should support the campaign—he or she already does. Instead, indicate why an additional donation is urgently needed. Be sure to solicit during the final days of the campaign, even if you think you have enough money. That is the time people are paying the most attention and have the highest level of emotional investment in the campaign, and are most likely to contribute.

Do not ask for too little. You can always reduce the request if the potential donor balks at the amount, but you will not get the donor to give more if he or she has already agreed to a lower amount.

Likewise, various fundraisers should coordinate their requests of donors. You do not want one member of the team to solicit and receive a $500 donation when another member is targeting that same donor for $2,500.

Lastly, do not be upset if one fundraising vehicle only breaks even (although if *all* your fundraising efforts only break even, you are in trouble). If a direct mail program costs $1,000 and brings in only

$1,000, you have actually gained some new donors that you can add to the candidate's permanent list, good prospects that can be solicited forever. Conservative groups have incredibly good lists, and this is how they created them.

GIVING LEVELS

Use a title for each giving level: "patron," "Governor's circle," "advocate," and others. Offer better premiums for each higher level of giving: a button or bumper sticker for the lowest level, invitations to private briefings with the candidate for members of the top giving levels (also a great way for these givers to network with each other), and various incentives in between. Also, if you publish a newsletter, list the members of the different contribution levels.

LEGALITIES

Under current federal law, an individual can contribute up to $1,000 for the primary, and $1,000 for the general election. Donors can contribute higher sums in other, perfectly legal ways, however.

For example, if the husband wants to contribute, perhaps the wife wants to give as well. That desire on the part of a spouse or other family member must be legitimate, though, otherwise such third-party giving is illegal. Some candidates and donors have gotten in trouble when contributions have been funnelled illegally through children; it is obvious to the state's attorney that four-year-old Johnny Jr. does not care who is elected to the legislature and would not have made a donation unless daddy was trying to get around the law.

The law may limit the amount of contributions to particular candidates, but not to political parties, so the donor can direct contributions there. If that results in the party paying for certain functions, such as voter registration drives, the individual campaign can save money and direct its own funds on other tasks.

The Supreme Court ruled in 1996 that a political party can spend as much as it desires on a candidate's election so long as the party and campaign do not discuss those expenditures, opening another avenue for campaign funding.

A trade organization, union, or company can contribute as much money to a political party as it wants, and that party can direct the money to the candidates of its choice.

G.O.P. Chairman Haley Barbour and House Speaker Newt Gingrich invited supporters to join a "Chairman's Advisory Board" for $5,000 per year for the privilege of meeting with party leaders. Senator Lloyd Bentsen also established a similar group a few years earlier.

"Issue ads" can be purchased by interest groups fighting your opponent's positions without having anything to do with your campaign. An example might be a pro-gun control ad targeting your National Rifle Association-backed opponent. As long as the interest group does not coordinate its efforts with your campaign, it is legal.

Unfortunately, contributions to campaigns, parties, and political action committees are not tax-deductible, so fundraisers should not mislead donors about deductibility.

HEADQUARTERS

"God is in the details."

—Mies Van der Rohe, architect

Whether your campaign headquarters is a rented office or the candidate's home, thoughtful planning will eliminate problems.

If you are leasing space, the lease should be for the length of the campaign—no shorter and, to save money, no longer. With today's glut of office space, that should not be a problem. Street level is better than upstairs—you want your office to be an advertisement for the candidate.

Get a space that has either a separate office or other space so staffers can meet in private.

Order phone lines and other utility services as soon as you lease your space.

Replace the locks, so the former occupant can not walk off with your fax machine and computers.

Buy window blinds, shades, or curtains and close them at night. Secure valuables; equipment should be in offices instead of in clear view of people on the street.

Locate the headquarters in a safe neighborhood, so both your workers and equipment are somewhat protected, preferably near public transportation and a highway.

Furniture should not be luxurious. Get donations or K-Mart specials, or shop at second-hand stores. Do not bother with anything more than cosmetic repairs to the office facilities, either. Do paint the place, though, so it is not depressing for staff.

The headquarters is a reflection of the candidate, so discourage foul language, alcohol consumption, and general slopiness.

Hire someone to be there at least part-time. People feel better if they do not reach an answering machine all the time.

Have at least one phone, fax, personal computer, and answering machine or voice mail. The office should also include a photocopier, which can easily be rented. Faxes and PCs can be rented, too, so decide whether rental or purchase is preferable. Most cost effective of all, of course, is donated equipment.

Have *good* maps of the district, both on the wall and for the footsoldiers and volunteers who will be walking the precinct.

Make sure the people at HQ know where to tell visitors to park. Decide whether to allow smoking or not, or if there is a designated smoking area.

Assign a staff member to turn off the computers, lights, air conditioning or heat, close the window blinds, turn on the phone answering machine and the alarm system (make sure you have one; temporary systems are available), and lock the windows and doors at day's end. Provide sets of keys only to people who really need them.

Determine who is going to clean the office and empty the trash— a staffer, cleaning person, or a janitorial service provided by the building—and how often. Do not assume a secretary or assistant will clean, as they should be engaged in more important work. If cleaning is provided by the building, make sure it is specified in the lease.

Have emergency phone numbers available so a staffer can contact the building manager or owner in case the heat quits, plumbing breaks down, or other problems arise.

The location of the headquarters may be important in sending a message to the voters. In a 1995 Chicago aldermanic run, incumbent Burt Natarus located the campaign headquarters on Taylor Street in an area that formerly had been part of another ward but that had been redistricted into his jurisdiction. This sent a message that he was concerned about his new constituents.

You may want to locate your headquarters in a part of the district in which the candidate is little-known to gain some visibility and show he or she cares about those forgotten constituents.

"If your competition is systematic about information management, and you aren't, chances are they can make you look dumb, out of touch, or just slow," says Duff Johnson, president, Document Solutions Inc.[48] Today, you cannot manage that information without the right computer hardware and software.

Until recently Macintosh and IBM-compatible personal computers could not easily communicate with each other, but there is now software that solves this problem.

Still, you are better off with the same platform throughout the campaign office. Although a Macintosh fan, I have to admit you may be better off with IBM-compatibles simply because they have a much larger share of the market. For graphics and layouts though, you cannot beat a Mac.

Make sure you have at least one modem, one CD-ROM drive (extensive political data now are available in this format), and one laptop. The laptop allows data to be entered and retrieved at the touch of a button outside the campaign office.

A variety of campaign-related software packages are on the market. For the low-budget campaign, they can be particularly useful as they may allow campaign staff to perform multiple functions. Some of the jobs computer software can handle are:

- Budgeting.
- Communications.
- Constituent response.
- Check printing.
- Donor tracking.
- Faxing.
- Financial disclosure.
- Fundraising.
- Forecasting.
- List/label generation.
- Managing contracts.
- Managing contributions.
- Managing contributor data.
- Managing finance/expenditure data.
- Managing voter data.
- Managing volunteer data.
- Payroll.
- Polling/market research.
- Questionnaire generation.

- Record keeping.
- Reference.
- Research.
- Targeting voters and precincts.
- Telephone dialing.
- Volunteer tracking.
- Writing.
- Zip code conversion.

Check with your local software dealer. *Campaigns & Elections'* annual "Political Pages" directory of political consultants, products, and services also can provide campaign software information. See also *APPENDIX NINE: MISCELLANEOUS RESOURCES.*

Explore the possibility of obtaining software from past campaigns or from the party, although be careful of legal restrictions on software transfer.

Demonstrate all software you consider for purchase, and ascertain availability of technical support for the product. If you can never reach anyone on the toll-free tech support line, do not buy the software.

Establish a local area network (LAN) for your campaign's computers. It should be organized so that one person cannot freeze or crash the entire network.

TELEPHONE

The number of candidates with unlisted phone numbers is astounding. If the candidate's phone number is unlisted, volunteers, voters, the media, and donors cannot contact him or her. If the candidate refuses to have a listed home number, make sure there is a campaign phone number that is listed with directory assistance—even if it is only for the duration of the campaign. The telephone number should appear on all campaign literature and in the media kit, and try to obtain an easy one to remember, like 555-NOV4.

Also, inform the state and local parties, as well as any party campaign organizations, of the telephone number. Prior to the November 1996 election, I phoned the Illinois Republican Party, the Republican Party of Cook County, and the State House G.O.P. Campaign to obtain the phone numbers of several Republican state legislative candidates. None of those organizations had them.

A great addition is an Automatic Number Identification or caller ID system that transfers to your database the phone number of everyone who calls.

For the campaign headquarters phone system, develop a standard greeting, such as "Mary Candidate for Alderman, Sally Smith speaking, how may I help you?" Post it by each phone along with a list of who is responsible for which campaign functions so all calls can be directed properly. The list also should include emergency numbers for the building manager or owner and for police and fire departments.

A pen, paper, and "while you were out" message pad should be located near every phone. Messages should be deposited immediately in receptacles designated by individual or function.

Also make sure there is an answering machine or voice mail. If it just rings and rings when no one is there, you are losing help, money, and credibility. People expect to get some sort of response, even if it only is voice mail, and they will call at all hours.

When you record your message, keep it short and play it back to verify that it sounds professional. Re-record it if it does not. In a 1996 Chicago congressional campaign, a leading candidate had a voice mail message on which children were screaming in the background. Record your message with silence or soothing music as background.

Within twenty-four hours, call back anyone who has left a message for any reason. If you wait longer than that, they will lose interest in providing assistance.

Make sure the phone system works. When one line is busy, does the call bounce to another line or to an answering machine, or does it just ring and ring or, worse, cut-off the caller? Will the calls actually transfer? Are there enough phone lines?

Have a short training session for everyone at the campaign headquarters on operating the system, with "cheat sheets" at every phone. It does not appear very professional when the respondant says "I do not know how to transfer," or again, cuts the caller off.

When the media phone, drop what you are doing and respond. This is a golden opportunity for free publicity—do not blow it. If you cannot respond immediately or if you need time to check facts or gather information, ascertain the reporter's deadline and then call back before that deadline.

Obviously, the telephone also can be used for campaigning, either for gathering information or for persuading the electorate to vote for your candidate, as well as for soliciting donations. See also *FUNDRAISING*, page 98.

Telephone campaigning used to be more effective than it is now. Before telemarketing was so prevalent, voters often enjoyed the dialogue with the campaign that a telephone call provided. Now, voters often categorize campaign calls as yet another nuisance.

There are two types of non-fundraising campaign telephone calls, according to Wally Clinton, president of the Clinton Group in Washington, D.C. There is the blind identification call, in which information on voter attitudes is gained through a brief survey given without identifying the candidate, and the persuasive identification call, in which the candidate is clearly indicated. [49]

If doing a blind identification call, make sure callers are not so incompetent that voters can easily identify which campaign is calling. In 1983 "blind" callers for incumbent Chicago Mayor Jane Byrne were sometimes so transparent and clumsy that they drove voters to look more favorably upon her opponent, Harold Washington.

Comuputer-assisted dialing and other technological advances have created a brand new phonebanking business used by almost all campaigns. These services have taken over a function that had been performed by volunteers in the past.

If you hire phone vendors, know if you will be charged per contact, or only per completed call; if you can listen in on the callers; and if you can change the caller's script while the phonebanking is ongoing, if you discover there is a problem.

Ever get one of those annoying telemarketing calls that features a pause after you pick up the receiver before a human actually starts speaking? Such a call is not only rude, but stupid as well. It indicates that the caller thinks his or her time is much more valuable than the voter's. According to consultant Anne Nordhaus of ANB Communications in Chicago, the technology exists so that this never has to happen; some telemarketers are just too cheap to employ it. Determine if your vendor is using technology that avoids this guaranteed irritant.

Before contracting with a phone vendor, demand to see the phone center while phonebankers are working and monitor a few calls. You will learn if the phoners are sloppy and poor speakers. If the vendor will not let you visit, use another company.

Inform the vendor that you will scrutinize the data the phoners gather for inconsistencies. This will help reduce data fabrication.

Some campaigns have started using 900 and 976 phone numbers, which result in charges billed to the caller being paid to the campaign. Obviously, this should not be the campaign's general number (nobody is going to pay *extra* to talk to your campaign), but should be an information line that provides a valuable service people are willing to pay for.

The phone can be used for polling throughout the campaign (see also POLLING, page 158) and for last-minute advertising and exhortations to voters (see also ADVERTISING, page 1). On election day, the telephone also should be used to remind voters to vote and to arrange rides to the polls.

MAIL

Have an outgoing mail box in your office and deliver outgoing mail to the post office daily. It also is a good idea to know your postal carrier and your local post office manager, for special situations and needs.

Purchase a bulk-mail permit to mail third class, but remember that your correspondence must be in zip code order. Also, bulk mail can take up to three weeks to be delivered, so do not bulk-mail your boffo campaign-clinching literature three days before the election, only to have it arrive a week later. This is one reason it is good to know the postal manager so he or she can indicate the optimal time to bulk mail.

If there is a lot of activity in your campaign headquarters, it might be a good idea to rent a post office box, just so bills and other important correspondence is not lost in the office paper shuffle.

FINANCIAL

Most campaigns are bound by financial disclosure laws that require the filing of reports detailing income and expenditures. It is likely the campaign also will have to file tax returns. Sometimes, special reports are required for particularly large contributions or for contributions close to the election date.

Start the process early. Establish the system for reporting from day one, and you will not have to scramble and backtrack. Secure the bank accounts and required tax ID numbers early.

All this requires detailed, daily recordkeeping, as well as understanding of all pertinent laws and requirements with the proper government agencies. Your political party can help, but do not rely on it completely. An Indiana state official who was considered her party's front-runner for a congressional seat in 1994 had to leave the race because her staff had not filed the correct paperwork.

Use receipts and invoices, as well as the services of an accountant or an attorney.

Do not do what one Illinois congressional candidate did in 1996. She intentionally did not raise as much money as she could have because she wanted to keep dollar totals below the minimum required to comply with legal requirements. Her victorious opponent did not follow the same strategy.

Aggregated contributions sometimes cause problems. If a donor provides several small donations, each below the floor amount of what legally needs to be itemized, but in the aggregate the amount exceeds that floor figure, the aggregated contribution has to be itemized. It is therefore best simply to itemize everything.

ISSUES

"Facts are to the mind what food is to the body."
—Edmund Burke, British statesman and orator

As a reporter, I have often asked candidates their positions on particular issues, only to find they did not have any. Do not be like 1996 presidential candidate Steve Forbes, whom voters quickly discovered had only one position on one issue: the flat tax. The joke was that if someone asked Forbes how his wife was, he would say "good, but not as good as the flat tax."

Brainstorm with your family, supporters, friends, associates, and staff on the issues and where you should stand on them. Some issues to consider:
- Abortion.
- Affirmative action.
- Agriculture/farming.
- Arts.
- Balanced budget/deficit reduction.
- Bilingualism.
- Campaign finance reform.
- Citizens/community commissions (formed as advisory bodies to offer community input and help you govern after you are elected).

- Civic participation/access to government.
- Civil liberties.
- Consumer affairs.
- Corporate tax breaks, incentives, and "welfare."
- Crime/safety.
- Culture.
- Death penalty.
- Development.
- Diversity, tolerance, and civility.
- Drug law enforcement/legalization.
- Economic development.
- Education.
- Energy.
- Environmental protection.
- Ethics.
- Flat tax.
- Foreign affairs.
- Free speech issues (modern ones concern the Internet and other forms of telecommunications).
- Gambling (lottery).
- Gay/lesbian issues.
- Government loans (student, business).
- Government reduction.
- Gun control.
- Healthcare.
- Housing/homelessness.
- Human rights.
- Hunger.
- Immigration.
- International affairs.
- Job creation.
- Labor/unions.
- Literacy.
- Medicare/Medicaid.
- Military.
- Minority/multicultural issues.
- Natural resource development
- Police.
- Poverty.
- Public sector/private sector partnerships.
- Race relations/civil rights.
- Reproductive rights/choice.
- Seniors/aging.
- Services: federal, state, local (and how electing the candidate will help voters receive their fair share).
- Small business.
- Tax incentives.

- Tax reduction.
- Technology.
- Term limits.
- Tort reform.
- Truth in sentencing.
- Upward mobility.
- Utility rates.
- Veterans.
- Welfare reform.
- Women's/family issues.
- Youth issues.

You do not need a position on all of these issues, but try to determine in advance which issues voters or the media expect you to address. The key to choosing issues upon which to take a position is to focus on the ones that are important to your constitutents.

Do not take a position or address issues that have nothing to do with the jurisdiction of the office you are seeking. If you are running for the state legislature, do not clutter your campaign with opinions on defense or the United Nations.

The candidate must be up on all *local* issues that concern voters, and must be sensitive to *larger* issues that affect local voters. As an example of the latter, if a significant portion of the district is Cuban-American, the candidate better be familiar with how American policy affects their homeland.

You may find you need to develop a position on a particular issue but are having trouble articulating one. If you do not use the services of a communication consultant, then local, state, and national interest and lobbying groups and associations may be glad to help. See also APPENDIX THREE: RESOURCES FOR KEY POLITICAL ISSUES. Associations exist that are concerned with almost every issue—and from every side of the question. For example, if you are against gun control, contact the National Rifle Association. If you support gun control, contact Handgun Control Inc.

To locate these associations, look in the telephone directory or visit the library reference collection or the Internet.

Humanize the issues when communicating them. According to *U.S. News & World Report*, Michael Deaver, executive vice president of Edelman Worldwide Public Relations and President Reagan's top image-maker, said

Fight bad policies by using examples of the ridiculousness of a policy...whether it's stupid OSHA rules, whether it's the welfare queen, whether it's the spotted owl putting people out of work—whatever side you agree with on all those things, those are the kinds of human examples that turn people on and reporters on.[50]

Emphasize how these issues affect the voters' friends and families.

Do not run a "single-issue" campaign. Single-issue candidates do not win. Sometimes they decide to make a kamikaze run just to "get the issue in front of the people," but this actually *harms* the issue more than helps it. For example, if the "environmental candidate" receives only thirty percent of the vote, the officials who are elected will conclude that only a minority cares about the environment and will focus on other issues they perceive people care more about.

MESSAGE

While the candidate should take stands or at least have opinions on a wide variety of issues, he or she must have a core message that is easy to understand—and must understand his or her own message. Mike Peterson, Iowa Democratic chair in 1996, said in reference to the Republican sweep two years before that, "The lesson we learned from 1994 is this: The more coherent and cohesive the message, the easier it is to sell the candidate."[51] The Republicans' 1994 "Contract with America" was simple, coherent, and cohesive—and it sold.

Contrast that message with that of Ted Kennedy who, when seeking the presidency in 1980, could not articulate why he was running. Consequently, he was trounced by Carter in the primaries.

According to Larry Sonis, vice president of public affairs for William Cook Public Relations of Jacksonville, Florida:

Staking out a clear position that moves voters, and sticking to it, is critical .... [E]lections are won and lost by getting across a winning message to people who have limited attention spans—not by advocating in detail the greatest position paper ever developed on the issue of the day.[52]

Political consultant David Axelrod wrote in the *Chicago Reader*:

By message, I mean an argument, much as a lawyer would develop a case or an argument for a courtroom—except in this case the jury is that electorate that you are trying to influence at the polls.[53]

Having a core message consisting of two or three themes at most is easy on the candidate and the campaign. They do not have to recall complicated information the voters will not remember anyway.

That core message should be something the voters care about and should be determined at the start, otherwise you will not know where the campaign is going. "The message is what drives elections," said Axelrod.[54]

The message also should make sense. The 1996 Republican candidate for Illinois' Cook County's recorder of deeds, Patrick Dwyer, included much information in his media kit about how his Democratic opponent, Jesse White, wanted to save the taxpayers money by eliminating the recorder's office. Dwyer's inexplicable message was that he was critical of this plan. White beat Dwyer sixty-five percent to thirty-one percent.

The following checklist may help craft the candidate's message:

- Who is the candidate and why is he or she running?
- What is his/her ideology or philosophy?
- What characteristics of the candidate appeal to the various constituencies and to the majority of the voters?
- What are the candidate's programs?
- What has/does/will the candidate do to benefit the constituency?
- Why are this office and candidate important enough to be acknowledged by the media and voters? What is the larger issue that makes this contest contest unusual?

Positions on issues should be heartfelt, not tailored to the opinion of the day. People like a candidate who believes in his or her convictions, even if they happen to disagree with those positions and even if the professionals advise the candidate to change direction. Poll after poll showed that most people disagreed with much of Ronald Reagan's outlook yet liked him and voted for him. You do not want to give anyone the opportunity to make a comment like one by conservative activist Grover Norquist on presidential candidate Bob Dole's constant position switching. Norquist wrote in *Campaigns & Elections*, "It seems as if Dole would wear a clown suit if that is what they wanted."[55]

An effective tactic is to link something that actually occurred in the candidate's life to his or her position on an issue, because it makes that position appear more legitimate. For example, a candidate whose car has been hit by a drunk driver can cerainly be an effective advocate for tougher DUI laws.

Make sure the candidate's positions on the issues are consistent with previous behavior. The candidate cannot claim to be an environmentalist and a preservationist if he bulldozed a prairie and an historic building to construct cheap condos. If the candidate's positions are consistent, examples should be emphasized in interviews and speeches.

The candidate's message should offer a contrast to the opponent's. If the opponent is a four-term incumbent, it is pointless to stress your candidate's vast experience. You can not beat the opposition on its home turf, so stress the candidate's fresh ideas.

It is vital that the candidate and campaign leaders be coordinated and speak with one voice, rather than behave like the Keystone Cops. Often candidates and campaign leaders tell the media differing stories. Or they pass the buck, with one official telling a reporter or potential supporter to call another campaign official, and that person telling the caller to contact the first one. Result: you lose your opportunity to get your message to the media, and you lose your potential supporter.

Have an outsider or a friend contact your campaign from time to time to gauge the response. Is a human or machine answering the phone, or does it just ring? Does your spokesperson sound articulate and organized, or harried or befuddled? If things are not working, your message is not getting across. The message being conveyed is that your campaign is a potential loser.

It is amazing how many candidates identify problems and go on and on about what is wrong in society or government without identifying solutions. Just as you would not hire someone for a job who did not have a clue about how to do the work, so the voters will not "hire" someone for elective office who has no ideas on how to solve problems. Identify problems *and* potential solutions.

The message should be in the candidate's own words. When preparing a speech, position paper, or advertisement, ask the candidate his or her opinions on the issues first, take good notes, and then base what is written around the candidate's response. It will be easier for the candidate to speak on and defend his or her own positions than positions slickly crafted.

Define your campaign's message early, because if you do not, the opposition will. Keep it in the context of historical tradition; if your message reflects that of a previous office-holder or your party's traditional stand (Democrats actively pursuing policies for the working person, Republicans promoting individual initiative, for example), emphasize that point.

If your message is a controversial one (pro-choice, for example), your position must be well-formed in advance so you can respond to the attacks. Do not be evasive. You can concede that opposing views are legitimate, but do not be bullied.

See also APPENDIX SIX: LANGUAGE MATTERS.

WEDGE ISSUE

A "wedge issue" is used to garner your candidate votes by dividing or frightening the electorate. For right-wingers, a wedge issue might be race. Blue-collar workers, who would normally vote for a progressive because of economic stands, might instead be frightened or incensed to vote for a right-winger if he is able to convince them that people of color threaten their jobs and livelihoods.

Progressives use wedge issues as well. Seniors who might normally vote Republican voted Democratic in 1996 because the Democrats were able to convince them that the G.O.P. was threatening Medicare and Social Security. For example, Arizona's electoral votes went to a Democratic presidential candidate for the first time since 1948.

As with negative campaigning, think long and hard before employing a wedge issue. Even if you win, you end up with a divided, angered, disillusioned constituency that is hard to govern. Also, you may have opponents in government who often bear such animosity toward you that it is impossible to reach compromises on issues.

Use of a wedge issue also can awaken the opposition and galvanize its voters. A few days before the presidential election of 1884, a prominent minister, the Reverend Samuel Dickinson Burchard, said in a speech, "We are Republicans, and don't propose to leave our party and identify ourselves with the party whose antecedents have been rum, Romanism, and rebellion."

When the good Reverand Burchard tried to use the specter of Roman Catholicism as a wedge issue, his words instead were a clarion call to Catholics to go to the polls and vote Democratic. James G. Blaine, the Republican presidential candidate who had the election all but sewn up, instead lost a squeaker to Democrat Grover Cleveland.

LEGAL ISSUES

God and the Devil were having a dispute over the border between Heaven and Hell that they just couldn't resolve. Finally, in exasperation, God said, "I'm going to sue you." The Devil replied, "Hah! Where are You going to get a lawyer?"

—Dave Allen, British comedian

You will not get through the campaign without the advice of an attorney, because various legal issues will arise.

What are the campaign finance laws? What is the legal limit for individual and business contributions? How much can the candidate contribute? Who is prohibited from contributing, such as corporations, foreigners, and companies that do business with the government? How much cash can be contributed? Which in-kind contributions are allowed, and which are not? How quickly must contributions be reported? What are the laws concerning loans? What must be done with funds remaining after the campaign? Are Federal Elections Commission or other state and local regulations applicable? If so, which ones?

If the candidate or a staffer already is an elected official or government employee, is it legal to work on the campaign in his or her government office? Is the candidate required to resign to run? Must the candidate actually be a resident of the district in which he or she is running, and if so, for how long?

What are the filing requirements? What financial and personal information statements must be filed? How many signatures are required on petitions? What format is proper for the petitions? Who can and cannot legally gather signatures on petitions? What are the deadlines? What ethics statements must be filed? What are the filing fees?

Are there any disclaimer requirements for advertising, literature, and other promotions, and is there a required wording? Are graphic images, words, or music planned for advertising protected by copyright? Are certain phrases libelous or slanderous?

What information about the opposition is the campaign legally entitled to receive? How do you file ethics, campaign finance, or other charges against the opposition?

Campaigns are just like any other business, so what business-related laws apply to the campaign?

What are the campaign's rights concerning recounts and other challenges to election results?

Can campaign funds left from old races be used for a new run? (A campaign cannot use funds remaining from a local campaign for a federal one, for example.)

For all these questions, you will need a lawyer. There is no way around it.

See also APPENDIX THIRTEEN: POLITICAL ACTIVITIES OF FEDERAL WORKERS.

FILING TO GET ON THE BALLOT

Always obtain double the number of signatures on your nominating petitions that the law requires because your opponents *will* challenge your petitions.

Make sure your petitions are identical and are arranged to conform to the letter of the law. If half of your petitions state your candidate's name is "Mary Smith" and the other half state "Mary B. Smith," half will be disallowed. Does the law require the candidate's zip code and county of residence on each petition? Better find out.

Know the deadline for filing the petitions with the board of elections and try to be the first candidate there—that means a couple of hours before the doors open. Depending on local laws, the early bird may get that all-important top ballot position.

The signatures on the candidate's nominating petition should be viewed by the campaign as a list of likely supporters and should be mined for votes, funds, volunteers, and more.

The signature-gathering process is the first test of your fieldworkers. Those who submit many petitions should be given greater responsibilities. Those who do not do their jobs can be weeded out.

It also is essentially the first announcement of the candidacy to most of the voters, so the signature-gatherers should have some campaign literature to hand out.

In addition, it is the first count of how many potential votes exist. A rule of thumb is that about sixty percent of people who sign petitions will vote for the candidate. If that sixty percent figure approaches the target you have calculated your candidate will need to win, the campaign already is in good shape. If not, you know you have some work to do.

Deciding whether to attempt to knock an opponent off the ballot for signature filing irregularities is a judgment call.

Sometimes, it is smart politics. In the 1996 Illinois Democratic primary, state senate candidate Ken Dunkin had one of his opponents removed from the ballot so he would be in a one-on-one contest against incumbent Senator Margaret Smith and have the anti-Smith vote all to himself.

Other times, however, it just makes your candidate look like he or she is hiding behind the law to try to limit the choices for voters. The campaign has to decide how the voters will react before deciding to file a legal challenge to an opponent.

TRADEMARK (AND OTHER RIGHTS) INFRINGEMENT

If your candidate has a name that also is found on a well-known corporate logo like "McDonald" or "Ford," you may want to capitalize on that fact. Be careful about trademark infringement, however.

Try to secure the company's permission. Atlanta mayoral candidate Bill Campbell did not receive Campbell's Soup's approval for his campaign advertisements that resembled soup labels. He then had the added expense of redoing his campaign materials.

Be aware that the use of logos or trademarks can backfire. One of Campbell's opponents described his positions as "warmed-over soup."

Use of music requires the payment of royalties as well, and often a determination of the recording artist's politics to avoid potential embarassment. In 1984, the Reagan campaign was using Bruce Springsteen's *Born in the U.S.A.* as a campaign theme, irritating the artist so much that he publicly indicated that he did *not* support Reagan's bid for the presidency.

Bob Dole's 1996 presidential campaign was embarassed when it was publicly criticized by Nike for using the phrase "Just don't do it" when referring to drug use, because the slogan was similar to Nike's "Just do it."

In both the Reagan and Dole cases, a quick check in advance could have avoided later problems.

RECOUNT

If you think your candidate was defeated by fraud, be aware that winning a recount is extremely difficult. To even get a recount will undoubtedly require legal action.

In addition, you will have to pay for it, and costs can be high. After John Kennedy's election in 1960, a recount was begun in Chicago, paid for by the Republican National Committee, to determine if there had been vote fraud. What the recount showed was that Kennedy's votes were legitimate, but that the fraud was actually indicated in the Cook County state's attorney's race. Despite the possibility that a recount might have put the G.O.P. candidate in as chief county prosecutor, the R.N.C. dropped the challenge because of the expense and difficulty.

Be prepared to rely on a backer with deep pockets or on a party organization with the resources and commitment if you plan to conduct a recount. It is better to use poll watchers and election judges to reduce the potential for fraud.

MANAGEMENT

"A manager is a person who does his/her work by getting other people to do theirs...True authority must be earned; the manager must deserve the allegiance of co-workers."
—Raymond Baumhart, S.J., former president, Loyola University[56]

No matter what your duties are in the campaign, if telling someone else what to do is part of your job, you are a manager.

The autocrat is dead. If you expect people to do a good job, you have to follow some rules that show people you respect them:

- *Communicate.* Tell people what is going on, and why. Make them feel they are part of the team. Particularly if changes have to be made in policy, tactics, personnel, or other similar areas, it is important to communicate *why.*
- *Be available.* You do not have to be available constantly, but you have to be accessible to staff, not shut up in your office. They need to receive decisions and explanations from you, and you will benefit from their input.
- *Provide realistic work assignments and time frames.* The workloads are huge and time constraints are severe in a campaign, but do not provide directives that are impossible to fulfill. Remember, *everything* is not an emergency.
- *Treat people like professionals, not like drudges.* Do not disregard the staff's professional expertise. You do not always have to agree with experts, but you should respect them.
- *Avoid mixed messages.* Do not tell your speechwriters to be controversial or creative and then jump all over them when they do not stick to the standard mom-and-apple-pie fare.

- *Follow chain of command.* For example, if you are the campaign manager and you want the media staff to do something, do not bypass the media relations director and give orders directly to the media relations intern. Such actions undermine the authority of the director and confuse the staffer. Also, be aware of the *unofficial* chain of command. Someone without an impressive title may actually cut the check or get to the candidate when that is what you need most.
- *Deal with a problem—do not just walk away—and weigh the interests of all parties.* For example, if the advance chief and the media pro have a disagreement, do not simply rule in favor of the last one to complain or the one who is in your face. Think through your decision carefully.
- *Always be diplomatic.* If you have to discipline or correct someone, do it in private. Focus on what they are doing right as well as what they are doing wrong to show them you understand they are generally doing a good job. Criticize the action, not the person, and stick to the issue at hand. Gently point out the negatives inherent in stupid ideas or suggestions. The person has an emotional investment in their ideas and should not be brusquely shot down.
- *Be positive.* "Seldom does a positive word come from her mouth," said one exasperated staffer of a public relations chief. "When she wants to see me, I know it's to criticize my work." This is not the reputation you want.
- *Provide direction, not just ideas.* The staff should understand what you want done and how to execute it. Do not give unclear direction and then criticize the staff's results. It is *your* job to help them succeed. There is never enough time for everything in a campaign, so if you do not create the conditions that allow staffers to do the task right the first time, when will they have time to do it again?
- *Do not show favoritism.* I once saw a cash-strapped operation hire a freelance photographer who was a friend of the public relations chief and pay the shutterbug an exorbitant fee for minimal work. The underpaid, overworked secretary found out and told the rest of the staff. Morale plummeted.
- *Protect your staff.* Take the heat for the mistakes of subordinates, and they will be loyal to you forever. But also let them know they will have to do better the next time.
- *Respect low-level staffers and volunteers.* Most high-level workers started at the bottom. President Franklin Roosevelt's secretary had an assistant. Most politicians were wise enough to stay on the secretary's good side, but they often ignored the assistant. Not Congressman Lyndon Johnson, though; he was courteous and respectful to both. When the secretary died and the assistant was promoted to her boss' spot, she

made sure LBJ had access to the president while others were left waiting. FDR ended up calling LBJ "my favorite congressman." Treat low-level staffers and volunteers with as much respect as those higher up, and you will keep their morale high and loyalty strong.

- *Put it in writing.* This removes all ambiguity and helps you discover where the breakdown occurred if something goes wrong.
- *Do not acquire a reputation as someone who cannot keep a secret or who gossips.* You will be both out of the loop on sensitive information and manipulated by people who want information leaked but do not want their fingerprints on it.
- *Make decisions based on the good of the campaign, not on what benefits you the most in the short run.* In the long run, what benefits the campaign *will* be what benefits you the most, because it will build your career as an indispensible cog in the machinery of winning campaigns.

TIME MANAGEMENT

There is never, ever going to be enough time, so you have to *manage* time. For guidance, I prefer a list compiled by time-management and public relations gurus Greta DeBofsky and Lou Williams for the Public Relations Society of America:

- Keep and update to-do lists and check those lists frequently.
- Do not do anything that your word processor, fax, modem, tape recorder, or another available device can.
- Avoid unnecessary memos.
- Hold planning and progress meetings.
- Do the necessary work before the fun work.
- Make deadlines.
- Do not start a project before thinking it through.
- Do not drop a project before it is completed.
- Delegate.
- Take careful notes.
- Keep in frequent touch with staff.
- Listen, for God's sake.[57]

My experience as a manager has taught me to avoid these time-wasters:

- A lack of or shifting priorities.
- Attempting to do too much/ineffective delegation.
- Visitors who are not there to conduct business.
- Clutter/losing things.

- Procrastination.
- Inability to say no.

MEDIA

"So I became a newspaperman. I hated to do it but I couldn't find honest employment."

—Mark Twain

You may not love the media, but you need them—and if you do not treat them right, they will bury you.

The campaign's media director should develop a media contact list, which includes not only the names of appropriate newspapers and broadcast outlets, but those reporters covering the political beat, beats concerning issues near and dear to the candidate's heart, and calendars of upcoming events. Lists of deadlines also should be included.

Whenever anyone from the campaign talks to the media, note the reporter's full name, affiliation, office phone number, home phone number, pager number, fax number, and e-mail address so the campaign can offer additional assistance if appropriate and can place the reporter on the media contact list. If the reporter has written about your campaign once, chances are he or she will do so again.

To reiterate an earlier point, only the candidate, the campaign manager, and designated media spokespersons should deal with the media. The campaign may decide to approve a family member or another staffer as media spokespersons as well. All questions from the media should be referred to the designated media spokespersons.

Much information is communicated by "news release." This is an announcement of news concerning the campaign, written by the campaign in a style much like a newspaper article, that is usually from one to three pages long (write more pages than this only in rare circumstances), double-spaced, with the date, campaign contact, and campaign phone number clearly indicated on the front page. The news release should be printed on one side of the paper only, and leave ample margin for reporters to make notes. Send news releases to appropriate persons on your media contact list. It is not necessary to send a cover letter with a news release.

Each page of the news release has a "slug" at the top that includes page number (in a three-page release, page numbers would be indicated as "Page one of three," "Page two of three") with a short title (if your candidate's name is "Jones." the title can be his or her name). Each page should have the word "more" at the bottom, except for the last, which gets the symbol "30" or "# # #" at the end, letting journalists know they have reached the end of the release. See also APPENDIX FOURTEEN: SAMPLE NEWS RELEASE.

You cannot just send a news release and expect it will get to the right person, no matter how small the media outlet. Find out who the right person(s) are, and target them. Do not be reluctant to send duplicate copies to different people in an organization.

Do not send too many different releases, because this taxes your time, and your real news may be missed among the reams of fluff. It also may irritate the media. One editor told me in 1996 that U.S. Senate candidate Al Salvi "faxes me about four press releases a day. Nobody wastes more of my fax paper than he does, and there's no way he's getting my endorsement." Salvi lost.

Do not disseminate useless information that puts your candidate in a negative light. In a 1996 Illinois congressional race at a time when the public was clamoring for campaign finance reform, a candidate's staff sent a release stating that she had raised more money than any of her rivals. She lost.

Short is good, and one-page releases are great. Omit needless words.

Faxing press releases or other information can be more effective and timely than mailing. A computer with fax capabilities allows you to broadcast to specific, targeted databases without someone having to stand at an independent fax machine.

But do not let the technology take control. Early in the evening of election day in November 1996, the Dole for President campaign accidentally faxed a news release conceding the election before Dole was ready to concede. Have a human being oversee the automatic fax function.

While it is acceptable for you to call to see if a release has been received, editors and reporters *hate* being asked if a release is going to run (releases often are pulled from publications at the last minute to make room for something late-breaking), and they *loathe* whiny sales pitches from media people who try to convince them to run a piece. If the media outlet asked *you* for the information, a follow-up call to see if it was received is not only courteous but efficient as well. Call to be helpful; do not call to be a pain.

You do have to pitch stories by telephone, and a phone call with a press release can be a great combination. But only if you follow the rules. A good set of rules is provided by the Community Media Workshop at Columbia College in Chicago.

- *Call at the right time,* to give the reporter time to discuss it with the editor and prepare to write it. Do not call when the reporter is "on deadline."
- *Be prepared: know whom you are calling and know your story.*
- *Make your calls near a fax machine.*
- *Be ready with specifics.*
- *Be persistent, but do not be a pest.* If it is obvious the outlet is not interested, quit while you are ahead before you make the candidate a pariah at the newsroom.
- *Offer to do more to make their job easier.*
- *Be pleasant and upbeat, not frantic, moralistic, or nagging.*[58]

Pay attention to the bylines or broadcast reports of related stories (pro and con), because to really make an impression with a reporter, reference to his or her earlier work can help enormously. Explain why you thought he or she would be the best one to talk to about the particular issue and ask if there is a colleague the reporter thinks would be interested.

You may wish to offer a story to one media outlet as an "exclusive"—information provided to the outlet before any other media receive it. One advantage is that an exclusive will likely get larger play in the favored outlet than it normally might or, in the case of a mediocre story, it might get play when it normally would be ignored. However, a disadvantage is that the other media might become upset with the campaign for favoring a competitor.

Candidates: do not expect the media director and staff to work miracles. They will do their best, but they do not control the media. "Put this on the front page of the *New York Times*" is *not* a reasonable request.

The Illinois Press Association recommends to its member media outlets to lead citizen focus groups and create a citizens' issues primer. Find out if your local media outlets run these. If they do, make sure your campaign is part of the process. If they do not, urge them to do so and offer assistance.

The campaign should be a source before it is a subject. Get to know the reporters who will be writing about the campaign and provide information to help them with their general reporting. For example, if the candidate is an agricultural expert, the campaign should establish a relationship with reporters on that subject long before the campaign begins.

Whenever the candidate or campaign members talk to the press, they should have other story ideas to pitch. Tip sheets sent to reporters at regular intervals can highlight the various subjects and messages the campaign wants to see disseminated.

Be creative and consider the different approaches that reporters (such as education, political, feature, columnists, commentators) might have on the same information. If you talk to more than one reporter at the same outlet on the same topic, however, *tell them,* so two journalists do not unknowingly work on the same story.

Part of being creative includes determining whom you know who may not be a direct media contact, but who does have media contacts and can put in a good word for your candidate.

Be proactive about contacting reporters when appropriate. You can develop a media list by searching in your area in media guides such as *Bacon's, Burrelle's,* or *Gale's,* which often are available in library reference collections. See also APPENDIX FIVE: MEDIA PUBLICATIONS AND SERVICES.

There also are media guides targeted to your area published by local organizations. (In Chicago, for example, the Community Media Workshop at Columbia College publishes *Getting on the Air and Into Print.* Determine if there is a comparable product in your area.) Or, just contact the local publications or broadcast outlets and ask for the political and calendar editors.

"If a politician starts complaining about [media] coverage and starts picking apart coverage, it means that campaign's in trouble," noted political consultant David Axelrod of Axelrod & Associates.[59] You never want to create that impression. Even if the reporter writes something you do not like, do not remove him or her from the press release list in a fit of pique or refuse to grant interviews. This only gives the reporter the opportunity to ridicule the candidate as a crybaby.

You can object to what you perceive as improper media coverage in a reasonable, rational manner, but never get emotional about it. *Campaigns & Elections* reported that ex-Honolulu Mayor Frank Fasi said to one newspaper's representative, "I don't need a story in your rag about the possibility of losing in the primary. [Expletive deleted] your newspaper and [expletive deleted] your editors."[60] This did not raise his standing with the voters. Bob Dole's anti-media tirades in the 1996 presidential race did not help him, either.

Do not display such paranoia. It is not that the media do not like you or your candidate; the media just generally are negative. "If it bleeds, it leads," often is their credo. So do not think just because the media concentrate on your candidate's negatives that they are biased. They are concentrating on everyone's negatives.

Do not go over the reporter's head to complain to the editor, who may attempt to placate you but likely agrees with the reporter. You will only guarantee that the reporter and probably the editor, too, will write something negative about the candidate the next time.

If you are speaking to a reporter, it is on the record. If you do not want what you are saying to be on the record, then simply do not say it. It is your job to be polished and professional with reporters at all times—that is good training for after you have achieved elective office.

Off-the-record causes several problems: the reporter and you may have completely different interpretations of which part of the interview was on the record and which was off; the reporter may ignore your wishes and print it anyway; or you may anger the reporter by giving him or her vital information and then preventing it from being used. As a reporter, I have conducted whole interviews with people only to be told at the end "this was all off the record" or asked "you're not going to print this are you?" Do this and, guaranteed, you have just made an enemy.

Do not provide your news only to one or two media outlets; aim for as wide a distribution as possible. Campaigns often make the mistake of consistently pitching news only to the biggest media outlet in town (which often is not interested) while ignoring smaller venues (which will print your news, and which are actually *read* by the voters). Mayor Harold Washington hired a community activist as a liaison to all the community newspapers in Chicago. It was a great strategic move that garnered much positive coverage in the neighborhoods to offset the bashing he received from the major media.

The campaign should be encouraged to interact with reporters from small outlets with the same diligence as a reporter from the *New York Times*. The local weekly shopper will likely cover your run for a an office down on the ballot more than the large media, and the voters will seek information on your electoral contest in the local outlets.

As your candidate's career advances, the reporters he or she has worked with will be advancing in their careers, too, to larger media outlets. Relationships made with a reporter from the community shopper can pay off handsomely later when he or she is on network television.

Do not overhype information, and do not bother the media with information that is not news. Is the information fresh, topical, different, unusual, unique? Then it is news. If it is not, do not waste your time pitching it. The media know what is news and what is not, and if you try to fool them into thinking a mundane story is something important, they will never take you seriously. A couple of pitchmen once said to my editor and me that if we covered their story in our local newspaper we would win the Pulitzer Prize. We covered it, but we were skeptical of everything they said and were aware of their penchant for hyperbole.

Possible news subjects:

- Call for governmental action on an issue.
- Candidacy announcement.
- Candidate's plans for dealing with hot issues after the election.
- Charges against opponent or the opponent's party.
- Criticism of opponent or government action.
- Endorsement announcements (endorsements of the candidate or the candidate's endorsement of other candidates).
- Poll results.
- Rebuttal of charges against the candidate.
- Response to a hot news story not directly related to the campaign (crime, a school crisis, or something similar).

News provided before the fact results in pre-event coverage, and if the object is to increase the size of an audience for an event (speech, rally, or similar), this is what is desired.

Television obviously relies heavily on visuals, and for anyone pitching a story to television (call the planning or assignment desk to do so), inform them of what interesting events will occur. Please be reasonable, though. If your candidate is running for water commissioner and is meeting with four people in a senior citizens' home, television is *not* going to cover this (nor will any other media).

News provided after the fact is of limited value and is a tough sell to any media outlet. An exception is photographs. Particularly in the case of community media, which never have enough photos, a news photo provided free is almost a guaranteed placement. It must be a good, interesting action news photo (a news photo is different than a facial publicity shot of your candidate, which should not be candid nor cluttered). The "firing squad" shot of five guys in suits is a sure bet to end up in the trash.

News items should contain the who, what, when, where, and why. A communication missing any one of these is useless.

Information should be provided as early as possible. Some publications have incredibly early deadlines. Learn the deadlines of the outlets you rely on most.

When a reporter calls, the candidate or media director should make him or her your number one priority. Make sure you get the reporter the information before deadline. If you do not, or if you respond too late, the story may not be published or broadcast at all, and you will not be contacted again.

If you need time to collect yourself or the information, make an agreement with the reporter that you will call back in five, ten, or thirty minutes. Then promptly return the telephone call.

In any case, the candidate and the campaign staff should be accessible to the media, otherwise they look incompetent or like they are hiding something.

You will *not* be allowed to review and approve a reporter's story before it goes to press. No halfway competent reporter will ever contemplate it, and to ask is an insult that will insure he or she does not write favorable copy about your campaign.

There is, however, one exception. If you have provided the reporter any complicated data, then you can offer the reporter the opportunity to verify the information with you later. In fact, whenever dealing with a reporter or editor, always offer to discuss the issue in more depth should the editor want to do a longer story.

Do not keep sending information to a particular publication after its deadline, because the reporter will not and cannot use it. Instead, start thinking about what can appear in the next edition.

The campaign should develop some special media events that would be fun and receive media attention. Do not assume if you are in a low-level contest that you cannot receive media attention. Barrie Tron, President Bush's director of public events and now president of Tron Communications in Arlington, Virginia, said even "if you're a candidate running for crossing guard or the metric conversion board, it doesn't mean you're relegated to cable access at 2:53 a.m."[61]

Tron offers several steps:

- *Define your goal.* Create an event that "aggressively and visually" promotes your agenda, such as the 1994 "Contract with America" event that featured G.O.P. congressional candidates signing contracts in front of the U.S. Capitol.
- *Draw the picture.* Tron sketches an actual drawing of the newspaper or television coverage desired, and then positions the event to foster that result.
- *Make it visual.* Include some action.
- *Beware of Mother Nature.* Make contingency plans for outdoor events.
- *Beware of acts of men.* If latebreaking news decreases interest in your event, try to hook into it.
- *Get the word out.* Do an agressive pre-event media relations campaign.
- *Get the best people.* Do not leave media events to second-line staff.
- *Be ready for a sequel.* If your event works, follow up.[62]

Hold media events on weekends, traditionally slow news days that will make your event stand out by comparison to other activities.

Rather than stage an elaborate event, the campaign also could invite the media to headquarters or specific site just as an information briefing on the candidate and campaign.

Whether the event is elaborate or small, make sure in advance that some friendly reporters plan to attend. In 1995, Congressman Michael Patrick Flanagan held a press briefing in Washington D.C., and nobody attended.

Also make sure you do not overpromise an event. In the 1995 campaign for mayor of Gary, Indiana, supporters of candidate Marion Williams organized a "10,000-man march." Less than 1,000 people participated. Williams lost.

The simplest media event is the news conference. Observe the guidelines for what news is (featured earlier in this section) to determine whether the news conference should even be held.

News conferences are more important for broadcast media than print media, so make your event visually attractive. Choose a location that is interesting visually or symbolically. If the candidate announces a new public transit initiative, for example, a train station is a much better place to hold a news conference than a meeting room.

The news conference begins with a memo sent at least three days before the event to the reporters whom you hope will attend, noting the time, location, and purpose of the news conference. Telephone in the intervening period to re-invite the reporters.

Refreshments should be available free to reporters at the press conference. There should be enough chairs for the number of reporters expected, but not too many—avoid the appearance of low attendance. A podium or table should be at the front. Charts and videotapes help make the news conference an interesting excperience.

Press packets should be given to reporters and a list of attendees kept by a staffer so the campaign can place them on the media contact list. Obtain this through a sign-in sheet.

The typical format for a news conference consists of the candidate making a statement on the main topic and then entertaining reporters' questions. The candidate's press secretary should assist with tough questions, although the press secretary should keep silent if the candidate is handling things well.

Reporters will not limit their questions to the main topic, so the candidate should be briefed and prepared with sample answers by the press secretary on a number of topics that are likely to arise.

When questions start to drag on and all business seems to have been accomplished, the candidate or press secretary should thank everyone and close the conference. (Do not do this to avoid tough questions, however; then it looks like your candidate is running scared.)

If a few reporters still need more information when most appear to want to leave, offer to meet with them individually after the conference is closed.

After the news conference, the press secretary should contact reporters who failed to attend. Ask if they want a summary or news release about the conference and if they are interested in interviewing the candidate. In this way, you may receive coverage from a media outlet that initially was not interested. Never berate the reporter for not attending the conference.

You also should contact reporters who did attend for any clarification or elaboration. But do not make that after-the-fact spin sound desperate, or else the media may think you are into damage control and focus on that instead of your candidate's actual message.

Do not neglect the little things. Let the candidate's high school, college, and other membership organizations know the candidate is running. You may receive coverage in their publications, or an invitation to speak.

Do not operate under erroneous assumptions. An African-American candidate did not want to talk to me because she said the newspaper I worked for had never endorsed an African-American candidate, when in fact the newspaper had *usually* endorsed African-Americans. A campaign manager once told me it would be useless for his candidate to talk to me because the opponent was my publisher's cousin. The publisher was not related to the opponent, and as a matter of fact usually found himself in disagreement with the opponent.

Even if you believe a media outlet has been unfair to your candidate in the past, speak with its reporters and provide what they need. The earlier reporting could merely have been sloppy and not indicative of the outlet's true opinion of the candidate. Or, the outlet's opinion could have changed. Or, the earlier reporting could have been the result of bias on the part of one reporter or editor who is not involved with the current campaign. View the media as a pipeline to the voters, which they are, rather than objects of contempt.

Do not lie to the media. When the lie is discovered, as it inevitably will be, you can count on all future coverage of your candidate to be negative—even from the rivals of the media outlet to which your campaign fudged.

Do not be like Richard Nixon and become paranoid about leaks, however, because leaks can work to your advantage. If you have some positive information about your candidate, try leaking it to one reporter. Chances are since it is an exclusive, he or she will use it. Or, use a leak as a trial balloon—for a policy change, for example. If the response is negative, the candidate can deny he or she ever favored it. If the response is positive, the candidate can support it.

Unless your candidate is running for a high-profile office, he or she is unlikely to appear on the network or affiliates' television or radio news broadcasts. However, with the proliferation of radio and cable television stations, it is easier than ever for candidates to be broadcast locally.

Try to arrange for your candidate to appear on the "talking heads" interview programs. Obtain a directory of radio and television programs (*Bacon's, Burrelle's,* and *Gale's* again are good sources, as well as your area's journalism, media, or communications professional organizations) and pitch a news angle to them. The fact that your candidate is running is not enough. It really is not news, because many candidates are running. His or her opinion on a hot topic, however, particularly if an expert, makes your candidate news.

Make sure you pitch a topic to a pertinent show. If your candidate is an environmentalist, do not pitch to your community's Rush Limbaugh broadcast clone. Make your pitch by letter and include your candidate's campaign biography and, if for television, a photo. Even better, include a videotape for television or a cassette for radio of your candidate, taped from a previous broadcast. (You can provide a homemade sample if your candidate has not yet appeared on television or radio.)

You have a better chance of getting your candidate booked if he or she shows more polish and passion than a thorough but boring command of facts and figures. Also, contact the station to verify the format of the show has not changed.

Do not dismiss public affairs shows or talk radio programs. They have devoted, well-informed audiences who vote. "The number of people who listen is much, much bigger than the number who call in," according to Bob Beckel, who ran Walter Mondale's 1984 presidential campaign. "It is a very efficient way to get your ideas in play."[63]

If your candidate is an expert on another topic, pitch him or her to shows that cover it. For example, in conducting public relations for a community group's street festival, I pitched one of the organizers to a radio show as an expert on street gangs, which he was. They booked him to talk about the gang problem, but he also plugged the street festival. Is your candidate a gardener, an author, a baseball expert? Pitch him or her to shows on those topics and have the candidate plug the candidacy, too.

Many radio interviews are not conducted in the studio but instead are over the phone. The candidate should stand while speaking on the telephone for a radio interview because the voice sounds more authoritative. (Add a longer cord to the phone if that makes it easier to speak while standing.)

The candidate should listen to the radio show before the interview, especially the weather and traffic reports. That way, he or she can tailor some comments to the particular show or day's events.

On television or radio, the candidate should refer to the host by name—and get the pronunciation correct.

Involve the viewers or listeners. The candidate should ask them to jot down your campaign headquarters number. The candidate also should ask the voters to cast their ballot for him or her.

After the show, thank the host and producer and follow with a thank-you note that also offers the candidate for future shows.

There is nothing to prevent a candidate from telephoning a call-in radio or television show and plugging his or her candidacy while stating an opinion on an issue. The candidate should stay composed if the host attacks, however. Such an attack even can be used to the candidate's advantage, as future ads can tout, "Mary Candidate took on Rush Limbaugh."

A noteworthy comment on the media comes from Michael Deaver in *U.S. News & World Report:*

> "Don't think about these people as journalists, because they aren't. They're in the entertainment business, and that's how you can get their attention. They want stuff that sells, that beefs up the bottom line—circulation and profits. Playing to that is how you can get yourself into print or on television or on the radio."[64]

"Be entertaining and controversial and repetitive," Beckel told *U.S. News & World Report.*[65]

Never miss an opportunity for free publicity. Why did Senator Ted Kennedy accept an invitation to speak to Jerry Falwell's Moral Majority a few years ago? Because it's never a waste of time to make news and try to change someone's opinion about you.

See also APPENDIX TWELVE: MEDIA TERMS.

INTERVIEWS/MEDIA APPEARANCES

Whether the candidate is being interviewed by print or broadcast media or "interviewed" by voters in a public forum, he or she should follow a few simple rules.

The candidate should arrive early and check the setting, as well as himself or herself in a mirror.

The candidate should know what he or she wants to say and then say it, no matter what questions are asked. The candidate should answer the reporter or voter's question, but then elaborate by making the point he or she wanted to get across all along. The candidate should never leave saying, "If only they had asked me X."

The candidate should dress well, even for a print interview.

Always have a glass of water and some lozenges handy in case of drymouth.

If seated, the candidate should not swivel or roll the chair, and should lean toward the interviewer slightly.

The candidate should never look at his watch during a media appearance. It indicates to the reporter and the audience that the candidate does not consider them to be as important as the next appointment. Instead, have an aide indicate to the candidate when it is time to leave.

On television, the candidate should never look off the set. There will be distractions that the television viewers will not see, and the candidate will just succeed in appearing shifty-eyed, like Richard Nixon in 1960.

Many interviews, particularly for races lower on the ballot, will occur over the phone. Do not insist that the reporter meet you in person; if he or she is asking for a phone interview, it is because there is no time for the reporter to visit you. If you make the reporter do so, you have not gotten on his or her good side. A phone interview is a win-win situation, because it takes up less of your time, too.

In any interview, do not say anything you would not want to appear in the media. Be careful; do not relax your guard. It is perfectly legal for a person to tape a phone conversation without telling you, so you are likely to be on tape during a phone interview. And, the interview is never over until the reporter leaves or hangs up. Many a candidate has been caught saying something damaging on audio or videotape when he or she thought the interview was over.

Be aware of the following interviewers' "tricks":

- Putting words in the subject's mouth via leading questions. Example:"Don't you think there are too many people abusing welfare?" Be careful if asked to agree with a statement, and do not give a "yes" or "no" answer. Instead, say something like, "I believe...," "The reality is," "The real issue is...," or something similar.
- Interviewer's silence, designed to intimidate you into saying something you should not. Just stay silent longer, and the interviewer will have to step in to fill the gap.
- Self-revelation. The interviewer tells something personal or

embarrassing about himself or herself, causing the interviewee to respond in kind.

• Repeating the same question several different ways in hopes of confusing the interviewee.

SPIN DOCTORING

Your campaign and supporters should be encouraged to respond to media reportage any way they feel most comfortable: fax, phone, letter, E-mail, whatever. Have response sheets ready to distribute to the media before a crisis arises, if you anticipate one may occur, or at least prepare them by the time or very quickly after an opponent makes an attack.

If you are not pleased with media coverage, be *very* courteous and considerate to its members nonetheless. Yelling at or criticizing reporters will put them squarely into the opponent's camp. Instead, clarify to reporters what you see as the facts in a pleasant and businesslike manner, and keep it short. An irate individual once kept me on the phone for twenty minutes complaining because a photo did not appear in a magazine I edited, a total waste of time for both of us, since I obviously could not place it in a publication that had already been distributed. I did not exactly bend over backwards to get any future items about him in the publication, either.

When you plan to contact a reporter, make a few notes to yourself in advance so you do not ramble.

Even more important than clarifying the negatives is complimenting the positives. Compliment reporters when they are doing a good job. The cliché about attracting more flies with honey than with vinegar holds true.

Your contacts with the media do not always get into print, but they are nonetheless valuable because your input has a behind-the-scenes effect on editorial content. It also helps develop long-term relationships with the media that can pay off later.

When bad news breaks, diffuse the situation by being as forthright as possible. Do not act shifty, uncomfortable, or as if you are hiding something, because people will think you are.

OP-EDS AND LETTERS TO THE EDITOR

Months or even years before the campaign starts, get in the habit of writing op-ed pieces and letters to the editor and sending them to local publications over the candidate's name (with his or her permission, of course). These will not only give the candidate visibility, but they also will establish him or her as a community opinion leader early on. You also can use them in your campaign literature and media kit later.

Most people do not realize that it is relatively easy to get a letter or even an op-ed piece printed in major media, and very simple to get such things printed in minor media such as neighborhood papers. Postings on the Internet are easy as well.

An op-ed submission or letter to the editor has a good chance of being published so long as it is typed, grammatically correct, and somewhat logical. Publications never actually receive enough letters or op-ed submissions, so if yours meet these criteria, you are in print. Do not make them too long, though. Review the letters and op-eds in the particular publication to determine the proper length.

Plenty of op-eds and letters to the editor that the news outlet received "over the transom" get printed, but for best results get to know the op-ed page editor or the editorial board in advance. The candidate may even become a semi-regular on the op-ed pages.

Respond to issues quickly. Do not take a week to write a perfect commentary on an issue that has been overshadowed by a dozen subsequent stories. Hammer it out and fax it.

Do not write emotional, extremist letters and op-eds that make the candidate look bizarre. Arguments should be reasoned, logical, and businesslike. Since the whole purpose is to get publicity, do not fail to sign the letter or op-ed. Do not request that the candidate's name be withheld.

Publications are unlikely to print your piece during the campaign if it is specifically about your campaign, but even during the campaign they are likely to print the candidate's opinion if it articulately deals with a hot issue and is not blatantly self-serving.

Op-eds and letters do not have to be written by the candidates. A piece written by a voter in support of a candidate or his or her position on an issue, or in opposition to the candidate's rival, can be highly effective.

Television and radio outlets also offer opportunities for guest and rebuttal commentaries. Contact each outlet to learn how the candidate or a supporter can get on the airwaves.

MEDIA KIT

"Reporters are not required to read you your Miranda rights."
—Christopher Matthews[66]

Provide the media with enough information in the media kit to do their jobs, and they may be less inclined to begin an adversarial relationship with the candidate.

The media kit should be a two-pocket folder. Expensive ones with the candidate's name on them are nice, but plain folders with stickers do just fine. Include in the media kit a glossy black-and-white photo of the candidate, a campaign biography, and short statements of the candidate's positions on the major issues. Include enough information to cover thoroughly what is important, but do not give the media too much to wade through, because they simply will not.

Include photocopies of other media coverage. "Media often feed on each other," according to *Getting On The Air & Into Print.* [67] Also include a campaign button. Everybody loves freebies, and the media person or a member of his or her family may wear it.

The campaign simply cannot afford not to have a media kit; it establishes credibility. If operating on a shoestring budget, prepare the inserts on a personal computer and photocopy them. The more information you provide the media in a neat, easy-to-read package, the more of it they will use in their coverage of the campaign.

BIOGRAPHY

The candidate's biography should be included in your media kit. None of your campaign literature should be excessively wordy, so the biography should be no longer than two pages. It should include:

- Accomplishments in business or community, place of worship, or government service.
- Address of campaign headquarters.
- Candidate's name.
- Religious membership/activity.
- Community service.
- Current job(s).
- Dates current and/or previous political offices were held.
- Educational level attained (unless it could be perceived as a negative. Holding a Ph.D. when running in a blue-collar

constituency might be considered a negative or a positive, depending upon the district.). Also include the names of schools attended.

- Honors and awards.
- Length of residency in area (if positive).
- Prestigious positions held in business or community, house of worship, or community service posts.
- Phone number of campaign headquarters.
- Political activity.
- Political party.
- Previous jobs that are relevant or prestigious.
- Military service.
- Marital status and children (unless marital status could be perceived as a negative, such as divorce when appealing to a conservative constituency).

Include reasonable information; no one needs to know about every school grade or every pat on the back you received from your boss. Make your biography a relevant, impressive cross-section of your accomplishments.

However, also include neutral information up front that, if left out, might become a negative because it could appear as if the candidate is hiding something. For example, in Chicago a gay candidate for alderman omitted that he had a son. When the information was revealed, it left supporters feeling slightly betrayed—not because he had a son, which did not cause a problem with his gay constituents, but because he seemed to be hiding it. In fact, his including that information might have helped him with his straight constituents.

Photo

It never ceases to amaze me how many campaigns do not have photos of the candidate available. A suitable photo is one thing that distinguishes a credible campaign from an amateur one.

Have available a good-quality photograph of the candidate's face. The photo should be taken by a professional photographer, but if you cannot afford one, contact the local college, high school, or a photography store and hire a student, with at least some training. If you have an amateur take your photo, you may end up with shadows, blurs, red eyes, or a bizarre expression.

The campaign's main publicity shot can be used both in media kits for outside publications and in campaign literature. It should not be a candid or include other people. The publication printing it will "crop" the photo to suit its space; candids and multiple-person shots with the contextual background removed will make the candidate look strange.

Ideally, have shots available in black-and-white glossy and color slide formats, which are most easily reproduced by publications. If you cannot afford both, opt for the black-and-white, since most local publications still do not use color photos. However, if you think local television stations will cover your candidate's race, then you must have color photos. A Polaroid will not do.

The best size for glossies is five inches by seven inches. You do *not* have to produce the photo in the size it will appear in the publication; the publication itself will resize the photo in the printing process.

Do not make the mistake of acquiring color glossies thinking newspapers can just print them in black-and-white. They can, but the photo then often has an overall dark appearance.

When a publication requests a photo, do not provide a photocopy of a photo, a fax of a photo, campaign literature with a photo, a negative, or a "screened" photo. These will not reproduce in a publication. Do not provide a photo of your candidate in out-of-date apparel, glasses, or hairstyle.

Have a sufficient number of copies available, as most publications will not return photos. Even if they do return the photos, it probably will not be before the end of the campaign.

Always have the name of the individual and the office he or she is seeking typed on a label affixed to the back of the photo. If the identification is on a separate sheet, it can (and usually does) get lost. Do not write the information on the back of the photo. Ink can smudge and bleed through, or leave pressure marks.

Well-financed campaigns or office-holders actually may want to send publications candid photos of the candidate at newsmaking events or with other dignitaries, as the more photos provided, the better the chance of one getting published. Do not use such news photos as a substitute for a quality facial shot, however.

ORGANIZATION

"The primary asset of any business is its organization."
—William Feather

Whether the candidates' troops are seasoned party precinct workers or idealistic volunteers, you will squander your campaign's precious human and financial resources if you do not organize them. See also *FUNCTIONS*, page 95.

If you do not develop an organization plan, some of your footsoldiers will get burned out working on too many projects, while others will leave the campaign because they are not being given enough work. Even a small staff can and should be organized.

The following list of successful organization points developed by the University of Illinois Alumni Association is an excellent start for organizing a campaign:

- Demonstrate a sense of purpose.
- Establish goals and objectives.
- Encourage a positive climate for interaction.
- Recognize individual personalities, skills, and experience within the group.
- Promote group participation and teamwork.
- Problem-solve.
- Delegate responsibilities.
- Evaluate effectiveness of activities.
- Review and revise goals and objectives.[68]

Start by recruiting former campaigns' pros and volunteers and with representatives of your core constituencies you create the organization. Then reach out to representatives from a more diverse base.

Dick Mell, a Chicago alderman sometimes described as a "political boss," keeps pertinent organization information in a thick three-ring binder, which includes a clear chain of command.

"This is what it's about—organization," Mell told a *Chicago Sun-Times* reporter. "The ward coordinator handles five area coordinators, and they command the precinct-level captains. Each precinct has three or four workers. We need to be sure of every vote."[69]

The field director (also called "field coordinator" or "precinct coordinator") should issue regular directives and communicate information to area coordinators (if the campaign has the luxury of that extra layer of workers), who pass it along to precinct workers. If there are no area coordinators, the field boss communicates with precinct workers directly. Precinct workers should in turn provide regular updates. This give-and-take not only allows you to focus on trouble spots, but it lets you know if the coordinators and workers are doing their jobs. They also keep the senior staff in touch with the workers. You do not want to lose workers because you are not paying attention.

Consider written office procedures for your campaign headquarters; regular working hours, so someone will be at the HQ to deal with the public and the media; regularly scheduled staff meetings with attendance required; sign-out sheets or a wallboard that indicate where key campaign people are and when they will be back; and schedule sheets, not only for individuals but for locations, such as conference rooms, to avoid conflicts. Keep rules simple, though, so people can actually follow them.

Have a regular pay schedule, and stick to it.

Create a structure that allows rapid communication and decision-making. *Do not* create a committee structure. Committees seldom accomplish anything with the speed needed in a campaign. The president of one of the universities I have worked for once told me that whenever he wanted to kill a proposal, he would send it to a committee. He would seldom hear about it again.

RELATIONSHIPS: RIGHTS AND RESPONSIBILITIES

Problems arise between a campaign professional and a candidate when either party overpromises what he or she can deliver, has unrealistic expectations, or a lack of commitment, and when there is misunderstanding.

These problems can be exacerbated when the personal, professional, and political relationships get out of balance. To maintain that balance, recognize that there may be an unwritten agenda in the relationship on the other person's part or on your part. All three of these types of relationships must be based on trust.

The candidate has the right to expect competent, professional skills and creative, imaginative, strategic, and proactive work from his or her workers. He or she in turn has the responsibility to be honest with the staff and to provide information and feedback.

The staffers, particularly the professionals, have the responsibility to be aware of the latest developments in political consulting. *Ameri-*

can *Psychologist* advises that they should limit their practice to their demonstrated areas of professional competence but work to develop innovative procedures and theories.[70]

Both candidate and staff must be responsive, provide reassurance, and inspire confidence. Each side needs reassurance that it will not be ignored, that it cares about the details, and that it will go the extra mile. Both candidate and worker should be reliable, consistent, accessible, and good listeners, and should communicate clearly. Availability and affability often are more important than ability.

Both must be aware that they need to be flexible because priorities change and crises occur. Before rushing to adopt a new strategy, however, ask if the campaign *can* change (economics, time, or the candidate's personality may prohibit that) or *should* change (perhaps the situation is not really a crisis).

A good professional relationship will allow and even encourage honest differences of opinion. Settle differences behind the scenes, but remember that in the end it is the candidate's reputation and future that are on the line, so he or she has the final say.

Never say you do not care about some aspect of the campaign. That will not inspire confidence in the candidate or in the workers.

STAFF

Nelson Rockefeller once said that politics "requires sweat, work, combat, and organization." By following a few rules for working with the staff, the campaign can get past personnel issues and concentrate on Rockefeller's requirements.

For paid staffers, create contracts or have them sign documents that delineate job duties, confidentiality, reasons for firing, and vacation policies.

That confidentiality statement is particularly important. A few years ago in Ypsilanti, Michigan, Frank Houston, a campaign worker for City Councilperson Geoffrey Rose, decided to run for Rose's seat himself. Armed with Rose's campaign voters list, Houston won the election. "I am dumbfounded, to put it mildly," Rose said in *Campaigns & Elections*. "I guess I'm too trusting."[71]

You also will need to determine whether staffers are independent contractors or employees whose wages must include withholdings for federal and state income tax, Social Security, and Medicare. Although it is more cumbersome, you are on more solid legal ground if staff are paid employees and taxes are witheld.

Paid and volunteer staff join with or quickly develop a personal attachment to the candidate, and it is required of the candidate that he or she return that affection. Candidates usually have massive egos, but they should never forget that it is the staff that is going to make or break the campaign. Happy, appreciated staff work better. People still are willing to put in a good day's work, and they are aching to make a contribution to an important cause in a world in which hard work seems to mean less and less. (A survey that asked if hard work paid off received a sixty-five percent affirmative response in 1969; by 1991, it dropped to thirty-two percent.[72])

Demonstrate to the staff that their hard work is appreciated. The candidate should mention and thank a few key workers at public or media appearances. He or she should send them thank-you notes and birthday cards or host a short birthday celebration, or offer a verbal thank-you for a job well done. Impromptu pizza parties are good. The candidate can invite a couple of staffers for a snack after a long day (although a one-on-one might start rumors of a romantic affair and is best to be avoided). How about asking some low-level workers for ideas or opinions? Not only will this puff-up their egos, but it may garner some valuable input, too.

Forget about buzz-phrases like "Total Quality Management" (TQM). If you get the staff to love what they are doing, you have TQM.

MEETINGS

In a busy campaign it is tough to find time to meet, but a regularly scheduled meeting is vital to keeping everyone productive.

Every meeting should have a purpose, and that purpose is not to take the place of phone calls or letters or to socialize. Lyndon Johnson's political career was nearly ended in 1948 when his political gurus were holding a meeting about how to handle the court fight over the disputed Democratic U.S. Senate primary and spent the time talking about the fun they had in previous campaigns. It required some of the younger, less experienced attorneys to silence them, take control of the meeting, and formulate a legal strategy that put LBJ in the senate.

Every meeting should start on time, otherwise you are wasting the time of those who arrived promptly. Everyone required to be there should be there, otherwise everyone will start skipping meetings. Latecomers and meeting-skippers should be reprimanded privately.

Do not let the people who like to hear themselves talk control the meeting. Consider establishing a time limit for discussions.

The University of Illinois recommends asking the following questions before scheduling a meeting:

- Why am I scheduling this meeting/what do we want to accomplish?
- Whom should I invite?
- What should I cover?
- How shall I communicate?
- Where will we meet?
- When will we meet?[73]

Meeting leaders, the University of Illinois stresses, should avoid arriving unprepared, appearing resentful of questions, monopolizing a meeting, chastising people publicly, permitting interruptions, going off on a different agenda, and losing control.[74]

Do not hold many unplanned meetings. *Everything* is not an emergency. Whether the meeting was scheduled or is *ad hoc*, be sure to give people some time, even if just a few minutes, to prepare.

Have someone take notes, so you can document the discussion.

Lastly, the meeting should result in decisions on actions to be taken, and by whom.

The late Mayor Richard J. Daley of Chicago said that he never walked into a meeting in which he was not reasonably sure of the outcome. Have at least a general idea of what the meeting's outcome is going to or should be. Otherwise, do not schedule it.

SCHEDULING (CALENDAR)

Keep the schedule and calendar on computer. Without much difficulty, the schedule can cover the candidate, all the other senior staffers, and the offices in campaign headquarters.

Schedule or calendar entries should include:

- Date.
- Day of week.
- Duties of staff and candidate at particular event.
- Hosts/sponsors of event.
- Location (including address).
- Miscellaneous information.
- Names of important people involved, and their functions.
- Phone number(s).

- Purpose of event.
- Travel directions.
- Time of start.
- Time of ending.
- Title of event.
- Who arrives when (different staffers may have to arrive at different times to deal with different functions).
- Who departs when.

One person should be the scheduling coordinator, with all approvals for scheduling coming through him or her to avoid conflicts. Create a scheduling request form for both outside and staff requests. The office manager or secretary should be responsible for entering the data. Do not rely on a volunteer who may not get around to it, leaving your candidate shuffling papers in the office when he or she is supposed to be meeting the mayor.

Print schedules weekly, daily, or as often as people need them. Distribute them to as many staffers and volunteers as needed.

Schedule sensibly, with the candidate going from one event to the next one nearby. Do not make the candidate travel back and forth across the district to events. The more time he or she spends in transit, the less time there is for garnering votes. Allow enough time to arrive at the next event on schedule, and do not schedule a particularly early event the morning after a particularly late one.

The scheduling coordinator or campaign manager should not commit to events scheduled in the last month of the campaign too early. You want to leave some flexibility and not be locked into speaking to a local club with eight members when the candidate could have been on a platform next to the governor.

The candidate should never be the one to decline an invitation. This dirty work—and the resulting heat and resentment—should be left to a staffer. If the candidate personally is asked to attend something, he or she should quickly refer the request to the scheduler.

The scheduler should provide a scheduling folder for the candidate every day. He or she should coordinate with the other senior campaign officials to include hard-copy briefing materials concerning specific messages or facts germane to each scheduled appearance for the candidate. If other people involved with the campaign are empowered to speak for the candidate, such as his or her spouse, they should receive scheduling folders as well.

Include in the folders the names and phonetic pronunciations of the contacts from the organizations the candidate will interact with that day, and some information about those organizations.

Scheduling coordinators also make the travel arrangements as well.

Often, the best scheduler is the candidate's spouse or another family member, because they can coordinate both political and private appointments and social obligations.

VOLUNTEERS

Campaigns constantly make the mistake of not using volunteers to the fullest extent possible. Often, campaigns seem to have trouble finding jobs for volunteers.

Volunteers can be an incredibly productive resource if used correctly. There are a million details that never get completed or that overtax the candidate and campaign leaders that can be accomplished by volunteers. No one to conduct opposition research? Send a volunteer to the library. Get a volunteer certified as a deputy registrar to register voters in your district. Have the volunteer write thank-you or congratulatory notes to newsmakers, reporters, donors, or anyone in your district whose support or friendship you need. Send the volunteer to distribute your campaign literature and make phone calls urging people to vote for your candidate. Encourage volunteers to host a coffee and meet-the-candidate session and organize their friends and neighbors to attend.

Some campaigns actually turn volunteers away. Never do this. Even if the volunteer is not particularly competent, be creative in finding some low-level task for him or her to perform. Disgruntled potential volunteers do not hesitate to tell their friends and family, your potential voters, how poorly they were treated.

On the other hand, interview volunteers just in case they may be there to sabotage the campaign on behalf of an opponent. At the very least, record the person's name, address, phone number, driver's license number, and Social Security number. This might scare off a spy, but it also is an invaluable resource for future campaigns.

Do not become paranoid about spies. Most information that gets out when you do not want it to comes from insiders with loose lips, not from planned sabotage. Encourage your people to think twice before talking, but do not crack down on them just for being human.

Believe it or not, free help is out there. Where do you get it? Some volunteers will contact you, but you will be amazed at how much help you can get if you just ask for it.

The first place to go is the list of volunteers who have helped the candidate on previous campaigns or other projects or who have helped the candidate's allies or ideological compatriots in previous campaigns. Retention is easier than recruitment.

Some places to get help: senior citizens homes or organizations have responsible, conscientious people; houses of worship do, too. Student organizations, such as the Young Republican National Federation or College Democrats, are filled with eager volunteers ready to help. (These younger volunteers also may be experts with computers or other electronic technology.) Members of the candidate's alumni associations, or other school organizations may be interested in helping a buddy. Community or activist organizations that hold the same views as the candidate also can be a source. Contact your local college for faculty and student organizations that might assist.

Stay-at-home spouses have some scheduling flexibility and know their own communities better than anyone. Teachers have their late afternoons available, and they are obviously educated. The aforementioned senior citizens not only often have time available but, remembering the momentous influence of government in the time of their youth (the New Deal, various wars), may be open to having the campaign rekindle their interest in political activity

Houses of worship are not only often good places to find volunteers—they are good places to mine for votes. Ask the pastor, priest, rabbi, or minister if you can speak to the congregation, get a message in the house of worship's bulletin, or have an announcement made from the lectern. At the very least, attend services and meet the congregation afterward. Ask to be placed on the calendar if the house of worship has education or lecture programs.

Youth groups, such as Camp Fire Boys and Girls, the Scouts, and others have teen programs that seek volunteer opportunities. Your campaign might be a good one, particularly if your candidate is strong on an issue near and dear to that organization.

Some campaigns even have attempted random calls or visits to voters in the district to find volunteers, but this is a low-yield strategy.

Suggest to potential volunteers, either verbally or in your literature, how they can volunteer. Some options:

- Working on election day.
- Working at campaign headquarters.
- Putting a sign in volunteer's yard or window.
- Canvassing a precinct for a candidate.
- Hosting a "meet the candidate" coffee for neighbors.
- Writing a letter to neighbors (the campaign should write and type the letter; the volunteer signs and mails or delivers copies. The campaign or the volunteer can make the photocopies, depending on campaign's cash status).
- Registering voters.
- Handling correspondence.
- Recruiting other volunteers.

Volunteers are too important to be shunted around. Someone from your campaign should be designated the volunteer coordinator, and a volunteer's duties should not be changed without the volunteer coordinator's approval. Otherwise, another staffer could reassign the volunteer to a task the volunteer hates, causing the task to go unfinished and the volunteer to be lost when he or she quits the campaign.

Determine what the volunteer wants from volunteering. Does he or she believe passionately in a particular issue your candidate advocates? Does he or she desire to eventually become a political consultant or a candidate? Is he or she using the experience to help get a job? Does he or she want to meet someone of the opposite sex? Is the person just bored? If your volunteer coordinator can determine what makes the person tick, he or she can better decide how to best utilize the volunteer.

Determine also what the volunteer likes to do. Some people are leaders; you want to put these people into organizing positions. Some are workers; they do not want to be boss, and they do not mind the grunt work. Some are donors; they want to be involved, but as minimally as possible. For them, providing a check or the prestige of their name to your campaign (on an endorsement list or fund- or friend-raising letter) is sufficient.

All of these types of individuals are valuable, and it is the job of the volunteer coordinator to slot them correctly. Make volunteering fun. Surprise volunteers with some sports tickets or a party.

INTERNSHIPS

Colleges and universities constantly seek to place students in internships—low-paying or unpaid positions in which students receive experience in the real world that will add to their resumes and help them secure jobs later. Not only are students good for free or low-cost help, but they bring fresh ideas that might be essential to energize a campaign.

Tap your local schools for students who can help. Do not limit your inquiries to the political science department, although that is a good place to start. Need a media director? How about the journalism department? An accounting intern can be obtained from the business department. Determine your needs, and call the chair of that particular academic department. Student organizations on campus, such as gender-based or ethnic organizations, issue-oriented groups, and the College Democrats or Republicans, also have capable, committed members who already have some experience your campaign needs.

Internships usually require a supervisor, either from the school's faculty or from the campaign, who will "grade" or evaluate the intern, as this is an academic experience for the student.

TRAVEL

For a campaign that requires inter-city travel, campaign staff have to make travel arrangements. This usually falls under the responsibilities of the scheduler.

Travel arrangements can include car rental, train, bus, taxi, or airplane tickets, and reimbursements for mileage (31.5 cents per mile is allowed by the IRS as of this writing). Travel plans should include specifically who in the campaign is travelling with whom, and by what conveyance (who is riding in what car, for example).

If the candidate is traveling by air, the scheduler should contact the airport's and the airline's customer service representative to smooth baggage checks and other potential travel-related problems. Someone also should be in charge of the baggage.

PARTY CHOICE

"He serves his party best who serves the country best."
— President Rutherford B. Hayes

Commonly held ideas, values, and positions on issues normally determine which party a candidate will choose—but not always.

As Daniel Bennett, Richard Nixon's 1968 campaign manager for Chicago, told me in an interview, choose your party also based on your family's history and your friendships.

Thus, if you are a conservative but come from a Democratic family or the people you know who are active in politics are Democrats, you might be better off becoming involved in politics as a Democrat rather than a Republican.

That is why—up until the 1990s, anyway—there always were conservative Democrats and liberal Republicans.

Prognosticators in the 1960s and 1970s argued that with the increasing importance of media, parties would become less relevant. As with rocket cars and vacations on Mars, they were wrong. With the communications and information glut, parties have become more important, because the only way harried voters can sort out candidates is via a party label. Or do you think a Rush Limbaugh "dittohead" would ever vote for a Democrat for president?

Independents and third-party candidates may make a splash, but they do not win. Does it matter if you are right if you do not win? It depends on your goal.

While it may be incredibly easy to be nominated by a "third" or minor party, these candidates rarely win general elections, and even getting on the ballot sometimes is difficult. "Attempts of groups that wish to run as 'third parties' are costly, time-consuming, and unbelievably frustrating," wrote Robert S. Ross in *American National Government.* [75]

There may be other reasons for running, however. Although I recommend against a kamikaze race just to get the candidate's name known, it is a strategy that sometimes works. A Libertarian Party activist's notoriety helped him receive the Republican nomination in a Texas congressional district in 1996.

Or, third-party races can serve to publicize ideas that are later co-opted by the Republicans and Democrats. In the late 1800s, the Farmer's Alliance Party's advocacy of railroad, agriculture, and trade reform propelled the issues onto the national agenda, and the Populist Party first brought forth the ideas of the progressive income tax and the secret ballot. Many positions championed by the Socialist Party in the 1920s and 1930s are now mainstream American values.

If a candidate is running a third party race to win, he or she faces certain disappointment. If there is another agenda that the campaign can achieve, however, it may be worth the effort.

POLLING

"The more we trust polls, the more likely they are to mislead us."
—Norman Solomon, media critic[76]

Despite media watchdog Norman Solomon's comment, more than $100 million is spent annually on political polling. In 1998, from three to five percent of candidates' budgets are devoted to polling, and the figure is rising. (If you are spending more than ten percent of your budget on polling, you are probably wasting money that could be spent better elsewhere.) Polling "is being used in races down to the county level," according to the *Chicago Sun-Times.*[77]

It is wise to keep Solomon's warning uppermost in mind when designing a poll. "Slight differences in question wording or in the placement of the questions in the interview can have profound consequences," according to David Moore, vice president of the Gallup Poll.[78] Solomon refers to a 1985 poll in which only nineteen percent of Americans thought that more money should be spent on "welfare," but sixty-three percent thought more should be spent on "assistance to the poor."[79] Other than the phrasing, it was the same question. If the wording of your question results in the wrong answers, your data will totally mislead you.

You do not necessarily need to spend money on a professional pollster to write questions. A college political science, business, or statistics professor may be able to do the job equally well at less cost. In fact, utilize faculty and students as much as possible.

Ideally, have the local, county, state, or national party organization fund your poll. Or, you may be able to piggy-back onto their polls.

There are several ways to conduct public opinion polls: telephone, street corner or mall surveys, informal conversation, mail surveys, or focus groups. If you cannot afford a professional polling or marketing organization, use your own volunteers or students from the local university—from the statistics, sociology, or marketing departments.

Determine if your polling venue is skewing your data. For example, 1948 polls that indicated Thomas Dewey was going to defeat Harry Truman often were telephone polls. The poorer people who were planning to vote for Truman did not have telephones and were eliminated. If you are polling in the upscale mall, you will probably be missing some lower income voters with different opinions.

If you do hire a professional pollster, ask if they just provide raw data or offer analysis and recommendations, too. Whom do they call—registered voters or all inhabitants of the community? (Sometimes you might want to call the latter to get the public's general opinion, whether they intend to vote or not.) Can you publicly attribute the data to the polling organization? (If the answer is "no" and the polling organization wants its name kept out of the media, you have to question whether the data is even accurate.)

Methods for determining public opinion need not be used only concerning issues and the candidate. They also can gauge reaction to print, direct mail, and television and radio ads.

Do not poll just to poll. The first order of business is to determine who is for and against your candidate and who is on the fence. You do not really care about the "horserace" when you are polling; instead, poll with the idea of finding *opportunities.* Definitely follow-up with the undecideds later in the campaign.Target your polls to discover if your candidate is weak among certain types of voters or in particular geographic areas. Then work on those weaknesses either by campaigning more aggressively among those voters or perhaps even changing the candidate. East Coast preppie George Bush acted more Texan in 1988 and got elected.

Polling also can determine the effectiveness of your opponents' strategies. For example, if the opponent accuses your candidate of not caring about "family values," but your polls tell you the voters are unconcerned about this issue because a toxic waste dump is the major issue, you do not have to waste resources on refuting this charge.

If you are conducting a mail poll, include a postage-paid business reply envelope or card. No one will pay to provide you with information.

The "blind identification" telephone call (see also HEADQUARTERS-TELEPHONE, page 112) can be an effective and low-budget method of gathering information.

Do not ever attempt to poll by phone on Friday or Saturday night; few people are home, and none of them are thinking about your candidate.

Different types of polls are:

- The benchmark poll, which is the first major information-gathering poll in the campaign.
- The tracking poll, which determines how the candidate compares with the other candidate.
- The brushfire poll, which helps determine public opinion on sudden, major developments in the campaign.
- The push poll, which attempts to sway voter opinion.

Some experts do not even consider the push poll a poll, but merely another form of negative campaigning. Questions are asked in a way that puts opponents in a bad light.

Tracking and brushfire polls require speed, so the telephone is the best method. When conducting multiple tracking polls, you can save money by "rolling" the sample. That means you poll only a portion of your entire list one night, poll a different portion on a subsequent night, and then "roll" the results together to form a representative sample for a "rolling-average tracking poll." This also eliminates alienating your sample voters because you have contacted them too often.

Or, ask one half of the sample one question, and the other half a different one. You acquire all the information you want, but you take up less of each voter's time.

You never need to poll more than 600 people to achieve a statistically valid sample.

The more questions asked and the more sophisticated the questions, the more information you will obtain and the costs will be greater. Professional benchmark and tracking polls are particularly expensive.

If the poll is too long, takes too much time, or features difficult questions phrased in jargon instead of normal language, each increases the likelihood of the voter hanging up the phone, walking away, or worse, getting mad at your candidate.

Rather than purchasing expensive lists from a pollster, you may want to use the voter lists available to you free (or inexpensively) from the local election board or party. The Internet can be a good source of polling information, not for your electoral contest specifically, but for public opinion on general issues.

Speak with your local phone company about Computer Assisted Telephone Interviewing (CATI) systems.

Polls help when making major decisions, but do not become so enamored of polls that you cannot make a decision without one.

Sophisticated polling is great, but it is still no substitute for common sense. Nationally syndicated columnist Molly Ivins visits the unemployment compensation bureau to discover what people are thinking. In 1992, she thought Bill Clinton was going to defeat George Bush despite the professional polls indicating the opposite. Harry Truman used to send a friend dressed as a farmer in a horse-drawn wagon to gauge public opinion. In 1948, he discovered that Truman would win the presidency when everyone thought he would lose.

A low-budget polling method is the focus group. Gather a few people (no more than ten) representative of the candidate's potential constituents, pay a minimum rate for their time, and ask them your questions. You can form a focus group yourself or hire college marketing students. If you hire a professional marketing firm, expenditures suddenly become large, but information derived also is more accurate. No matter who conducts it, a focus group will not mirror public opinion exactly, but it will provide at least some valuable data.

Do not attempt to cover more than ten issues in a focus group, and do not ask more than five questions concerning each issue. Also, observe the listeners' body language. If a respondent is saying that race is not an issue, but his body language indicates he cannot stand that member of a minority group sitting next to him, you know his responses are suspect.

Professional firms experienced in running focus groups often have facilities equipped with two-way mirrors that allow observation of the participants.

Try to write questions that actually elicit information, and do not skew your questions to get the answers you want (then you just are seeking validation, not insight). If you ask people if too much money is being spent on government entitlement programs, they will say yes. If you ask if spending on Medicare, Medicaid, and Social Security for ill, low-income grandparents should be cut, they will say no. Essentially, though, it is the same question.

All your poll's questions should not be answerable with a mere yes or no; try to write open-ended questions that actually elicit new information.

Positive poll results should be communicated to the media and potential endorsers and donors. Even an unsophisitcated poll performed by your own staff can amass results that can generate some free publicity following a news release on the poll numbers. Some unscrupulous candidates have released "poll results" from polls that never were actually taken, and unfortunately, media have sometimes been suckered into printing them.

What if the polls indicate your candidate is in trouble? Do not panic. If it is early in the campaign, your candidate's low ratings usually represent a lack of name recognition, and you can work on that. If it is later in the campaign, polling can indicate why your candidate is weak and how to work on those negatives. Remember, "voters make up their minds like they do for a major purchase; it takes time," said Nancy Todd of the Todd Co.[80]

Also remember that after all this science, people lie. Not everyone who says he or she will vote for the candidate will actually do so. That is why when the polls indicate your candidate is ahead, he or she has to run as hard as if he or she were actually behind. Just ask Mike Dukakis. In fact, polls consistently indicate that more people will vote for the progressive candidate than actually do cast their ballots for progressives on election day, so a good rule of thumb is to subtract about three percentage points from a progressive's poll numbers to arrive at more accurate results.

Just cannot afford to poll, but want to get some information on peoples' opinions and lifestyles anyway? Try the National Opinion Research Center (NORC) in Chicago. The center has extensive social research information and conducts the "General Social Survey" annually to measure trends.

RESEARCH

"The old cliché is 'information is power.' The new cliché is 'knowing where to get information is power.' 'It' is out there somewhere; you need to know where to find it."
— Lou Williams, president, L.C. Williams & Associates [81]

Research can take many forms: polling, examination of voter data, or study in the library or on the Internet, and more. "It's fun, but be ready to dedicate some time," Lou Williams noted.[82]

The ultimate goal of research is to understand what the voters are like, what their attitudes are, what their awareness levels are, and what their needs are. With good research, you can develop a campaign that speaks to their needs.

Research attempts to determine:

- Who are the target voters, what are their demographic characteristics, and where do their interests lie.
- What the voters currently are aware of and believe and how persuadable they are.
- "Hot-buttons."
- The right media.
- The right message.
- The right tactics.

A few research tips:

- Ask precise questions.
- Be courteous.
- Be prepared. Learn as much as you can on your own so you are well-informed when you ask an outside source.
- Find everything you can. Do not stop at one source; try to get independent confirmation.
- Keep exact records. Many researchers fail to indicate the source of the information. If you make this mistake, you either have to duplicate the research or not use the information.
- Use lists.
    Phone lists.
    Voter lists.
- Use the following sources:
    The Internet.
    Libraries.
        Public.
        Universities/colleges.
        Library of Congress.
        If your local library does not have the information try interlibrary loan.
    The media (old newspapers, magazines, film libraries).
    Public records (credit reports, tax, real estate, court, police, public hearings, governmental bodies, and similar items). Can be found in municipal facilities, court facilities, state archives, and similar repositories.

A Comprehensive Guide to Electoral Success | 163

Universities/colleges.
The public relations department can provide a list
of the institution's experts.

When photocopying at the library or other research centers, either bring a lot of change or ask staff if you can pay when you are finished copying.

See also Appendices Three, Four, Five, and Seven for research resources.

Researching the Opposition

"Never underestimate the ability of elected officials to say and do dumb things," said political consultant Terry Cooper. Those dumb things are likely on the record someplace. Finding them is called opposition research.

Opposition research is not used only for negative campaigning. Innumerable times candidates have told me they do not know anything about a particular opponent. If you do not know whom you are running against, you really do not know why you are running.

Call a friendly reporter to get the basic facts about your opponent. Or, have a staffer call the opponent's campaign or the opponent. The staffer can indicate he or she is gathering information for a possible volunteer effort, newspaper article, school assignment, or whatever.

There is little that is cloak-and-dagger about opposition research. It usually consists of examination of newspapers and public records, such as transcripts of meetings and tax, court, business, and motor vehicle records to determine your opponent's past actions and positions.

Fact-check the opponent's literature, ads, and credentials. If he said he went to Harvard, you can ascertain if that meant he earned a degree or if he only participated in an aerobics mini-course.

Have someone from your campaign tape your opponent's statements and speeches and look for items you can refute. It is even better when the opponent claims he or she never said it and you can prove otherwise. George Bush once claimed he never called Ronald Reagan's financial plans "voodoo economics" and looked ridiculous when media proved he did.

"Clipping" and broadcast monitoring services such as *Bacon's* and *Burrelle's* (see also Appendix Five: Media Publications and Services) can provide articles and transcipts about the opponent from publications and radio and television broadcasts. The services can, of course, provide citations to your candidate as well.

In monitoring broadcast media, these services provide transcripts at approximately one dollar per page plus addional monitoring costs. The broader the search, the more expensive, so the search can run into some serious money. You may want to limit the search either by subject (ask for everything the opponent says on, for example, the minimum wage) or by particular broadcast outlet, or both.

If you want to discover on which broadcast outlets the opponent is scheduled to speak, have a college student contact the opponent's campaign and indicate he or she is in a broadcast journalism course, and for a class assignment would like to listen to as many of their candidate's campaign appearances to track media bias.

As someone active and known in the community, your opponent is likely to be involved with nonprofit, charitable, and tax-exempt agencies. That includes clubs, banks and credit unions, civic associations, foundations, hospitals, insurance companies, museums, nursing homes, professional associations, schools, trade organizations, and unions. Many organizations are not-for-profits. Believe it or not, *Quill* reports, even the National Football League, Ocean Spray, and Land O'Lakes have nonprofit status.[83]

Researchers should be aware of the Internal Revenue Service's Form 990, which *Quill* described as "the ultimate public record."[84] Similar to the 1040 but much longer and more detailed, the 990 is required of all nonprofit, charitable, and tax-exempt agencies. The confidential finances of these organizations can be found in the 990, and this can be used to determine if your opponent's involvement with a nonprofit is proper. Be aware of the following: Are nonprofits spending too much on administrative costs as compared to its expenditures on services? How does your opponent's salary at the nonprofit compare to other nonprofit compensation? Where are the nonprofits investing? Are travel and expense accounts suspiciously high? An IRS regional center's tax-exempt compliance officer will provide a photocopy of any nonprofit's 990.

Check your opponent's list of campaign contributors. If you are running for water district commissioner and he is receiving contributions from the county's biggest polluter, you have an instant issue.

It also does not hurt to have the campaign do "opposition re-search" on your own candidate, to look for vulnerabilities. This lets you head off problems and prepare responses to potential attacks.

Research of public records does not have to be opposition-based only. You can use those same public records to determine information on crime and demographic trends, and other issues that can be useful to your campaign.

To get certain government information, you may need to file a Freedom Of Information Act request. See also APPENDIX SEVEN: FREEDOM OF INFORMATION ACT .

RESOURCES

"...man's judgment is no better than his information."
—Robert P. Lamont

Even the most severely underfunded campaign has access to a wealth of resources.

COLLEGES/UNIVERSITIES

Local colleges and universities can be a great asset. Need an intelligent analysis of a specific issue? Talk to a professor who already may have written a paper on it and be looking for a way to get his or her thoughts into the mainstream. For example, if you want a plan on balancing the budget, talk to an economics professor.

You do not have to wander around the college to find an expert. Simply contact the media relations department, whose personnel are likely to have a list of professors and their areas of expertise.

Schools also are great places to find campaign volunteers, interns, and students with other specialized skills, such as video. If you want to produce a video but can not afford a professional service, try to hire a student in the communications or video department.

Talk to the political science and social work departments, as well as student activist organizations like the Young Republicans and College Democrats.

Your local college or university will have a library (and an inter-library loan program) and Internet access. Use them.

LIBRARIES

Libraries are your greatest resource for free information; you can find literally anything. If you want to develop a position on an issue, you will be able to find a relevant article, book, or an Internet site. Tell the librarian what you are looking for, and you are on your way.

If you discover that you can not find the information you need even with the librarian's help because everything is on computer and you are computer illiterate, enlist the aid of a student. Their generation knows its way around a computer like the 1950s generation knew its way around a station wagon.

LISTS

The late DePaul University Dean Austin M. Flynn was the academic who said, "Garbage data produces garbage conclusions."

Today, lists exist that are categorized by almost every subject imaginable. They are indispensible in fundraising. Keep in mind the late Dean Flynn's warning, however: ask tough questions of those providing the lists to understand the age of the data, how it was gathered, and in which format(s) it is available.

Begin by creating your own list of the candidate's friends, business associates, fellow religious congregants, and other acquaintances. For a complete rundown of basic sources for the campaign's key list, see also FUNDRAISING, page 98.

Then, go to outside list sources. Some lists can be obtained just for the asking, while others must be rented. Only the campaign can determine if the cost of the particular list is likely to be exceeded by monies generated by using the list. Do not be reluctant to request the organization providing the list to conduct the mailing for you, either. While a commercial organization selling you a list obviously has no reason to subsidize your mailing, the P.T.A. or Sierra Club might.

Parties and candidates from previous runs can provide lists of donors, volunteers, and more for free or for a minimal cost. Voting records and other government lists also are available free or at low rates.

List brokers can provide names based on magazine subscriptions (the progressive candidate might want to buy a list from the *Nation* or the *Progressive*; the conservative from the *National Review* or *New Criterion,* for example) by zip code, so you have to purchase only the names of people in your district. These can be expensive, however. To find a list broker, examine *Direct Marketing Market Place* or *Literary Market Place* (found in many libraries), or see also Appendix Eight: List Brokers. List brokers often can download lists to your computer.

You may be able to cross-reference data. For example, if your candidate is a dentist, lists of dentists are available for purchase from dental associations, local dental societies, commercial magazines that deal with dentistry, list brokers, and other sources. You can cross-reference the list of dentists with a list of donors or a list of voters, and more. This may be expensive and not yield many matches; however the matches it does yield may be worth their weight in gold. List brokers can cross-reference, but it also can be done at a college computer department or by a campaign worker who is computer literate.

Some list brokers provide "database enhancement," such as socio-demographic or other subject "overlays" for creating detailed profiles. They also provide "merge/purge" services to eliminate duplicate names and addresses (do this yourself to save money). In addition, they may offer "mapping" services so you do not receive lists of voters outside your district, and "selects" based upon age, income, or other criteria.

Lists are available for virtually any subject, e.g., by profession, income, age, recreational preference, reading habits, education, religion, lifestyle, and much more, categorized by a wide variety of variables (name, gender, phone number, and zip code).

You may want to obtain a Washington, D.C.-based list of members of your party, targeted by giving levels, profession, or interest in a particular issue, from a list broker or political party. You may be able to find a hook as to why people from outside your district will donate money. For example, when liberal reformer Harold Washington ran for mayor of Chicago in 1983 and 1987, he raised money throughout the country. He was running against Chicago's Democratic machine, and he was able to solicit funds from liberals who remembered the 1968 Democratic Convention and wanted to break the Chicago organization's power, even though these donors lived elsewhere.

It is better to obtain a list electronically than on paper so you can add it to your electronic database. The ideal list includes name, salutation (does William Jones like "Dear William," "Dear Bill," "Dear Buddy," or what?), address, city, zip code, home and work phone numbers and fax numbers, job, and donation history.

Make sure any voter list a vendor provides has recently been phone-matched. The list should not be too old and should have been improved through the National Change of Address (NCOA) computer program, which lists all address changes over the previous thirty-six months. Lists that have been zip-code corrected, zip-plus-four appended, and carrier-route coded and appended also are desirable.

Ask what electronic format the list is in, if it can be appended easily, and the legal or contractual constraints on the file's use.

Some lists can be provided on CD-ROM. Aristotle Industries of Washington, D.C., offers CD-ROMs with voter lists, names and addresses of licensed drivers, campaign contributors, and mail routes.

EXPERTS

"An expert is someone who is afraid of learning something new, because if he did, he wouldn't be an expert anymore," said President Harry Truman. While there is nothing more valuable than expert help or advice, the campaign should not be a slave to the experts' opinions.

Sometimes the candidate's or staff's gut feeling or heartfelt commitment is more important than the advice of a dozen experts. Use common sense in following experts' advice, and do not be afraid to question that advice. To obtain expert help, check with other candidates from current or previous campaigns, party organizations, or local colleges.

THE INTERNET

While it certainly does not hurt your candidate to be on the Internet, it is not mandatory at this point either, although that is likely to change as more people become comfortable with the technology. Still, it currently makes more sense to devote scarce resources to conventional communications.

If you want to be on the Internet and are a technological illiterate (like most of us), find a computer science student from the local high school or college to help you establish a web site.

Merely being on the Internet is a great way to get free publicity—from the Internet itself, as well as from media coverage regarding your site.

As when buying anything, *caveat emptor*—buyer beware. Make sure the technology can do something conventional campaigning cannot. Otherwise, why get it? Know what you are buying—otherwise, do not buy it. Do not buy technology or equipment just because it is the latest available—the old technology might be fine for your needs, and the new hardware will become outmoded quickly.

Neither the candidate nor the staff should spend a lot of time surfing the Internet. It is a tool, not a toy. If the candidate is a tech-head, you have to get him or her off the computer and out campaigning.

Illinois congressional candidate Danny Davis used the Internet wisely in his 1996 campaign. As alderman and county commissioner he had represented low-income areas, so in his run for congress he established a home page on the World Wide Web as a way to communicate with residents of the affluent sections of the congressional district, developing a connection to people with whom he had none previously.

Undoubtedly in the future, every candidate will have a home page. Here are a few tips found in *Writing Concepts* from consultant Jeff Herrington of Jeff Herrington Communications in Dallas. [85]

- *Keep quotations short.* "Probably no more than one short sentence."
- *Use lots of bullets.* Lists are more appropriate for the Internet than for print.
- *Get to the point.* "People go online to retrieve facts fast, not to read."
- *Rely on words, not graphics or design.* A graphic may take considerable time to download, the person may become angry with the candidate, or just not wait.

In addition, the home page should contain a short biography of the candidate, a photo (but make sure it does not take forever to download), information from news releases, and the candidate's stand on issues.

The Internet allows even the smallest campaign to provide a daily update for the public and the press. It also allows rapid response to a negative attack or other surprise development.

The Internet also allows you to interact with intelligent constituents. In 1994, U.S. Senator Barbara Boxer of California placed a healthcare survey on the World Wide Web and averaged more than 100 responses per day.

Consider also holding a chat session between the candidate and Internet users.

If the campaign has a web page, it must publicize it on all advertising materials. The page must be updated frequently, and a staffer must be assigned to the task. Surfers want new material constantly, so if the campaign does not have the resources to update the web page, forget it.

The Internet can be valuable not only for disseminating information, but for obtaining it as well. Federal Election Commission reports are published on the Internet, providing information about political action committees (PACs) that may be useful to your fundraising.

The Internet also contains freebies such as databases, graphics, type fonts for your campaign literature, and more.

Increasingly, the Internet will prove indispensible for the research you must perform on voters, demographic and social trends in your district, the opposition, and more. Lexis/Nexis™ is only one of the online database services that researchers will find helpful. It offers the ability to track any federal or state bill and any citation to a particular organization, issue, and/or candidate; access congressional testimony; monitor campaign finance activity; and analyze congressional voting.

In conducting Internet research, however, you can quickly ring-up charges. Be focused, and do not waste time surfing. Consider an Internet service that offers unlimited use for a flat rate.

If you are not connected to the Internet and cannot afford or do not wish to be, your local library, university, and perhaps the local high school can be your entrance ramp to the information highway.

HISTORY

"The only thing new in the world is the history that you don't know," President Harry Truman was fond of saying. Americans are a people with an unfortunate lack of interest in history. This allows politicians to reopen issues that people thought were settled long ago, because younger generations often are oblivious of many past philosophical and political battles.

The balanced budget now is a mantra, but how many people are aware that *every* attempt to balance the budget in American history has been followed by severe economic depression? The argument that a minimum wage creates no economic benefits and engenders job loss was proven to be inaccurate during the New Deal, yet in the 1990s no one remembers the counter-arguments. Anti-regulation fervor is at fever-pitch because the abuses that originally required government regulation have been forgotten.

Historical knowledge also allows the campaign to develop that all-important coherent message. If you know where you have been, you can more easily articulate where you are going—and why.

History also shows which political tactics have worked and which have failed. Bill Clinton before 1998 demonstrated an amazing resiliency, bouncing back to win whenever it looked as if his career were over. He is one of the few recent presidents to have read the biographies of *every* president, and undoubtedly he gathered a few pointers along his scholarly journey. Discussing issues with a faculty member at your local college could be quite productive.

Newt Gingrich was a history professor and was able to translate his historical knowledge into an ideology understood, embraced, and advocated by enough voters to put him and his ideological fellows into power. That is the supreme example of the value of history as a resource for achieving elective office today.

SPEECHES

"The nice thing about being a celebrity is that, if you bore people, they think it's their fault,"

—Henry Kissinger, former Secretary of State

Since your campaign's candidate is not Henry Kissinger, his or her speeches must not put the audience to sleep. Keep the speeches simple and short. The day of the five-hour diatribe ended around the time of the Lincoln-Douglas debates. Omit the statistics and add references to real people and real situations. Also, do not ever assume the audience is as interested in the details of the issue as the candidate.

Know something about your audience, e.g., gender balance, ethnicity, sexual orientation, age. It is hard to make an intelligent speech without this basic information. Tailor speeches to the audience. The candidate may be a strong advocate of Social Security, but it is pointless to talk about this issue to a high school crowd.

You should type the candidate's speech, but if the candidate uses a full text, he or she should not flop pages so that they are sloppily hanging over the front of the lectern. A better idea is not to staple the pages, so the candidate can smoothly move one page over to the side as he or she completes it. Make sure pages are numbered, so if they become out of order they can be collated easily. Have a second copy of the speech available in case the first one gets lost, perhaps one in the car and another in the candidate's briefcase or with an aide.

Use a larger typeface for the speech so the candidate can more easily read it, and double-space it so last-minute changes and edits can be included. Read the speech aloud once as a dry run, because sometimes what looked good on paper sounds strange, or sometimes a phrase turns out to be awkward.

If the candidate prefers not to speak from a full text, prepare three-by-five-inch cards with talking points.

A good opening is a story about something the candidate shares with the audience. This quickly establishes a common ground. The worst possible opening is tapping the microphone or asking "Is this on?" (Your advance work should have already made sure that it is.)

Personalized information, about what the candidate or other people have accomplished in comparable situations, always is preferable to dry statistics. Real-life examples also build credibility. Metaphors, similes, and anecdotes are what people remember. Rhetorical questions are good, because they involve the audience.

It is great to mention a personal reference specifically tailored to a particular audience, but make sure the information is correct. When Senator George McGovern spoke to Gordon Tech High School students in Chicago in 1972, he pronounced all of the Polish priests' names flawlessly and received a standing ovation. Mayor Harold Washington, however, when addressing a DePaul University crowd once pronounced the name of beloved basketball coach Ray Meyer "Ray Mayors," causing both ill-will and ridicule. Make sure you get it right. In fact, not only in speeches but in any situation, the candidate should be briefed on correct pronunciation of the important players' names.

Parallel structure does well in creating a sense of rhythm. Jesse Jackson's use of this structure always makes his speeches effective.

Ronald Reagan was undoubtedly the greatest political speaker of the latter part of the twentieth century. Perhaps the number one attribute of his speaking success was his use of what communications professors Michael Weiler and W. Barnett Pearce call "ceremonial discourse": the ability to use patriotic, family, and moral themes to "prove" his ideas were right and cut-off debate from his detractors by making them look opposed to these values.[86]

Through the 1980s, conservatives were successful with this technique while progressives, inexplicably, did not even try. However, themes such as equality, helping others, and not letting work dominate life to the point of hurting families can be used to craft a progressive speech employing "ceremonial discourse" with equal effect to positive conservative themes.

The candidate should make eye contact with the audience and speak clearly and loudly enough but not so loud as to be annoying. This takes practice, and taping or videotaping the candidate practicing or presenting actual speeches and analyzing the tapes is an excellent aid. The speaker should never read word for word from the speech, and should look at the audience.

The candidate also should speak slowly and avoid drumming fingers, tapping a pen, or jingling coins or keys. He or she should forego touching hair, an ear, or face during a speech. *U.S. News & World Report* printed a photo of five presidents, Nixon, Ford, Carter, Reagan, and Bush, talking to each other at the opening of the Reagan Library. While the other four look erect and confident, Bush is shown fiddling with his ear, making him look nervous.

The speaker should avoid coffee, tea, or alcohol before speaking, as they dry the salivary glands.

If the candidate loses his or her place in a speech, he or she should relax and take the time necessary to regroup. It will seem like a long time to the candidate, but really will only be a few seconds and the audience will likely not even notice. Pauses are fine; "umms" and "urrs" are terrible.

If the speaker blanks out, he or she should repeat what was just said. The audience will think it is emphasis. If the candidate still can not remember the next part of the talk, the candidate should just skip ahead to another part of the speech.

Today it is better to show instead of tell, so include some graphics in the presentation via flip charts or overheads. Ross Perot used this tactic very effectively in his 1992 presidential campaign. Do not expect the visuals to carry the message, however—the speech still is important. If you include handouts, pass them around after the speech, so people are not fiddling with them while the candidate is talking.

It also is not a bad idea to move around a little, instead of using the podium as a shield. A little movement establishes rapport with the listeners. If the microphone is stationary though, stay put.

Lastly, close the sale: the candidate should ask for the audience's votes. Then ask for questions and comments. If the candidate is asked one to which he or she does not know the answer, that is fine; he or she should promise to get back to the person later with the answer, and then someone from the campaign should do so. An aide should get the person's address or phone number.

If there are no questions, either an aide should ask a previously prepared one, or the candidate should have a rhetorical question or comment ready. You do not want to end a great speech with an awkward silence.

Look for public speaking opportunities; do not think that the invitations are going to roll in. Develop a list of organizations in your district that might be interested in hearing the candidate speak. Does your candidate have something to say on healthcare? A local seniors organization, or medical, dental, or nurses group might be interested, and these are the types of people who vote and contribute.

The campaign should videotape the candidate's speeches to critique them and help the candidate practice for future speeches. The tapes also may be valuable for sound bites and potential footage for television or videocassette commercials.

Public speaking gets easier and speakers get better with practice, so the candidate should be out there as much as possible.

STRATEGY

"...political campaign tactics, a subject that enchants journalists but either bores or disgusts millions who lack White House press passes."
—Russell Baker, journalist[87]

One type of newspaper or broadcast report you never want to see is one about your campaign strategy. The campaign should be talking to the press and the public about the candidate, his or her ideas, and the issues—not about the brilliance of the campaign strategy.

For one thing, public discussions of campaign strategy take the focus off your candidate, where it belongs, onto the campaign staff, where it does not. Republican political consultant Roger Ailes in the 1990 Illinois U.S. Senate contest actually held a press conference in which he, not candidate Lynn Martin, attacked opponent Paul Simon. "That was unprofessional and ludicrous, and hurt his candidate more than Simon," wrote political consultant David Axelrod in the *Chicago Reader*. "And it hurt him [Ailes]—I think he looked foolish."[88]

For another, the strategy you think may be so brilliant may not be. Presidential candidate Bob Dole in 1996 actually told the media that his campaign strategy would be to run as a Washington outsider. Since he had been in congress for forty years, the strategy did not look particularly smart.

The media wants to cover the horserace, and you will be tempted to brag. Resist the urge.

ANALYSIS

Opera diva Grace Moore said, "Analyzing what you haven't got as well as what you have is a necessary ingredient of a career." To learn what you've got and what you don't before beginning the campaign, do a SWOT analysis. SWOT, according to Joe Williams, CEO of Joe Williams Communications Inc. in Bartlesville, Oklahoma, stands for:

- Strengths.
- Weaknesses.
- Opportunities.
- Threats.[89]

Analyze these aspects of the candidate and the campaign before deciding to make the big commitment.

You must analyze facts such as previous voter turnout, the number of votes it has taken to win a particular office in the past, what the margins of victory were, and how much money was spent.

PLANNING

It may sound Zen-like, but crises do not arise from events themselves. They arise from your not having planned for them.

Ask yourself where the campaign is, where you want it to go, and how you are going to get it there. Also ask whom you are trying to influence, what you want them to do, and how you are going to get them to do it. That is planning.

Planning is crucial, and do not ever go into a campaign without some sort of plan. The candidate and campaign team should develop a plan early: how much money is going to be spent, what groups are going to be targeted for campaigning, how to attract volunteers, what alliances and endorsements are going to be sought, and other related items. In fact, just about everything in this book can be included in your plan.

Of course the plan will change throughout the course of the campaign, but having one will allow you to be proactive rather than reactive.

Planning should address objectives, possible problems, and possible solutions and their several consequences. Planning also should prioritize, because the campaign will not have enough human or financial resources and must make decisions on where to deploy them to do the most good.

According to Michael Deaver in *U.S. News & World Report*,

> One of the things that most people do not do when they get into this is to sit down and develop a strategy. They should set it all down: where do you want to be, what is an endgame for you—and then figure out all the ways you can get there. Another key is to make priorities with the amount of time you have got. Keep your message as simple as possible and stick to your strategy.[90]

That will keep your campaign from jumping from tactic to tactic—a sure path to losing.

Inform all the campaign's key players about the plan—do not keep anyone in the dark. This will encourage them to work together, even if some members of the team disagree on certain points. They must agree with the plan publicly, although they should be encouraged to express ideas and better solutions privately.

A written plan allows easy reference, but give it only to trusted staffers so it does not fall into the hands of the opposition.

The following is a checklist for the planning process:

- Assemble data; determine what data still is needed.
- Analyze previous plans (from other campaigns, candidate's business operations plans, similar sources).
- Analyze candidate's strengths and weaknesses.
- Analyze the competition's strengths and weaknesses.
- Analyze voters (demographics and trends); determine whom to target.
- Determine potential and available funding.
- Determine rough expenditures.
- Determine availability of other resources (volunteers, alliances, endorsements, other).
- Determine organizational structure.
- Determine message: why the candidate is running.
- Determine tentative campaign plans and projects; include options that may not be engaged in immediately but may become necessary later (damage control for potential problems).
- Group and assign priorities.

- Develop schedules.
- Determine standards or benchmarks by which you can assess performance.
- Assess performance and alter plans if necessary.

TARGETING

No campaign has enough resources, so targeting makes the best use of limited resources.

Estimate the turnout, the numbers of voters favorable toward your candidate and what their turnout is likely to be, and then calculate how many swing voters there are and how many of them are needed. Take the number of votes cast in the last election, and divide by the number of registered voters; the result is the percentage of turnout.

Then determine the approximate number of voters favorable toward your candidate during the last election (looking at votes for candidates ideologically compatible with yours if your candidate never ran before) and divide that by votes cast; the result is the likely performance of your voters.

If the last election had a particularly hot issue that skewed turnout, like a school bond issue or presidential race, you might want to examine the numbers from two elections ago to get a better indication of what behavior is likely to repeat in this year's election.

Target few resources to your party or ideology's voters and concentrate on the swing voters. Look at data to try to isolate swing precincts. For instance, if a certain precinct went for your party's candidate for governor two years ago and its candidate for senator four years ago by eighty percent, you do not have to pay a lot of attention to it. A precinct that went for the Senate candidate by sixty percent but provided only forty percent to the gubernatorial candidate, however, is a swing precinct and must be targeted. It has a "persuasion percentage" of twenty percent. The higher the persuasion percentage, the more you target your campaign efforts there.

Targeting also allows you to avoid expending efforts on voters opposed to your candidate. Not only is this a waste of time and money, it can actually galvanize the opposition. "Soft" support for Carol Moseley-Braun in her 1992 Illinois U.S. Senate run became strong support when the campaign of her opponent, Rich Williamson, became increasingly offensive to women.

Target your communication efforts to the particular group. The campaign obviously should not be talking to students about retirement issues, or be speaking about abortion policy on a radio talk show whose audience is senior citizens.

POSITIONING

To "position" the candidate, the campaign must meaningfully differentiate the candidate from his or her opponent(s) among core target groups.

You first must identify the voters and their perceptions of issues and the candidate; develop a positioning theme (message); build understanding of the candidate's beliefs and characteristics among target groups; change the beliefs of those in disagreement, opposition, or ignorance; and develop action plans for leveraging that positioning. Reinforce the candidate's strengths and reframe the weaknesses so they become irrelevancies or even positives.

PUBLICITY

It may sound cynical, but one of President George Bush's campaign manuals advised his handlers that it is not what the candidate does, it is what he *appears* to do that counts.[91]

Campaign publicity efforts should aim continually to increase the candidate's visibility and strengthen his or her image among the voters, the media, and interest and support groups as a viable, exciting, influential, credible, and electable leader.

The candidate should be marketed as an individual who gives the public a voice in and access to the governing process.

Publicity efforts should aim to support the campaign by attracting more campaign volunteers, funding, and media attention. A little "theatre" for the sake of publicity does not hurt.

REPETITION

Studies show it takes from three to ten communications of a message before people even understand the message is for them, let alone before it actually sinks in. Do not be afraid to repeat your message.

RECYCLING

Recycling has nothing to do with taking out the trash, but has everything to do with avoiding trashing your campaign's precious time. The facts and preparation you put into one area should be recycled into others. The points researched for a candidate for a public or broadcast appearance, for example, should be used in campaign literature, advertisements, letters to the editor, op-ed pieces, and vice versa. Do not re-invent the wheel every time.

COORDINATION

Many people from the campaign will be asked questions by the media and the public: the candidate, the campaign staff, the candidate's family, and the footsoldiers. Make sure they all agree on the facts to be conveyed. Even more important, make sure they are not making conflicting statements.

Only the candidate, the campaign manager, and designated media spokespersons should respond to the media. The campaign may decide to approve a family member or another staffer as additional media spokespersons. All questions from the media to anyone else involved with the campaign should be referred to the designated media spokespersons.

Meetings should be held, daily if necessary but at least at regular intervals and as early in the day as possible, to create schedules for major players in the campaign. Review what went right, what went wrong, what was accomplished, what should have been accomplished but was not, and what needs to be completed. Make lists to use at the next meeting.

Share the big picture with staff. It is easier for people to perform their tasks—especially tasks they may not particularly like—if they understand the overall strategy. Be sure that all staff understand the big message. Keep them briefed. Too easily, staffers can become consumed by their own jobs and miss important information concerning other areas of the campaign. Also, an uninformed staff guarantees bad morale. You do not have to share the most sensitive information with staff, but do keep them informed about everything else.

I once heard a candidate tell his campaign manager, in the presence of the publisher of a local newspaper, to get his ad to the publication the next day. Two weeks later, it still had not arrived, and the campaign barely handed it in before the election. Obviously, the staff was not following through or coordinating.

While everything does not have to be coordinated with the candidate, as a staffer do not ever neglect to inform the candidate about something important. Your candidate being unpleasantly surprised by a situation that you should have coordinated in advance is one of the worst situations you can create. The goal is "no surprises," so when in doubt, share your information with the candidate.

BRIEFING

When he was vice president, Dan Quayle once used Black dialect in a speech to the National Association for the Advancement of Colored People. Obviously, no one briefed him that this was not a good idea. This wretched incident proves that there is no detail small enough to ignore when briefing the candidate. Regular briefings are just good strategy.

The candidate not only should be briefed on major issues but should be briefed on issues of concern to the particular audiences or media outlets before which he or she will appear.

Voters and media manage to embarrass politicians with this ploy all the time: they ask a question that every normal person knows the answer to but that out-of-touch candidates do not, making the candidate look foolish. Such questions include:

- How much does a loaf of bread cost?
- What is the price of a dozen eggs?
- How much is a gallon of milk?
- What does a gallon of gas cost?

Also, the candidate should be briefed on current events and popular culture. In November 1995, a Portland, Oregon, television station managed to embarrass all of the state's U.S. Senate candidates not only by asking those basic questions but asking, "Who is the prime minister of Canada?" and "Can you point out Bosnia on a globe?" None of the candidates did a good job. And of course, during the 1996 campaign, Bob Dole was surprised to discover that the Dodgers had left Brooklyn—thirty-eight years earlier.

While the candidate should be briefed on the basics, it is less of a sin to admit he or she does not know something than to make a ridiculous guess. You do not want your candidate to look as foolish as former Chicago Alderman Adeline Keane who, when asked about how to break down language barriers for Latino students, replied that they should be taught Latin.

If the candidate is surprised by a question to which he or she does not know the answer, the candidate should offer to get back to the person with the answer. An aide should then take the questioner's name and phone number or address and be sure to follow-up. A candidate should be frank about not having an answer readily available—do not try to fudge if you do not know something.

When asked a question by a New Hampshire resident concerning federal laws' impact on snowmobiling during the 1980 presidential campaign, candidate John Anderson chose to ridicule the questioner instead of admitting that he did not know the answer. While this tactic may work for New Orleans Saints Coach Mike Ditka in dealing with the media, it did not work for Anderson, and unless your candidate is a football superstar, it will not work for him or her either.

Brief the candidate in the way he or she prefers: in person, on tape, or via one-page memos with the most important facts highlighted. Staff should always provide hard-copy briefing materials and place them in the day's scheduling folder.

Do mock question-and-answer sessions in advance with the candidate for events such as debates, speeches, and media interviews. It was in one of these that a member of Senator Lloyd Bentsen's staff surprised him with a question comparing his vice-presidential rival Dan Quayle to President John Kennedy, inspiring Bentsen to come up with the "Senator, you're no Jack Kennedy" line that was one of the Democrats' few bright spots in the 1988 campaign. Briefings should be part of the schedule, not squeezed in around other events.

PACING

The battle between the 1969 Chicago Cubs and New York Mets serves as a great example of how a political campaign should be paced. The Cubs, who led the whole year until overtaken by the Mets in September, celebrated every victory like it was a circus and mourned every loss like a Greek tragedy. They expended too much energy and emotion too early and too often and were burned out at the end. The Mets slowly and steadily built momentum, with manager Gil Hodges trying different lineups and strategies early and coalescing everything late for the team to come on strong at the end.

The early stages of the camppaign are for acquiring funding and staff, strategizing, and building ties with the community. The later stages are for the big blitz. So do not worry if your candidate does not take an early lead. "Starting early does not mean treating each day like Election Day," according to *Campaigns & Elections*.[92]

The big blitz at the end can overcome an opponent's early lead, so save some money and energy for it. In the 1996 congressional campaign, the Democrats front-loaded their campaigning and led in the polls all year. The Republicans blitzed at the end when the Democrats were running on empty and were able to retain congress by getting most of the last-minute undecided voters.

INCUMBENTS

While it is always preferable to run for an "open" seat, a seat held by an incumbent can be won by a challenger; it happens all the time. The incumbent may have lost the zest for campaigning and passion on the issues, providing a real opportunity for a challenger. The incumbent may be running in a recently redrawn district, so many constituents may have no history of voting for that candidate. Just ask former Congressman Dan Rostenkowski, who was beaten by unknown Republican Michael Flanagan in a newly redrawn congressional district in Illinois in 1994. (Of course, the federal indictment against Rostenkowski might have had *something* to do with his loss, too.)

People love an underdog and love to be part of an upset—voters will shift to upset the incumbent just for the fun of it.

If your candidate is a challenger, show how he or she represents the future, and make the incumbent defend his or her record. Incumbents often fail to understand how their district has changed; the challenger can appeal to new voters and deal with new issues.

On the other hand, if your candidate is an incumbent, he or she has to show some zest, passion, and interest in and understanding of the future.

Beating an incumbent is all about change. Since people generally do not like change, they have to be persuaded.

People initially focus on what they can lose with any change, so the challenger has to focus on what they can gain. People also feel isolated when contemplating change, so the challenger has to persuade them that he or she and all the other voters are going through the same feelings and have decided to change anyway. People can handle only so much change, which is why radicals seldom get elected. People agreed with the post-1994 election Republican-dominated congress in wanting to reduce bureaucracy and try to balance the budget, but those representatives' attempts to restrict Medicare and environmental laws were more than people could accept. Keep the gentle pressure for change, otherwise people will revert to their old ways.

Even though they generally do not like change, sometimes voters seek it. Candidates of change also have to position themselves as reliable and not radical. Bill Clinton in 1992 was able to portray himself as an agent of desired change who was non-threatening and stable, despite G.O.P. attempts to portray him as extreme.

Conversely, the candidate of stability must be portrayed as open to progress. The 1992 Clinton campaign successfully painted President George Bush as unyielding and unchanging. "When I see a calendar and think of yesterday, I think of George Bush," Clinton advisor James Carville said in the documentary film *The War Room*.

Sometimes it takes serious challenges during several elections to "soften up" an incumbent for the kill, but often the giant-killer turns out to be someone other than the candidate who weakened the incumbent originally. Former Chicago Alderman Dick Simpson "softened up" Rostenkowski with two hard-fought campaigns against the congressman, but unfortunately for Simpson it was unknown challenger Flanagan who finally knocked off the embattled House chairman.

A sleazy tactic used by parties is having an incumbent nearing the end of their career resign in the middle of their term due to age, infirmity, or scandal. That allows the party or the pols in power, instead of the voters, to choose the successor. The appointee then has all the advantages of incumbency at the next election.

If you believe something like this is on the horizon, harp on the media to expose it. That may force the party and pols, for public relations' sake, to appoint a blue-ribbon chairwarmer who promises not to seek re-election, instead of a pol who will hold onto the office for several years. Your campaign also can use this issue as one to spark a petition drive to prevent mid-term appointments to elective offices, gaining your candidate exposure on a clean-government issue.

DIRTY TRICKS

For centuries, people have been admiringly quoting the unethical "dirty tricks" tactics of Niccolo Machiavelli delineated in his book, *The*

Prince. They neglect to mention that Machiavelli never worked in politics again after he wrote the book.

Simply, do not perform dirty tricks. They seldom work, they usually are discovered, and they make your campaign look not only immoral but incompetent.

Norman Fink, senior counsel at John Grenzebach & Associates, recommends two rules. Follow the "ulcer rule": if it feels bad, do not do it. Unethical action erodes not only other people's confidence in you, but your self-confidence as well. In addition, follow the "just this once" rule: if something is not proper at any other time, it is likely to be improper "just this once" as well. [93]

Dirty tricks also can land you in jail, as many of Richard Nixon's minions from the Committee to Re-Elect the President discovered.

Campaigns can get *very* dirty. The candidate must seriously consider this issue in a district that is controlled by a political machine, gangs, organized crime, or another powerful group or individual.

Chicago's old First Ward for many years was considered to be controlled by organized crime. When attorney Richard Murray was considering an insurgent run for alderman in 1983, he was told by a veteran political operative, according to the *Chicago Reader,* "See, the precinct captains in the First run the gangs. They'll tell them to harass you, harass your car. They will harass your workers at night. Your response is to be as follows. Get a high school football team. Have 'em wear 'Murray' jackets when they go shopping. Pay them to go shopping a lot. Word gets around" that the good guy has his own tough-guy supporters.[94]

Candidates and workers have been shot, offices and cars have been bombed, and family members have been threatened. There was even an attempt to kidnap Harry Truman's daughter when he was starting out in politics—in rural Missouri in a so-called "simple" era.

The candidate might want to run anyway but must consider the consequences.

OVERCONFIDENCE

Scottish philosopher David Hume said it best: "When men are the most sure and arrogant, they are commonly the most mistaken...."

History is full of examples of campaigns that thought they had the election in the bag and ended up going home instead of to city hall, the legislature, the state house, or the White House.

The 1948 Dewey-Truman electoral contest is the best example, with Mike Dukakis and his early seventeen-point lead over George Bush a close second. Even the Carter-Reagan matchup saw Carter with nearly a two-to-one lead over Reagan in the polls late in 1979.

Democratic political activist Jean Lachowicz commented when Bill Clinton's early lead over Bob Dole dropped in early August in the 1996 presidential race, "That's good. I don't *want* to see Bill Clinton with a thirty-point lead. I want him to run as if he were behind."

Always run as if your candidate is ten points behind but gaining. Even the 1984 Reagan campaign ran this way against Walter Mondale, quickly shifting into crisis mode to sharpen Reagan's speaking style after his mediocre performance in his first debate with Mondale, and sending the president to Mondale's home state of Minnesota the last weekend of the campaign to try to eke out every single possible vote. The result: landslide. The reason: they did not take it for granted.

ZENITH

Win or lose, after the conclusion of the campaign, there are a few things to do.

Thank everyone involved; not only staff and volunteers, but contributors as well—and put it in writing. That written thank-you unfortunately may also have to be one final solicitation for funds to help retire the campaign debt.

Return all leased and borrowed equipment if your candidate lost, or transfer it to the government office if the campaign was successful and the equipment still is required. Close all operations that you will not need anymore, such as facilities, phone lines, and Internet page— or again, transfer them over to the new operation. Have all campaign signs removed from the district.

Organize lists of voters, volunteers, and contributors for the next campaign—or for that of an ideological compatriot who can use them in a future campaign.

Perhaps after it is all over you will want to record what went right and what went wrong, who worked out well and who dropped the ball, and what you learned. Do not wait. Make notes while everything still is fresh in your mind. It will pay off, because this will be the beginning of your campaign bible for the next election.

ENDNOTES

[1] Sorauf, Frank J. *Party Politics in America.* Boston: Little, Brown, 1976, p. 249.

[2] *Campaigns & Elections,* Dec./Jan 1996, p. 49.

[3] Simon, Roger. "Media Frenzy Turns Political 'Ad' Into News," *Liberal Opinion Week,* June 17, 1996, p. 28.

[4] Campaign Training Workshop, Leadership 2000 Conference, Democratic Leadership for the 21st Century, Chicago, Illinois, Oct. 16, 1993.

[5] Kirk, Jim. "Ad Spending Picks Up Pace at 11th Hour," *Chicago Sun-Times,* March 18, 1996, p. 39.

[6] Steward, Janet Kidd. "Campaigns Ice the Cake for Industry," *Chicago Sun-Times,* March 18, 1996, p. 29.

[7] *op. cit.,* Leadership 2000 Conference, Oct. 16, 1993.

[8] "How to Influence Press Coverage," *U.S. News & World Report,* Feb. 19, 1996, p. 54.

[9] Simpson, Burney. "Rainbow Machine," *Campaigns & Elections,* June 1996, p. 35.

[10] "Washington Whispers," *U.S. News & World Report,* March 11, 1996, p. 22.

[11] Persinos, John F., and Tom Russell. "Life of the Parties," *Campaigns & Elections,* Dec./Jan. 1996, p. 29.

[12] "Speak Up! You Can be Heard!," *U.S. News & World Report,* Feb. 19, 1996, p. 51.

[13] Stillwell, Scott, and Dick Roling. "NPOs Guard Tax Exempt Status," *NFC Notable$,* Summer, 1996, p. 1.

[14] Hazelwood, Dan N. "Targeting Persuasion Mail," *Campaigns & Elections,* Sept. 1995, p. 33.

[15] "Mad About You," *Campaigns & Elections,* Oct./Nov. 1994, p. 29.

[16] "Negative Messages Prove 'Tricky and Risky' for Business," *Writing Concepts,* March 1996, p. 1.

[17] Allen, Cathy. "Women on the Run," *Campaigns & Elections,* Oct./Nov. 1995, p. 28.

[18] Running for Office," *DePaul University Magazine,* Spring 1996, p. 4.

[19] Shepherd, Chuck. "News of the Weird," *Chicago Reader,* July 5, 1996, section 4, p. 1.

[20] *op. cit.,* "How to Influence Press Coverage" p. 54.

[21] *Ibid.,* p. 57.

[22] Germond, Jack, and Jules Witcover. "Exit Gramm," *Liberal Opinion Week,* Feb. 26, 1996, p. 24.

[23] "Most Amazing Winners of '94," *The Political Speaker,* Feb. 1995, p. 1.

[24] Boswell, Thomas. *Why Time Begins On Opening Day.* New York: Penguin Books, 1984, p. 84.

[25] *Ibid.,* p. 103.

[26] Miller, Bryan. "The Art of the Campaign." *Chicago Reader,* July 12, 1991, p. 18.

[27] Women in Communications Inc., Chicago Chapter. *22nd Annual Career Conference Handbook.* Chicago, 1986.

[28] "For the Record," *National Review,* Nov. 11, 1996, p. 5.

[29] Barone, Michael. "The New America," *U.S. News & World Report,* July 10, 1995, pp. 20-21, 23.

[30] Lehigh, Scot. "New Collar," *Chicago Reader,* Dec. 6, 1985, p. 16.

[31] Hornung, Mark. "A Few Rules for Racial Appeals," *Crain's Chicago Business,* Jan. 16, 1989, p. 22.

[32] Custer, Charley. "The Education of Richard Murray, Candidate." *Chicago Reader,* March 4, 1983, p. 24.

[33] Simpson, Dick. *Winning Elections.* New York: HarperCollins, 1996, p. 67.

[34] *Ibid.*

[35] *op. cit.,* Leadership 2000 Conference, Oct. 16, 1993.

[36] Thompson, Chic, head, Creative Management Group, "Using Creativity as the Key to Competence in Changing Times," Seminar for Chief Publications Officers, Council for Advancement and Support of Education, Chicago, Illinois, March 17-19, 1993.

[37] *Ibid.*

[38] "Off the Record," *Campaigns & Elections,* Aug. 1994, p. 70.

[39] Buruma, Ian. "Taiwan's New Nationalists," *Foreign Affairs,* July/Aug. 1996, p. 84.

[40] "Language: A Key Mechanism of Control," *Extra! Update,* Feb. 1995, p. 3.

[41] *op. cit.,* "Mad About You, " p. 29.

[42] *Ibid.*

[43] *op. cit,* Simpson, p. 148.

[44] "Off the Record," *Campaigns & Elections,* Aug. 1995, p. 70.

[45] "Off the Record," *Campaigns & Elections,* July 1994, p. 70.

[46] Persinos, John F. "Pushing the Envelope," *Campaigns & Elections,* June 1994, p. 20.

[47] "Rules to Break and to Keep in Writing Direct Mail," *Writing Concepts,* June 1996.

[48] Johnson, Duff. "Political Information Management," *Campaigns & Elections,* Oct./Nov. 1996, p. 50.

[49] Clinton, Wally. "Telephone Campaigning," *Campaigns & Elections,* Oct./ Nov. 1995, p. 33.

[50] *op. cit.,* "How to Influence Press Coverage," p. 57.

[51] *op. cit., Campaigns & Elections,* Dec./Jan. 1996, p. 28.

[52] Sonis, Larry. "Understanding Direct Democracy," *Campaigns & Elections,* Dec./Jan. 1995, p. 63

[53] *op. cit.,* Miller, p. 16.

[54] *op. cit.,* Leadership 2000 Conference, Oct. 16, 1993.

[55] "Off the Record, " *Campaigns & Elections,* Sept. 1995, p. 70.

[56] Baumhart, Raymond, S.J. "It's Not Easy Being a Manager and a Christian," *Loyola Magazine,* Fall 1990, p. 4-9.

[57] DeBofsky, Greta, corporate vice president, public relations, Quintessence Incorporated, and Lou Williams, president, L.C. Williams & Associates Inc., "Time Management," Management Directions '89, Public Relations Society of America, Chicago, Illinois, Feb. 28, 1989.

[58] The Community Media Workshop. *Getting On The Air & Into Print (6th edition).* Chicago: Columbia College, June 1996, p. 90.

[59] *op. cit.,* Miller, p. 14.

[60] "Off the Record," *Campaigns & Elections,* Dec./Jan. 1995, p. 78.

[61] Tron, Barrie. "Staging Media Events," *Campaigns & Elections,* Dec./Jan. 1996, p. 50.

[62] *Ibid.*

[63] *op. cit.,* "How to Influence Press Coverage," p. 57.

[64] *Ibid.*

[65] *Ibid.*

[66] "Off the Record," *Campaigns & Elections,* Aug. 1996, p. 78.

[67] *op. cit.,* The Community Media Workshop, p. 2.

[68] *Volunteer Handbook 1995-1996,* Urbana: University of Illinois Alumni Association, 1995, p. G-3.

[69] Oclander, Jorge. "In Mell's World, It's Politics as Usual," *Chicago Sun-Times,* March 23, 1996, p. 21.

[70] "Specialty Guidelines for the Delivery of Services by Industrial/Organizational Psychologists," *American Psychologist,* 36(6), 1981, pp. 664-669.

[71] "Campaign Screw Up 103," *Campaigns & Elections,* June 1994, p. 10.

[72] *op. cit.,* Council for Advancement and Support of Education conference.

[73] *op. cit., Volunteer Handbook, 1995-1996,* p. H-2.

[74] *Ibid.*

[75] Ross, Robert S. *American National Government.* Chicago: Rand McNally, 1972, p. 63.

[76] Solomon, Norman. "Polls Give Numbers, But Truth Is More Elusive," *Liberal Opinion Week,* May 20, 1996, p. 30.

[77] *op. cit., Chicago Sun-Times,* March 18, 1996, p. 29.

[78] *op. cit.,* Solomon, p. 30.

[79] *Ibid.*

[80] *op. cit.,* Leadership 2000 Conference, Oct. 16, 1993.

[81] Williams, Lou, president, L.C. Williams & Associates Inc., "Analyzing and Tracking Issues," Jesuit Advancement Administrators National Conference, Loyola University of New Orleans, New Orleans, June 29, 1993.

[82] *Ibid.*

[83] Winternitz, Felix. "990 & Nonprofits." *Quill,* April 1995, p. 40.

[84] *Ibid.*

[85] "Use Special Techniques When Writing Online Materials," *Writing Concepts,* May 1996, p. 2.

[86] Weiler, Michael, and W. Barnett Pearce, eds. *Reagan and Public Discourse in America.* Tuscaloosa: The University of Alabama Press, 1992, p. 11.

[87] Baker, Russell. "Ado About Dole," *Liberal Opinion Week,* May 27, 1996, p. 24.

[88] *op. cit.,* Miller, p. 34.

[89] Williams, Joe. "On Becoming a Strategic Partner with Management." *Communication World,* March 1996, p. 31.

[90] *op. cit.,* "How to Influence Press Coverage," p. 57.

[91] McPartlin, Brian, advisor to President Bill Clinton, workshop, Leadership 2000 Conference, Democratic Leadership for the 21st Century, Chicago, Oct. 16, 1993.

[92] "The 50 Things Not to Do in a Political Campaign," *The Best of Campaigns & Elections,* 1996, p. 31.

[93] Fink, Norman S. "The Capital Campaign in Year 2000," Jesuit Midwest Advancement Conference, Loyola University Chicago, Chicago, June 18-20, 1990.

[94] *op. cit.,* Custer, p. 22.

APPENDIX ONE

SAMPLE ITINERARY FOR SPEAKERS AT A POLITICAL DINNER

Mary Candidate: the candidate
George Washington: master of ceremonies from the host organization
John Adams: a member of the clergy
Sally Organization-President: head of organization hosting the dinner
Joe Warhero: a well-known supporter of the sponsoring organization or of the candidate

• When all attendees are seated for dinner, master of ceremonies George Washington provides a few words of welcome. Then George Washington invites John Adams to offer the invocation. John Adams asks the audience to stand and bow their heads. When John Adams recites invocation, George Washington withdraws from podium.

• John Adams offers invocation, then withdraws from podium.

• Dinner is eaten.

• As dessert is served, George Washington comes to the podium. He introduces Sally Organization-President and invites her to join him on the podium.

• When Sally Organization-President comes to the podium, George Washington stays at the front and picks up plaque to present to Mary Candidate.

• Sally Organization-President introduces Mary Candidate and invites her to the front. George Washington stands by.

• Mary Candidate comes from the side by George Washington. George Washington hands her the plaque and shakes her hand. Then, Sally Organization-President shakes Mary Candidate's hand. Both George Washington and Sally Organization-President withdraw from podium.

• Mary Candidate speaks.

• When Mary Candidate finishes her talk, she stays at podium and invites George Washington and Sally Organization-President to join her at the podium to recognize Joe Warhero.

• George Washington steps to the podium, and Mary Candidate and Sally Organization-President stay at front but behind George Washington. Sally Organization-President picks up plaque for Joe Warhero.

• George Washington invites Joe Warhero to come to the front. Joe Warhero comes up from the side by Sally Organization-President. Sally Organization-President hands Joe Warhero the plaque and shakes his hand, Mary Candidate shakes his hand, and George Washington shakes his hand. Sally, Mary, and Joe then leave podium.

• George Washington thanks the audience for attending, reminds attendees that there will be a photo opportunity with Mary Candidate in the foyer, and adjourns the gathering.

APPENDIX TWO

EVENT PLANNING CHECKLIST

Auction/raffle
Audiovisuals:
    Sound system
    Televisions with VCRs
Budget
Coat storage/racks:
    Paid or free
    Claim tickets
Consumables:
    Liquor (determine whether bar is cash or free; if beer and wine
        are free but if mixed drinks are paid; if there will be wine with
        the meal)
    Soft drinks
    Meal
Contracts:
    Drink
    Entertainment
    Food
    Location
    Other
Date:
    Avoid conflicts
Decorations:
    Balloons
    Banners/posters
    Centerpieces
    Flowers
Donors who can provide free items:
    What they can provide
Entertainment:
    Music
        Band/disc jockey
        Dancing
        Other performers

Other
    Comedian
    Guest speakers
    Storyteller
Equipment:
    Determine what is needed
Financial:
    Establish the budget and the price
First-aid kit
Format
    Snacks and drinks
    Coffee and drinks
    Buffet
    Sit-down meal
Giveaways
Host committee:
    Creation
    Choose a chairperson
    Define members' responsibilities
    Stewardship-make sure members are fulfilling their
        responsibilities
Location:
    Contract (be aware of hidden costs, cancellation fees, etc.)
    Determine size, space, and time needed
    Handicapped accessibility
    Lighting
    Sightlines
    Sound
    Lodging
Identify and notify moderator, other speakers
Invitations:
    Develop printing and mailing schedule
Insurance
Itinerary
Mailings:
    Determine how many and of what type ("save the date" card,
        invitation, flyer, reminder)
    Determine whether bulk mail or first class
    Determine if you are conducting a confirmation mailing

Thank-you and follow-up notes
Mailing list:
Candidate's
Host organization's
Map
Media relations:
News release
Accommodations for television, radio
Arrange interviews with speakers
Photographer
Miscellaneous:
Certificates
Gifts
Paper
Paper clips
Plaques
Scissors
Stapler
Writing implements
Parking
Printed materials:
Select designer
Select printer
Program of events:
Determine itinerary
Provide itinerary to speakers
Establish time limits
Registration:
Attendee lists
Cashbox with change
Greeters
Handouts
Name badges
Sign-in cards or sheets
Table and chairs
Wastebasket
Seating:
General seating
Reserved seating

Head table
VIPs
Signage
Staff
    Determine duties
Sound system
Speaker:
    Obtain the speaker (usually the candidate)
    Obtain speaker's biography and photo for advertising
    Negotiate honoraria and expenses if speaker is not the candidate
    Confirm the speaker
Special needs
    Dietary restrictions
    Handicapped access
Telephone:
    Invitation calls
    Reminder calls
Transportation
Verify arrangements
Volunteers:
    Determine duties
Water and glasses

APPENDIX THREE

RESOURCES FOR KEY POLITICAL ISSUES

ARTS AND CULTURE

Conservative:
Family Research Council, 700 13th St. N.W., Suite 500, Washington, DC 20005, (202) 393-2100, e-mail (through web site), <http://www.frc.org>.

Traditional Values Coalition, 139 C St. S.E., Washington, DC 20003, (202) 547-8570, fax (202) 546-6602, e-mail tvcmedia@erols.com, <http://www.traditionalvalues.org>.

Progressive:
Artists for a Hate Free America, P.O. Box 12667, Portland, OR 97212, (800) 3WHAT-2-DO, (503) 335-5982.

Global WARM (Women's Art Registry Minnesota), 2402 University Ave. W., St. Paul, MN 55114, (612) 649-0059, fax (612) 649-0708.

CENSORSHIP

Conservative:
Morality in Media, 475 Riverside Drive, Suite 239, New York, NY 10115, (212) 870-3222, fax (212) 870-2765, e-mail mimnyc@netcom.com, <http://www.netcom.com/~mimnyc>.

National Coalition for the Protection of Children & Families, 800 Compton Road, Suite 9224, Cincinnati, OH 45231, (513) 521-6227, fax (513) 521-6337, e-mail nvpus@nationalcoalition.org, <http:www.eos.ncp/ncpcf>.

General/Neutral:
Alliance for the Arts, 330 W. 42nd St., Suite 1701, New York, NY 10036, (212) 947-6340, fax (212) 947-6416, e-mail afta@ix.netcom.com, <http://allianceforarts.org>.

American Library Association Intellectual Freedom Committee, 50 E. Huron St., Chicago, IL 60611, (312) 944-6780, fax (312) 280-4227, e-mail jkrug@ala.org, <http://www.ala.org>.

Progressive:
Anti-Censorship and Deception Union, Porter Square, P.O. Box 297, Cambridge, MA 02140, (617) 499-7965.

Artists for a Hate Free America, P.O. Box 12667, Portland, OR 97212, (800) 3WHAT-2-DO, (503) 335-5982.

CHILDREN'S ISSUES

General/Neutral:
Children's Defense Fund, 25 E St. N.W., Washington, DC 20001, (202) 628-8787, fax (202) 662-3510, e-mail cdfinfo@childrensdefense.org, <http://www.childrensdefense.org>.

CIVIC INVOLVEMENT

Conservative:
The Reason Foundation, 3415 S. Sepulveda Blvd., Suite 400, Los Angeles, CA 90034, (310) 391-2245, fax (310) 391-4395, e-mail gpassantino@reason.org, <http://reason.org/aboutreason2.html>.

Progressive:
Alliance for National Renewal, 1445 Market St., Suite 300, Denver, CO 80202-1728, (303) 571-4343, fax (303) 571-4404, e-mail ncl@cfn.net, <http://www.ncl.org/ncl>.

CIVIL LIBERTIES

Conservative:
Americans for Tax Reform, 1320 18th St. N.W., Suite 200, Washington, DC 20036, e-mail info@atr.org, <http://www.atr.org/>.

Progressive:
American Civil Liberties Union, 122 Maryland Ave. N.E., Washington, DC 20002, (202) 544-1681, fax (202) 546-0738, <http://www.aclu.org>.

COMMUNICATIONS

General/Neutral:
ANB Communications, 3632 N. Central Park Ave., Chicago, IL 60618-4107, (773) 866-0024, fax (773) 866-0025, e-mail anbcomm@interaccess.com.

CONFLICT RESOLUTION

General/Neutral:
The Carter Center, 1 Copenhill, Atlanta, GA 30307, (404) 420-5100, fax (404) 331-0238, e-mail nsingh@emory.edu.

DEMOCRATIC PARTY AND RELATED ORGANIZATIONS

Democratic Leadership Council and Progressive Policy Institute, 518 C St. N.E., Washington, DC 20510, (202) 546-0007, (202) 544-5002, e-mail cazoano@dlcppi.org, <http://www.dlcppi.org>.

Democratic National Committee, 430 S. Capitol St. S.E., Washington, DC 20003, (202) 863-8000, fax (202) 863-8081, e-mail dnc@democrats.org, <http://www.democrats.org>.

Digital Democrats, P.O. Box 75848, Washington, DC 20013 (202) 554-8586, e-mail digitals@webcom.com, <http://www.webcom.com/~digitals>.

National Jewish Democratic Council, 503 Capital Court N.E., Suite 300, Washington, DC 20002, (202) 544-7636, fax (202) 544-7645, e-mail njdconline@aol.com, <http://www.njdc.org>.

ECONOMIC DEVELOPMENT/REFORM

Conservative:
American Policy Center, 13873 Park Center Road, Suite 316, Herndon, VA 22071, (703) 925-0881, fax (703) 925-0991, e-mail apc@americanpolicy.org, <http://www.americanpolicy.org/>.

America's Future, 7800 Bonhomme, St. Louis, MO 63105, (314) 725-6003, fax (314) 721-3373, e-mail frd@accessus.net, <http://users.accessus.net/~eamiller/af>.

Atlas Economic Research Foundation, 4084 University Drive, Suite 103, Fairfax, VA 22030-6812, (703) 934-6969, fax (703) 352-7530, e-mail atlas@atlas,fdn.org, <http://www.atlas.fdn.org>.

Foundation for Economic Education, 305 Broadway, Irvington-on-Hudson, NY 10533, (914) 591-7230, fax (914) 591-8910, freeman@westnet.com, <http://www.fee.org>.

Future of Freedom Foundation, 1350 Random Hills Road, Suite 800, Farifax, VA 22030, (703) 934-6101, fax (703) 803-1480, e-mail 75200.1523@compuserve.com, <http://www.fff.org/freedom/daily>.

General/Neutral:
Accion International, 120 Beacon St., Somerville, MA 02143, (617) 492-4930, fax (617) 876-9509, e-mail info@accion.org, <http://www.accion.org>.

Business Executives for National Security, 1615 L St. N.W., Suite 330, Washington, DC 20036, (202) 296-2125, fax (202) 296-2490, e-mail bensdc@org.com, <http://www.bens.org>.

Center for the Defense of Free Enterprise, Liberty Park,12500 N.E. 10th Pl., Bellevue, WA 98005, (206) 455-5038, fax (206) 451-3959, <http://www.eskimo.com/"rarnold/wiseuse.html>.

Progressive:
Center on Budget and Policy Priorities, 820 1st St. N.E., Suite 510, Washington, DC 20002, (202) 408-1080, fax (202) 408-1056, e-mail: center@center.cbbp.org, <http://www.cbpp.org>.

Foundation for a Civil Society, 477 Madison Ave., 6th Floor New York, NY 10022, (212) 223-6530, fax (212) 223-6534, e-mail info@fcsny.org.

Earthtrade Inc., 150 Broadway, 1814 Franklin St., 6th Floor, Oakland, CA 94612, (510) 987-7222, fax (510) 836-1621, e-mail bam@progressive-asset.com.

National Jobs For All Coalition, 475 Riverside Drive, Suite 554, New York, NY 10115-0050, (212) 870-3449, fax (212) 870-3454, e-mail njfac@ncccusa.org

Southwest Network for Environmental and Economic Justice, P.O. Box 7399, Albuquerque, NM 87194, (505) 242-0416, fax (505) 242-5609, sneej@igc.org.

EDUCATION

General/Neutral:
North Carolina Center for the Advancement of Teaching, NCCAT/WCU, Cullowhee, NC, 28723-9062, (704) 293-5202, fax (704) 227-7363, e-mail smithda@www.wcu.edu, <http://www.nccat.org>.

ELECTION MONITORING

General/Neutral:
The Carter Center, 1 Copenhill, Atlanta, GA 30307, (404) 420-5100, fax (404) 331-0238, e-mail nsingh@emory.edu.

ELECTRONIC PRIVACY

General/Neutral:
Electronic Privacy information Center, 666 Pennsylvania Ave. N.E., Washington, DC 20003, (202) 544-9240, fax (202) 547-5482, e-mail info@epic.org, <http://www.epic.org/>.

ENVIRONMENT

Conservative:
Frontiers of Freedom Institute, 1100 Wilson Blvd., Suite 1700, Arlington, VA 22209, (888) 8-RIGHTS, (703) 527-8282, fax (703) 527-8388, e-mail freedom@ff.org, <http://www.townhall.com/ff/>.

Heartland Institute, 800 E. Northwest Highway #1080, Palatine, IL 60067, (847) 202-3060, fax (847) 202-9799, e-mail think@heartland.org, <http://www.heartland.org>.

Independence Institute, 14142 Denver West Pkwy., Suite 185, Golden, CO 80401, (303) 279-6536, fax (303) 279-4176, e-mail webmnger@i2i.org, <http://i2i.org/WhoIsII.htm>.

The Advancement of Sound Science Coalition, P.O. Box 18432, Washington, DC 200365, (800) 369-6608, fax (800) 251-5253, e-mail tassc@apcoassoc.com, <http://www.tassc.org/about.html>.

General/Neutral:

Environmental Defense Fund, 1875 Connecticut Ave. N.W., Suite 1016, Washington, DC 20009, (202) 387-3525, fax (202) 334-6049, e-mail members@edf.org, <http:// www.edf.org>.

Environmental News Network, P.O. Box 1996, Sun Valley, ID 85353, (208) 726-3649, fax (208) 726-2476, e-mail curtis@enn.com, <http://www.enn.com/>.

Illinois Environmental Council, 319 W. Cook St., Springfield, IL 62704, (217) 544-5954, fax (217) 544-5958, e-mail iec@eosinc.com, <http:// www.prairienet.org/~isen/>.

League of Conservation Voters, 1707 L St. N.W., Suite 750, Washington, DC 20036, (202) 785-8683, fax (202) 835-0491, e-mail lcv@lcv.org, <http:// www.lcv.org>.

National Audubon Society, 700 Broadway, New York, NY 10063, (212) 979-3000, fax (212) 979-3188, e-mail jau@audubon.org, <http:// www.audubon.org>.

National Wildlife Federation, 1400 16th St. N.W., Washington, DC 20036, (202) 797-6800, fax (202) 797-6646, e-mail action@nwf.org, <http://www.nwf.org/ nwf>.

The Nature Conservancy, 1815 N. Lynn St., Arlington, VA 22209, (703) 841-5300, fax (703) 841-1283, e-mail (through web site), <http://www.tnc.org>.

Western Organization of Resource Councils, 2401 Montana Ave., #301, Billings, MT (406) 252-9672, fax (406) 252-1092, e-mail billings@worc.org, <http://www.worc.org>.

Wilderness Watch, Box 9175, Missoula, MT 59807, (406) 542-2048, fax (406) 542-7714, e-mail wildwatch@igc.apc.org, <http:// www.wildernesswatch.org>.

Progressive:

Earth Island Institute, 300 Broadway, San Francisco, CA 94133, (415) 788-3666, fax (415) 788-7324, e-mail earthisland@earthisland.org, <http:// www.earthisland.org>.

Greenpeace, 1436 U St. N.W., Washington, DC 20009, (202) 462-1177, fax (202) 462-4507, e-mail greenpeace@usa.greenpeace.org, <http:// www.greenpeace.org/~usa>.

Sierra Club, 85 2nd St., 2nd Floor, San Francisco, CA 94105, (415) 977-5500, (415) 977-5797, e-mail information@sierraclub.org, <http:// www.sierraclub.org/>.

Southern Utah Wilderness Alliance, 1471 S. 1100 E., Salt Lake City, UT 84105, (801) 486-3161, fax (801) 486-4233, e-mail suwa@suwa.org, <http:// www.xmission.com/~suwa/suwa.html>.

FIREARMS

Conservative:
National Rifle Association, 11250 Waples Mill Road, Farifax, VA 22030, (703) 267-1000, e-mail (through web site), <http://www.nra.org>.

Progressive:
Handgun Control Inc., 1225 I St. N.W., Suite 1100, Washington, DC 20003, (202) 898-0792, fax (202) 371-9615, <http://www.handguncontrol.org>.

FREEDOM OF INFORMATION ACT

General/Neutral:
FOIA Group Inc., 1090 Vermont Ave. N.W., Suite 800, Washington, DC 20005, (202) 408-7028, fax (202) 347-8419, <http://www.cais.net/foia/>.

Freedom of Information Center, University of Missouri, 127 Neff Annex, Columbia, MO 65211, (573) 882-4856, fax (573) 884-4963 e-mail robert_anderson@jmail.jour.missouri.edu, <http://www.missouri.edu/~foiwww/>.

Freedom of Information Clearinghouse, P.O. Box 19367, Washington, DC 20036, (202) 588-7790.

National Center for Freedom of Information Studies, Loyola University Chicago, 820 N. Michigan Ave., Chicago, IL 60611, (312) 915-6548, fax (312) 915-7095, e-mail malleyn@luc.edu.

GANGS

General/Neutral:
Barrios Unidos, 313 Front St., Santa Cruz, CA 95060, (408) 457-8208, fax (408) 457-0389, e-mail barrios@cruzio.com.

GOVERNMENT INFORMATION

General/Neutral:
Coalition on Government Information, c/o American Library Association Washington, 110 Maryland Ave. N.E., Washington, DC 20002, (202) 628-8410, fax (202) 628-8419, e-mail aah@alawash.org, <http://www.ala.wash.org>.

OMB Watch, 1731 Connecticut Ave. N.W., 4th Floor, Washington, DC 20009, (202) 234-8494, fax (202) 234-8584, e-mail ombwatch@rtk.net, <http://www.rtk.net>.

HEALTH

Conservative:
American Council on Science and Health, 1995 Broadway, 2nd Floor, New York, NY 10023-5860, (212) 362-7044, fax (212) 362-4919, e-mail whelan@acsh.org, <http://www.acsh.org/>.

General/Neutral:
The Carter Center, 1 Copenhill, Atlanta, GA 30307, (404) 420-5100, fax (404) 331-0238, e-mail nsingh@emory.edu.

Doctors Without Borders, 11 E. 26th St., Suite 1904, New York, NY 10010, (212) 679-6800, (212) 679-7016, e-mail dwb@newyork.mss.org, <http://www.dwb.org>.

League of Conservation Voters, 1707 L St. N.W., Suite 750, Washington, DC 20036, (202) 785-8683, fax (202) 835-0491, e-mail lcv@lcv.org, <http://www.lcv.org>.

Progressive:
Mark Hagland & Associates, 440 W. Barry Ave., Suite 202, Chicago, IL 60657, (312) 248-2305, fax (312) 248-2318, e-mail MHagland@aol.comm.

HUMAN RIGHTS

Conservative:
Center for Individual Rights, 1233 20th St. N.W., Suite 300, Washington, DC 20036, (202) 833-8400, fax (202) 833-8410, e-mail CIR@MAIL.WDN.COM., <http://www.wdn.com/cir>.

General/Neutral:
The Carter Center, 1 Copenhill, Atlanta, GA 30307, (404) 420-5100, fax (404) 331-0238, e-mail nsingh@emory.edu.

Human Rights Watch, 485 5th Ave., New York, NY 10017-6104, (212) 972-8400 fax (212) 972-0905, e-mail hrwnyc@hrw.org, <http://www.hrw.org>.

National Immigration Forum, 220 I St. N.E., Suite 220, Washington, DC 20002, (202) 544-0004, fax (202) 544-1905, <http://www.immigrationforum.org>.

Political Research Associates, 120 Beacon St., Suite 202, Somerville, MA 02143, (617) 661-9313, fax (617) 661-0059, e-mail publiceye@igc.apc.org, <http://www.publiceye.org>.

Progressive:
Southwest Network for Environmental and Economic Justice, P.O. Box 7399, Albuquerque, NM 87194, (505) 242-0416, fax (505) 242-5609, e-mail sneej@igc.org.

HUNGER

General/Neutral:
American Express' Charge Against Hunger, Greg Tarmin, TRS Communications, American Express Tower, World Financial Center, New York, NY 10285-4800, (212) 640-4428.

LAW

Conservative:
Federalist Society, 1015 18th St. N.W., Suite 425, Washington, DC 20056, (202) 822-8138, fax (202) 296-8061, e-mail fedsoc@radix.net, <http://www.fed-soc.org/>.

Progressive:
Foundation for a Civil Society, 477 Madison Ave., 6th Floor New York, NY 10022, (212) 223-6530, fax (212) 223-6534, e-mail info@fcsny.org.

MEDIA

Conservative:
Accuracy In Media, 4455 Connecticut Ave. N.W., Suite 330, Washington, D.C. 20008, (202) 364-4401, fax (202) 364-4098, e-mail ar@aim.org, <http://www.aim.org.>.

General/Neutral:
Cultural Environment Movement, 3508 Market Street, Philadelphia, PA 19104, (215) 387-5202, (215) 387-1560, e-mail cemad@libertynet.org., <http://www.cem-net.org>.

Poynter Institute, 801 3rd St. S., St. Petersburg, FL, 33701, (813) 821-9494, fax (813) 821-0583, e-mail info@poynter.org, <http://www.reporter.org/poynter/home/index.htm>

Reporters Committee for Freedom of the Press, 1101 Wilson Blvd. #1910, Arlington, VA 22209, (703) 807-2100, fax (703) 807-2109, e-mail rcfp@rcfp.org, <http://www.rcfp.org/rcfp>.

Progressive:
Fairness and Accuracy in Reporting (FAIR), 130 W. 25th St., New York, NY 10001, (800) 847-3993, (212) 633-6700, e-mail fair-info@fair.org, <http://www.fair.com/fair/>.

MILITARY

General/Neutral:
Center for Defense Information, 1600 Massachusetts Ave. N.W., Washington, D.C. 20005, (202) 862-0700, fax (202) 862-0708, e-mail info@cdi.org, <http://www.cdi.org>.

MISMANAGEMENT

General/Neutral:
Citizens Against Government Waste, 1301 Connecticut Ave N.W., Suite 400, Washington, DC 20036, (800) BE-ANGRY, (202) 467-5300, fax (202) 467-4253, e-mail webmaster@cagw, <http://www.govt-waste.org/>.

Conservative:

American Conservative Union, 1007 Cameron St., Alexandria, VA 22314, (703) 836-8602, fax (703) 836-8606, e-mail acu@conservative.org, <http://www.townhall.com/conservative>.

America's Future, Inc., 7800 Bonhomme Ave., St. Louis, MO 63105, (314) 725-6003, fax (314) 721-3373, e-mail frd@accessus.net, <http://members.accessus.net/~eamiller/af>.

Cato Institute, 1000 Massachusetts Ave. N.W., Washington, DC 20001-5403, (202) 842-0200, fax (202) 842-3490, e-mail Cato@cato.org, <http://www.cato.>.

Heritage Foundation, 214 Massachusetts Ave N.E., Washington, DC, 20002-4999, (202) 546-4400, fax (202) 546-8328, e-mail dickson@heritage.org, <http://www.heritage.org>.

General/Neutral:

The Carter Center, 1 Copenhill, Atlanta, GA 30307, (404) 420-5100, fax (404) 331-0238, e-mail nsingh@emory.edu.

Center for Public Integrity, 1634 I Street N.W., Suite 902, Washington, DC 20006, (202) 783-3900, fax (202) 783-3906, e-mail contact@publicintegrity.org, <http://www.publicintegrity.org>.

Congress, U.S., Senate Dirksen Building Mailroom, Basement 28, Washington, DC 20510 (202) 224-3121. Phone this number to be connected with individual congressional representatives, who have their own fax numbers and e-mail addresses

Institute for Policy Studies, 1601 Connecticut Ave. N.W., Suite 500, Washington, DC 20009, (202) 234-9382, fax (202) 387-7915, e-mail ipscom@igc.apc.org, < http://www.igc.org/ifps>.

National Council of Churches, 475 Riverside Drive, Room 850, New York, NY 10115, (212) 870-2227, fax (212) 870-2030, e-mail carol_fouke.parti@ecunet.org <http:www.ncccusa.org>.

The President of the United States, The White House,1600 Pennsylvania Ave., Washington, DC 20500, (202) 456-1414, fax: (202) 456-2461, e-mail president@whitehouse.gov, <http://www.whitehouse.gov>.

Urban Institute, 2100 M St. N.W., 5th Floor, Washington, D.C. 20037, (202) 833-7200, fax (202) 331-9747, e-mail paffairs@ui.urban.org, <http://www.urban.org>.

The Vice President of the United States, The White House, 1600 Pennsylvania Ave., Washington, DC, (202) 456-2326, fax: (202) 456-7044, e-mail vice-president@whitehouse.gov, <http://www.whitehouse.gov>.

Progressive:
Liberals United, 118 Westshore Blvd, Tampa, FL 33609, (813) 651-4472, fax (813) 661-9361, e-mail libsunited@aol.com, <http://www.idir.net/%7Elieberals/who.html>.

People for the American Way, 2000 M St. N.W., Suite 400, Washington, DC 20036, (202) 467-4999, (202) 293-2672, e-mail pfaw@pfaw.org, <http://www.pfaw.org>.

Public Citizen, 1600 20th St. N.W., Washington, DC 20009, (202) 588-1000, fax (202) 588-7796 e-mail public_citizen@citizen.org. <http://www.citizen.org/public_citizen/litigation/litigation.html>.

Working Assets Online, 701 Montgomery St., 4th Floor, San Francisco, CA 94111, (415) 788-0777, e-mail wald@wald.com, <http://www.wald.com>.

NATIONAL SECURITY

General/Neutral:
American Friends Service Committee, 1501 Cherry St., Philadelphia, PA 19102, (215) 241-7000, fax (215) 241-7247, e-mail rbyler@afsc.org, <http://www.afsc.org>.

National Security Archive, George Washington University, 2130 H Street N.W., Suite 701, Washington, DC 20037, (202) 994-7000, fax (202) 994-7005, e-mail nsarchiv@gwis2.circ.gwu.edu, <http://www.seas.gwu.edu/nsarchive/>.

NUCLEAR ENERGY

Conservative:
Nuclear Energy Institute, 1776 I St. N.W., Washington, DC 20006-3708, (202) 739-8000, fax (202) 785-4113, e-mail media@nei.org, <http://www.nei.org>.

Progressive:
Nuclear Information and Resource Service, 1424 16th Street N.W., #404, Washington, DC 20036, (202) 328-0002, fax (202) 462-2183, e-mail nirsnet@igc.apc.org, <http://www.nirs.org>

PEACE AND FREEDOM

Conservative:
Hoover Institution, Stanford University, Stanford, CA 94305-6010, (650) 725-7293, fax (650) 725-8611, e-mail mandy@hoover.stanford.edu, <http://www.hoover.stanford.edu>.

General/Neutral:
Doctors Without Borders, 11 E. 26th St., Suite 1904, New York, NY 10010, (212) 679-6800, (212) 679-7016, e-mail dwb@newyork.mss.org, <http://www.dwb.org>.

Progressive:
ACORN, 739 8th St. S.E., Washington, DC 20003, (202) 547-2500, fax (202) 546-2483, e-mail dcnatacorn@igc.apc.org, <http://www.acorn.org>.

PEOPLE WITH DISABILITIES

General/Neutral:
Chicago Lighthouse, 1850 W. Roosevelt Road, Chicago, IL 60608-1298, (312) 666-1331, TDD (312) 666-8874, fax (312) 243-8539.

POLITICAL ACTIVISM

Conservative:
Conservative Political Action Conference, 1007 Cameron St., 2nd Floor, Alexandria, VA 22310, (800) 752-4391, fax (703) 836-8606, e-mail moskal@cpac.org, <http://www.cpac.org>.

Empower America, 1776 I St. N.W., Suite 890, Washington, DC 20006, (202) 452-8200, fax (202) 833-0388, e-mail fluet@erols.com, <http://www.townhall.com/empower/html/about/eamissn.html>.

Progressive:
Democratic Leadership for the 21st Century, P.O. Box 3726, Chicago, IL 60654, (312) 527-3366; fax (312) 527-3369, e-mail dl21c@aol.com, <http://miso.wwa.com/~jase/dl21c>.

Minnesotans for a Democratic Majority, P.O. Box 65801, St. Paul, MN 55165-0801.

POLITICAL REFORM

Conservative:
Cascade , 813 S.W. Alder, Suite 300, Portland, OR 97205, (503) 242-0900, fax (503) 242-3822, e-mail info@cascadepolicy.org, <http://www.cascadepolicy.org>.

General/Neutral:
Center for Responsive Politics, 1320 19th St. N.W., Suite 700, Washington, DC 20036, (202) 857-0044, fax (202) 857-7809, e-mail info@crp.org, <http://www.crp.org>.

Committee for the Study of the American Electorate, 421 New Jersey Ave. SE, Washington, DC 20003, (202) 546-3221, fax (202) 546-3571.

Congressional Accountability Project, P.O. Box 19446, Washington, DC 20036, (202) 296-2787, fax (202) 833-2406, e-mail gary@essential.org, <http://www.essential.org/orgs/CAP/CAP.html>.

Maine Voters for Clean Elections, P.O. Box 7692, Portland, ME 04112, (207) 773-3274, fax (207) 780-0142, mainevoter@aol.com.

Missouri Alliance for Campaign Reform, 4144 Linden Blvd., Room 504, St. Louis, MO 63108, (314) 731-5312, fax (314) 731-2729, e-mail pkharvey@aol.com.

U.S. Public Interest Research Group, 218 D St. S.E., Washington, DC 20003, (202) 546-9707, fax (202) 546-2461, e-mail pirg@pirg.org, <http://www.pirg.org>.

Progressive:
Center for Voting and Democracy, P.O. Box 60037, Washington, DC 20039, (301) 270-4616, fax (301) 270-4133, e-mail fairvote@compuserve.com, <http://www.igc.org/cvd>.

POLITICAL RESOURCES

General/Neutral:
American Association of Political Consultants, 900 2nd St. N.E., Suite 204, Washington, DC 20002, (202) 371-9585, (202) 371-6751, e-mail aapcmail@aol.com, <http://www.theaapc.org>.

ANB Communications, 3632 N. Central Park Ave., Chicago, IL 60618-4107, (773) 866-0024, fax (773) 866-0025, e-mail anbcomm@interaccess.com.

Political Resources, Inc. P.O. Box 3177, Burlington, VT 05401, (800) 423-2677, fax (802) 864-9502, e-mail PolResInc@aol.com, <http://PoliticalResources.com>.

PUBLIC POLICY

Conservative:
Eagle Forum, P.O. Box 618, Alton, IL 62002, (618) 462-5415, fax (618) 462-8909, e-mail eagle@eagleforum.org, <http://www.eagleforum.org>.

Progressive:
Policy Studies Organization, University of Illinois, 361 Lincoln Hall, 702 S. Wright St., Urbana, IL 61801, (217) 333-4401, fax (217) 244-5712, e-mail s-nagel@uicu.edu, <http://www.staff.uiuc.edu/~s-nagel/>.

RACIAL EQUALITY

Conservative:
Center for Equal Opportunity, 815 15th St. N.W., Suite 928, Washington, DC 20005, (202) 639-0803, fax (202) 639-0827, e-mail Comment@ceousa.org, <http://www.ceousa.org/abceo.html>.

Progressive:
Project Change, Levi's Plaza, 1155 Battery St., San Francisco, CA 94111, (415) 501-7420, fax (415) 501-6575, e-mail sstrong@levi.com.

Conservative:
Acton Institute for the Study of Religion and Liberty, 1612 Ottawa N.W., Suite 301, Grand Rapids, MI 49503, (616) 454-3080, fax (616) 454-9454, e-mail info@acton.org, <http://www.acton.org>.

The Advocates for Self-Government Inc., 1202 N. Tennessee St., Suite 202, Cartersville, CA 30120, (770) 386-8372, fax (770) 386-8373, e-mail advocates@self-gov.org, <http://www.self-gov.org/>.

American Association of Christian Schools, P.O. Box 2189, Independence, MO (816) 795-7709, fax (816) 795-7462, e-mail aacs@aacs.org, <http://www.aacs.org>.

Christian Coalition, 1801-L Sara Drive, Chesapeake, VA 23320, (757) 424-2630, fax (757) 424-9068, e-mail letters@cc.org, <http://www.cc.org/>.

Rutherford Institute, P.O. Box 7482, Charlottesville, VA 22906, (804) 978-3888, fax (804) 978-1789, e-mail tristaff@rutherford.org, <http:www.rutherford.org/>.

Traditional Values Coalition, 139 C St. S.E., Washington, DC 20003, (202) 547-8570, fax (202) 546-6602, e-mail tvcmedia@erols.com, <http://www.traditionalvalues.org>.

General/Neutral:
American Jewish Committee, 165 E. 56th St., New York, NY 10022-2746, (212) 751-4000, fax (212) 319-0975, e-mail pr@ajc.org, <http://www.ajc.org>.

Interfaith Alliance, 1511 K St. N.W., Suite 738, Washington, DC 20005, (202) 639-6370, fax (202) 639-6375, e-mail TIAlliance@intr.net, <http://www.tialliance.org>.

Religious Action Center of Reform Judaism, 2027 Massachusetts Ave N.W., Washington, DC 20036, (202) 387-2800, fax (202) 667-9070, e-mail 74637.277@compuserve.com, <http://www.cdinet.com/RAC/>.

Progressive:
Americans United for Separation of Church and State, 1816 Jefferson Place N.W., Washington DC 20036, (202) 466-3234, fax (202) 466-2587, e-mail amerunited@aol.com, <http://www.au.org>.

Catholics for a Free Choice, 1436 U St. N.W., #301, Washington, DC 20009-3916, (202) 986-6093, fax (202) 332-7995, e-mail cffc@igc.apc.org, http://www.igc.org/catholicvote>.

National Jewish Democratic Council, 503 Capital Court N.E., Suite 300, Washington, DC 20002, (202) 544-7636, fax (202) 544-7645, e-mail njdconline@aol.com, <http://www.njdc.org>.

People for the American Way, 2000 M St. N.W., Suite 400, Washington, DC 20036, (202) 467-4999, (202) 293-2672, e-mail pfaw@pfaw.org, <http://www.pfaw.org>.

People of Faith, c/o the Rev. David Dyson, Lafayette Ave. Presbyterian Church, 85 S. Oxford St., Brooklyn, NY 11217, (718) 625-7515, fax (718) 693-3367, e-mail POF@igc.apc.org.

Women's Alliance for Theology, Ethics, and Ritual (WATER), 8035 13th St., Silver Spring, MD 20910, (301) 589-2509, fax (301) 589-3150, e-mail mary.hunt@hers.com, <http://www.hevs.com/water>.

REPUBLICAN PARTY AND RELATED ORGANIZATIONS

Republican National Committee, 310 1st St., Washington, DC 20003, (202) 863-8500, fax (202) 863-8820, e-mail info@rnc.org, <http://www.rnc.org>.

National Federation of the Grand Order of Pachyderm Clubs, 7306 Wise Ave., Suite 100, St. Louis, MO 63117, (314) 645-4467, fax (314) 644-6776, e-mail www@pachyderms.org, <http:www.pachyderms.org>.

Republican Liberty Caucus, 611 Pennsylvania Ave., Suite 370, Washington, DC 20003, (410) 679-8898, fax (410) 679-8898*51, <http://www.rlc.org>.

Republican National Hispanic Assembly, 600 Pennsylvania Ave. S.E., Suite 300, Washington, DC 20003, (202) 608-1400, fax (202) 608-1427, e-mail rnha1@aol.com.

TECHNOLOGY

Conservative:
Hudson Institute, P.O. Box 26-919, Indianapolis, IN 46226, (317) 545-1000, fax (317) 545-9639, <http://www.a1.com/hudson/abouthd.html>.

General/Neutral:
Center for Science in the Public Interest, 1875 Connecticut Ave. N.W., Suite 300, Washington, DC 20009-5728, (202) 332-9110, fax (202) 265-4954, e-mail cspi@cspinet.org, <http://www.cspinet.org>.

Progressive:
Center for Democracy and Technology, 1634 I Street N.W., Suite 1100, Washington, DC 20006, (202) 637-9800, <http://www.cdt.org/>.

URBAN ISSUES

General/Neutral:
The Carter Center, 1 Copenhill, Atlanta, GA 30307, (404) 420-5100, fax (404) 331-0238, e-mail nsingh@emory.edu.

VIOLENCE

General/Neutral:

Family Violence Prevention Fund, 383 Rhode Island St., Suite 304, San Francisco, CA 94103, (415) 252-8900, fax (415) 252-8991, e-mail fund@igc.apc.org, <http://www.fvpf.org>.

VOLUNTEERISM

General/Neutral:

Association of Volunteer Administrators of Metropolitan Chicago, 560 W. Lake St., Chicago, IL 60661-1499, (312) 906-2494.

Impact Online, 715 Colorado Ave., Suite 4, Palo Alto, CA, (650) 327-1389, fax (650) 327-1395, e-mail respond@impactonline.org, <http://www.webcom.com/iol/welcome.html>.

Points of Light Foundation, 1737 H St. N.W., Washington, DC 20006, (202) 223-9186, (800) 59-LIGHT, <http://www.pointsoflight.org>.

VOTER PARTICIPATION/INFORMATION

Conservative:

College Republican National Committee, 600 Pennsylvania Ave. S.E., Suite 300, Washington, DC 20003, (202) 608-1413, fax (202) 608-1429, <http://www.crnc.org>.

National Federation of Republican Women, 124 N. Alfred St., Alexandria, VA 22314-3011, (703) 548-9688, fax (703) 548-9836, e-mail nfrw@worldweb.net, <http://www.nfrw.org>.

General/Neutral:

Democracy Network, Center for Governmental Studies, 10951 W. Pico Blvd., Suite 206, Los Angeles, CA 90064, (310) 470-6590, fax (310) 475-3752, e-mail westenCGS@aol.com, <http://www.democracynet.org>.

League of Conservation Voters, 1707 L St. N.W., Suite 750, Washington, DC 20036, (202) 785-8683, fax (202) 835-0491, e-mail lcv@lcv.org, <http://www.lcv.org>.

League of Women Voters, 1730 M St. N.W., Washington, DC 20036, (202) 429-1965, fax (202) 429-0854, e-mail lwv@lwv.org,   <http://www.lwv.org/~lwvus/>.

Project Vote Smart, Northeastern University, 102 The Fenway, Cushing Hall, Room 17, Boston, MA 02115, (800) 622-SMART, fax (617) 373-5485 or (617) 373-5699, e-mail comments@vote-smart.org, <http://www.votesmart.org>.

Progressive:

Common Cause, 1250 Connecticut Ave. N.W., 6th floor, Washington, DC 20035, (202) 833-1200, fax (202) 659-3716, e-mail 753.3120@compuserv.com, <http://www.commoncause.org>.

Voters for Choice, 2604 Connecticut Ave. N.W., Washington, DC 20008, (202) 588-5200, fax (202) 588-0600, e-mail vfc@igc.apc.org,

WELFARE REFORM

Conservative:

The Future of Freedom Foundation, 11350 Random Hills Road, Suite 800, Fairfax, VA 22030, (703) 934-6101, fax (703) 352-8678, e-mail: freedom@fff.org, <http://www.fff.org/freedom/info/fff.html>.

Progressive:

Horizons Initiative, 90 Cushing Ave., Dorchester, MA 02125, (617) 287-1900, fax (617) 287-0898, e-mail horizonsin@aol.com, <http://www.brighthorizons.com>.

WOMEN'S ISSUES

Conservative

Republican Network to Elect Women (RENEW), 1555 King St., Suite 300, P.O. Box 507, Alexandria, VA 22313-0507, (703) 836-2255, <http://members.aol.com/gorenew>.

Women in the Senate and House (WISH List), 3205 N St. N.W., Washington, DC 20007, (202) 3422-9111, e-mail thewishlist@aol.com, <http://www.thewishlist.org>.

Progressive

Women's Wire, 1820 Gateway Drive, Suite 150, San Mateo, CA 94404, (415) 378-6500, (415) 378-6599, <http://www.women.com>

Voters for Choice, 2604 Connecticut Ave. N.W., Washington, DC 20008, (202) 588-5200, fax (202) 588-0600, e-mail vfc@igc.apc.org.

APPENDIX FOUR

MY FAVORITE GOVERNMENT INTERNET SITES

Americans Communicating Electronically, <http://www.sbaonline.sba.gov/ace/guide96.html>, connects to more than 100 federal government gopher sites.

American University Campaign Finance Web Site, <http://www.soc.american.edu/campfin/>, information about campaign contributions.

Center for Public Integrity, <http://www.publicintegrity.org>, issues, accountability, miscellaneous information.

Center for Responsive Politics, <http://www.crp.org>, indicates contributors to candidates, miscellaneous political information.

Counterpoint Publishing, <http://www.tlp.com/counterpoint2.html>, federal and state regulations.

Federal Election Commission, <http://www.fec.gov>, information about campaign contributions.

Fedworld, <http://www.fedworld.gov/>, connects to 150 federal electronic bulletin board services.

Internet Sources of Government Information, <http://www.cs.ruu.nl/wais/html/>, a complete guide of government information Internet sites.

Library of Congress Information System, <http://www.loc.gov/>, unlimited information.

Political Resources, <http://PoliticalResources.com>, a variety of political resources, lists, job postings, and a calendar.

SunSite, <http://wss-www.berkeley.edu/unix/faa/>, a gateway to information stored in computers around the world, White House, CIA information and more.

The White house, <http://www.whitehouse.gov>; e-mails publications@whitehouse.gov; President@whitehouse.gov; Vice.President@whitehouse.gov; First.Lady@whitehouse.gov; faq@whitehouse.gov (for alternate sources of government information). The White House is the single point of access to all government information available electronically on the Internet.

Appendix Five

Media Publications and Services

Bacon's Media Directories, 332 S. Michigan Ave., Chicago, IL 60604, (800) 621-0561, (312) 922-2400, fax (312) 922-3127, <http://wwwbaconsinfo.com>.

Beach, Mark. Editing Your Newsletter: How to Produce an Effective Publication Using Traditional Tools and Computers. Cincinnati: Writer's Digest Books, 1995. (800) 264-6305.

Bruno, Michael H. (editor). Pocket Pal: a Graphic Arts Production Handbook. Memphis, Tennessee: International Paper Co., 1989. (901) 763-6000.

Burrelle's Media Directories, 75 E. Northfield Road, Livingston, NJ 07039, (800) 876-3342, fax (800) 898-6677.

Gale Research Inc., 645 Griswold St., 835 Penobscot Building, Detroit, MI 48226-4094, (800) 877-GALE, (313) 961-2242, fax (313) 961-6815, galeord@gale.com, <http://www.gale.com>. One of the largest information publishers in the world, Gale has an extensive catalog of reference and information directories.

Parker, Roger C.. Desktop Publishing and Design for Dummies. San Mateo, California: IDG Books. (800) 762-2974.

Pattison, Polly. 101 Ways to Save Money on Newsletters, Flyers, Brochures, Posters, Catalogs, Letterheads, Annual Reports & Practically Anything You Print. Newsletter Resources, 1995. (800) 264-6305.

Stopke, Judy. 31 Trends in Graphic Design: Some That Work and Some That Don't. Promotional Perspectives, 1994. (313) 994-0007.

Video Monitoring Services (Radio/Television Reports), 212 W. Superior, Chicago, IL 60610, (312) 649-1131, fax (312) 649-1427, and (312) 649-1527, e-mail (through web site), <http://www.vidmon.com>.

Wheildon, Colin. Type and Layout: How Typography and Design Can Get Your Message Across-or Get in the Way. Strathmoor Press, 1995. (800) 217-7377.

APPENDIX SIX

LANGUAGE MATTERS
[A GOPAC MEMO]

Language: A Key Mechanism of Control *

As you know, one of the key points in the GOPAC tapes is that "language matters." In the video *"We Are a Majority,"* Language is listed as a key mechanism of control used by a majority party, along with Agenda, Rules, Attitude and Learning. As the tapes have been used in training sessions across the country and mailed to candidates, we have heard a plaintive plea: "I wish I could speak like Newt."

That takes years of practice. But we believe that you could have a significant impact on your campaign and the way you communicate if we help a little. That is why we have created this list of words and phrases.

This list is prepared so that you might have a directory of words to use in writing literature and mail, in preparing speeches, and in producing electronic media. The words and phrases are powerful. Read them. Memorize as many as possible. And remember that, like any tool, these words will not help if they are not used...

CONTRASTING WORDS

Often we search hard for words to help us define our opponents. Sometimes we are hesitant to use contrast. Remember that creating a difference helps you. These are powerful words that can create a clear and easily understood contrast. Apply these to the opponent, their record, proposals and their party

decay... failure (fail)... collapse(ing)... deeper... crisis... urgent(cy)... destructive... destroy... sick... pathetic... lie... liberal... they/them... unionized bureaucracy... "compassion" is not enough... betray... consequences... limit(s)... shallow... traitors... sensationalists...

endanger... coercion... hypocrisy... radical... threaten... devour... waste... corruption... incompetent... permissive attitudes... destructive... impose... self-serving... greed... ideological... insecure... anti-(issue): flag, family, child, jobs... pessimistic... excuses... intolerant...

stagnation... welfare... corrupt... selfish... insensitive... status quo... mandate(s)... taxes... spend(ing)... shame... disgrace... punish (poor...)... bizarre... cynicism... cheat... steal... abuse of power... machine... bosses... obsolete... criminal rights... red tape... patronage...

OPTIMISTIC POSITIVE GOVERNING WORDS

Use the list below to help define your campaign and your vision of public service. These words can help give extra power to your message. In addition, these words help develop the positive side of the contrast you should create with your opponent, giving your community something to vote *for!*

share... change... opportunity... legacy... challenge... control... truth... moral... courage... reform... prosperity... crusade... movement... children... family... debate... compete... active(ly)... we/us/our... candid(ly)... humane... pristine... provide...

liberty... commitment... principle(d)... unique... duty... precious... premise... care(ing)... tough... listen... learn... help... lead... vision... success... empower(ment)... citizen... activist... mobilize... conflict... light... dream... freedom...

peace... rights... pioneer... proud/pride... building... preserve... pro-(issue): flag, children, environment... reform... workfare... eliminate good-time in prison... strength... choice/choose... fair... protect... confident... incentive... hard work... initiative... common sense... passionate[95]

*As preparation for the Republican landslide of 1994, GOPAC, Newt Gingrich's political organization, issued a memo to Republican candidates on the importance of words, entitled "Language: A Key Mechanism of Control." The memo is reprinted with permission of GOPAC, Tinabeth Burton (202-484-2282).

APPENDIX SEVEN

FREEDOM OF INFORMATION ACT

GUIDEBOOKS

House Report 104-156: *A Citizen's Guide on Using the Freedom of Information Act.* U.S. House of Representatives, Subcommittee on Government Management, Room B-373, Rayburn House Office Building, Washington, DC 20510.

How to Use the Federal FOIA. Reporters Committee for Freedom of the Press, 1101 Wilson Blvd. #1910, Arlington, VA 22209, (703) 807-2100, fax (703) 807-2109, e-mail rcfp@rcfp.org, <http://www.rcfp.org/rcfp>.

Using the FOIA: A Step-by-Step Guide. American Civil Liberties Union, 122 Maryland Ave. N.E., Washington, DC 20002, (202) 544-1681, fax (202) 546-0738, <http://www.aclu.org>.

INTERNET

<http://www.best.com/~schmitz/IUFOG/Foia/foia-sample.html> has sample FOIA request letters.

<http://www.epic.org> offers information from the Electronic Privacy information Center, 666 Pennsylvania Ave. NE, Washington, DC 20003, (202) 544-9240, fax (202) 547-5482, e-mail info@epic.org.

APPENDIX EIGHT

LIST BROKERS

Aristotle Industries, 205 Pennsylvania Ave. S.E., Washington, DC 20003, (202) 543-8345, fax (202) 543-6407, <http://www.aristotle.org>.

Cahners Direct Marketing Services, 1350 E. Touhy Ave., Des Plaines, IL 60018, (800) 323-4958, (847) 390-2361, fax (847) 390-2779, <http://www.cahners.lists.com>.

Chicago Association of Direct Marketing, 435 N. Michigan Ave., Suite 1700, Chicago, IL 60611, (312) 670-2236, fax (312) 670-2236, e-mail cadmhq@aol.com. Not a list broker per se, but an industry expert on list brokerage and related marketing issues.

Best Mailing Lists Inc., 888 S. Craycroft Road, Tucson, AZ 85711, (520) 745-0200, 1 (800) 692-2378, fax (520) 745-3800, e-mail best@bestmailing.com.

Metromail, 2122 York Road, Oak Brook, IL 60521, (630) 574-7663, fax (630) 574-3823.

MGT Associates Inc., 11111 Santa Monica Blvd., Suite 620, Los Angeles, CA 90025, (310) 473-7550, fax (310) 473-1616.

Names and Addresses Inc., 5200 W. 73rd St., P.O. Box 39139, Edina, MN 55439, (612) 941-6332, fax (612) 941-6362.

Appendix Nine

Miscellaneous Resources

AIM Report, Accuracy in Media, 4455 Connecticut Ave. N.W., Suite 330, Washington, DC 20008, (202) 364-4401, fax (202) 364-4098, e-mail ar@take.aim.org, <http://www.aim.org>, conservative media critic attempting to correct left-wing media bias.

The Almanac of American Politics, P.O. Box 46909, St. Louis, MO 63146, (800) 424-2921, fax (202) 739-8540, <http://www.cloakroom.com>, contains biographies of federal officials, voting and financial records, maps, and more.

American Spectator, 2020 N. 14th St., Suite 750, Arlington, VA 22201, (800) 524-3469, fax (614) 382-5866, e-mail amspc@ix.netcom.com, <http:// www.savers.org/heritage/links>, investigative reporting and commentary with a conservative view.

Bireley, Robert. *The Counter-Reformation Prince.* The University of North Carolina Press, 1990. Focuses on six political thinkers of the 16th and 17th centuries whose philosophies of ethical political leadership and statecraft were put into practice with great success by government officials opposed to the Machiavellian philosophy.

Campaigns & Elections, 1511 K St. N.W., #1020, Washington, DC 20005-1450, (202) 638-7788, <http://www.camelect.com>. The bible of politics; it also offers an annual political services guide, "The Political Pages," a directory of resources for every campaign need: direct mail, fundraising, media, opposition research, polling, products, political consulting, list services, and much more.

Community Information and Education Service, Office of Continuing Education and Public Service, University of Illinois at Urbana-Champaign, Suite 202, 302 E. John St., Champaign, IL 61820, (217) 333-1444, fax (217) 333-9561, publications and audiotape series on local government issues.

Compuserve, 5000 Arlington Center Blvd., P.O. Box 20212, Columbus, OH 43220, (800) 848-8990, e-mail (through web site), <http://www.compuserve.com>, a database company with many services.

DataTimes, 14000 Quail Spring Parkway, Suite 450, Oklahoma City, OK, 73134, (800) 642-2525, e-mail info@datatimes.com, <http://www.datatimes.com>, a database company that provides coverage of major and minor publications.

Directory of News Sources, National Press Club, 529 14th St. N.W., Washington, DC 20078-1450, (202) 662-7525, fax (202) 662-7512, e-mail (through web site), <http://npc.press.org>, lists hundreds of organizations that provide valuable information.

Extra!, 130 W. 25th St., New York, NY 10001, (212) 633-6700, fax (212) 727-7668, <http://www.fair.org/fair/>, media criticism attempting to correct right-wing bias.

Horowitz, Lois. *Knowing Where to Look: The Ultimate Guide to Research.* Cincinnati: Writer's Digest Books, 1984. A how-to book on research.

Knight/Ridder Information, 2440 El Camino Real, Mountain View, CA 94040-1400, (800) 334-2564, fax (415) 254-7070, <http://www.krinfo.com/>, a technical/scientific database company that provides access to more than 425 databases.

Lexis-Nexis, 9443 Springboro Pike, Miamisburg, OH 45342, (800) 544-7390, fax (513) 847-3097, e-mail steven.edwards@lexis-nexis.com, <http://www.lexis-nexis.com>, the largest database of legal information and publications.

Liberal Opinion Week, 108 E. 5th St., Vinton, IA 52349, (319) 472-2313, fax (319) 472-4811, progressive commentary on the week's news.

Mother Jones, 731 Market Street, Suite 600, San Francisco, CA 94103, (415) 357-0509, fax (415) 665-6696, [employee's name]@motherjones.com, <http://www.motherjones.com/info/info.html>, a publication promoting progressive change.

National Opinion Research Center, 1155 E. 60th St., Chicago, IL 60637, (773) 753-7500, fax (773) 753-7886, e-mail depoyph@norcmail, <http://www.norc.uchicago.edu>. A national survey research organization that conducts social research in the public interest, including the "General Social Survey" every year to profile American society.

National Review, 150 E. 35th St., New York, NY 10016, (212) 679-7330, fax (212) 696-0309, <http: www.sbsc.org/nationalreview>, a publication promoting conservative change.

The Political Market, The Washington Post, 1150 15th St. N.W., Washington, DC 20071-9100, (202) 334-6000, fax: (202) 334-4311, <http://www.washingtonpost.com>, a directory of political services and products.

Political Resource Directory, Political Resources Inc., P.O. Box 3177, Burlington, VT 05401, (800) 423-2677, fax (802) 434-5127, <http://PoliticalResources.com>, a comprehensive guide to political services.

Ripon Forum, The Ripon Society, 501 Capitol Court N.E., Suite 300, Washington, DC 20002, (202) 546-1292, fax (202) 547-6560, e-mail riponsoc@aol.com, twice-monthly Republican commentary.

Utne Reader, 1624 Harmon Place, Minneapolis, MN 55403, (612) 338-5040, e-mail editor@utne.com, <http://www.utne.com>, a digest of the best of progressive thought.

Weiler, Michael, and W. Barnett Pearce. *Reagan and Public Discourse in America.* Tuscaloosa: The University of Alabama Press, 1992. Communications and political professionals' analyses of the Reagan communications techniques.

APPENDIX TEN

DEMOCRATIC NATIONAL COMMITTEE

The Democratic National Committee, 430 S. Capitol St. S.E., Washington, D.C. 20003, (202) 863-8000, fax (202) 863-8081, dnc@democrats.org, <http://www.democrats.org>, offers a variety of valuable services.

- Candidate training. The DNC offers the Democratic National Training Institute, how-to materials, and workshops.

- Targeted in-state services. These include coordinated polling, database development, voter targeting assistance, phone banks, state party contributions, and national contributions.

- Planning and consulting services. These include operations plans, campaign plans, direct voter contact plans, voter registration plans, fundraising consulting, communications consulting, and computer systems consulting.

- Communications and media services. The DNC provides some production of cable television shows, media production, generic advertising, public service announcements, press briefings, and newsletters and publications.

Through its Democratic Policy Commission:

- Policy roundtables. An examination of policy issues and proposals.

- "Democratic Spotlight." A clearinghouse of innovative solutions to problems available to candidates throughoutthe country.

- Candidate briefing materials.

APPENDIX ELEVEN

REPUBLICAN NATIONAL COMMITTEE

The Republican National Committee, 310 1st St., Washington, DC 20003, (202) 863-8500, fax (202) 863-8820, e-mail info@rnc.org, <http://www.rnc.org>, offers a variety of valuable services

- Candidate training seminars held throughout the country.

- Planning and consulting services. Similar to those of the DNC, they are offered for House of Representatives candidates through the House Congressional Campaign Committee, for U.S. Senate candidates through the Senate Congressional Campaign Committee, and for local candidates through individual state Republican committees.

- Communications and media services. Similar to those of the DNC, although in more of an advisory rather than hands-on role. However, the RNC's TV studio is second to none.

- Policy briefings.

It is through publications that the RNC particularly excels, with the following handbooks and manuals available:

- *The Redbook.* Designed for candidates at the local level.

- *The Local Party Leadership Manual.* Focuses on the roles and responsibilities of local party chairs and creating a local party plan. An abridged version known as *The Summary* also is available.

- *The Complete Guide to Voter Programs.* Five books on data processing, phone banking, direct mail, election day, and more.

- *Candidate Recruitment Workbook.* Includes information on analyzing the district and the opposition and in engaging local community and financial leaders.

- *Precinct Organization.* Information on planning, recruiting and training volunteers, canvassing, and more.

- *Targeted Voter Registration.* Information on locating potential voters, registration, and getting them to the polls.

- *Reach Out and Touch the Voter.* Describes how to establish a phone bank.

APPENDIX TWELVE

MEDIA TERMS

ANGLE. The main reason, focus, or aspect of a story.

ADVERTISEMENT, ADVERTISING. Publicity paid for by the campaign. As opposed to a *NEWS* or *FEATURE* story, which is "free publicity."

ATTRIBUTION. Statements of opinion in a news story credited to someone. "Not for attribution" is *BACKGROUND* given to a reporter for which the source is not to be quoted, but very often this is of little use to the reporter. Do not attempt to squirm away from standing behind a statement by arguing it is "not for attribution."

BACKGROUND, BACKGROUNDER. Information not to be quoted that provides information to help the reporter gain a greater understanding of a subject.

EMBARGO. A story provided to the media with the understanding that they may release it only at a certain time or date. Possible problem: one member of the media may ignore the embargo, causing the other members of the media to be upset with the campaign for providing that reporter with an "exclusive."

EXCLUSIVE. A story provided to one member of the media in advance of all other members.

FEATURE STORY. "Soft" news treatment that provides more human interest and less criticism on a topic or individual than *NEWS*.

LEADING QUESTION. One that puts the reporter's words in the interviewee's mouth. Example: "Don't you think there are too many people abusing welfare?" If you do not agree with the words the reporter is putting in your mouth, instead of answering with a "yes" or "no," answer with "My opinion is...."

NEWS, or *HARD NEWS*. New items of information of interest to the public.

NEWS RELEASE (PRESS RELEASE). An article prepared by the campaign and sent to the media. The media are not expected to use it word-for-word (if they do, so much the better), but instead employ it as a point of departure for their own individual stories.

"NO COMMENT." Indicates to reporter and reader that you are hiding something. Some sort of answer must be given—preferably one thought of in advance.

OFF THE RECORD. Do not even bother. Some reporters will not respect it, and others will get angry that you gave them information and then will not allow them to use it. If you don't want to go on the record, do not say it in the first place.

"PUFF" PIECE. A fawning news article about the candidate. You are very lucky if you get one of these.

SLANT. The reporter's subjective opinion injected into the story.

SPIN. The campaign's attempt to draw attention away from some negative aspect and onto a positive aspect.

APPENDIX THIRTEEN

POLITICAL ACTIVITIES OF FEDERAL WORKERS

The Hatch Act, which describes allowed and prohibited political activities of federal workers, was amended in 1993 to expand civil servants rights to participate in political campaigns. The following describes what is permitted and prohibited under current law.[*]

ALLOWED

Attendance at political fundraising events

Display of campaign material on a private vehicle occasionally used for public business; however, if the vehicle frequently is used for public business, such display is prohibited

Identification as a host or speaker on a fundraising invitation, so long as it does not say that host or speaker is soliciting contributions

Mailing of campaign literature that asks for contributions

Monetary contributions to political organizations

Phone banking

Service as an officer of a political campaign, fundraising organization, or committee, but without soliciting or receiving contributions

Solicitiation of contributions for a multi-member federal employee/labor PAC from a fellow employee who is a member of the PAC, so long as the soliciting party is not directly or indirectly the employee's supervisor

Solicitation of political volunteer services from a non-subordinate

Speechmaking at a fundraiser, if the speech does *not* ask for contributions

PROHIBITED

Conducting political activity while at work or on the premises

Displaying campaign literature on federal premises, on federal business, or in uniform

Forcing an employee to contribute

Participation in any political activity if a member of the CIA, FBI, or FEC (Federal Election Commission)

Solicitation of contributions by signed letter

Solicitation of contributions from the public

Solicitation of services from a business

---

[*] See "Inside Politics," *Campaigns & Elections*, Sept. 1996, p. 9.

Mark J. Valentino for State Representative - 19th District

For release: immediately
Date: March 1, 1998
For more information contact: Anne M. Nordbi, (312) 996-8495
Page one of two

Valentino Endorsed by Near West Side Village Association

The Near West Side Village Association (NWSVA), the leading community service organization in Cleveland's Near West Side neighborhood, has given its highest unqualified endorsement to Mark J. Valentino in his race for the Republican nomination for State Representative in Ohio's 19th District.

"Mark's record of community service is second to none, and through his work as publisher of the *Near West News,* he has been a vital partner in the Near West Side Village Association's efforts to improve life in the neighborhood," said William J. Baxter, executive director of the Near West Side Village Association.

Valentino's neighborhood activities also have included active membership on the education and finance councils of Notre Dame Parish.

-more-

Through his work on the *News*, Valentino is familiar with and has been influential on the leading issues facing the Near West Side community, including fighting the rising crime rate, easing parking woes, and balancing gentrification with the needs of longtime residents.

"Valentino supports legislation to ban assault weapons and to revoke the gun rights of domestic abusers, and to increase state-supported student loans and scholarships for college students," Baxter noted. "He's an active, visible member of the community who will fight for what's best for us down in Columbus."

The NWSVA was established in 1978 to provide a forum and activist action concerning neighborhood issues. It represents more than 700 dues-paying area residents and lobbies governmental officials and local business leaders for actions that will benefit the community.

-30-

Appendix Fifteen

Sample Direct Mail Piece

Bill Baxter
U.S. Congress
Fighting <u>with you</u> to end gun violence

July 29, 1996

John Q. Public
123 Milwaukee Ave.
Kenosha, WI 53142

Dear John:

What I read today in our community paper, the *Journal*, sickened me.

One of our neighbors was shot in the leg during an attempted robbery on Damen near Sawyer. Gangbangers shot at a 16-year-old who was helping a neighbor <u>carry her groceries</u> near Hoyne and Pratt. Two punks put a gun to the head of a 54-year-old man *coming home from work* near Wood and Michigan, and took all his money.

And this is considered one of the city's <u>safer</u> neighborhoods.

What has our Congressman, John Smith, *one of the 73 freshman Republicans Newt Gingrich is so proud of*, done about gun violence?

Last year the Republican-dominated congress, the one that wants to <u>repeal</u> the ban on assault weapons, had uncharacteristically voted in the House

Judiciary Committee to outlaw cop-killer bullets—
the kind that can *rip through* a "bullet-proof"
vest.

That is, until John Smith <u>changed his vote</u>. Originally in favor of the ban, John *flip-flopped* on a
second vote, and a "recommendation" to "study" the
bullets was passed instead.

What is there to "study"? **Cop-killer bullets kill
cops—and kids.**

Smith even told the *Kenosha Gazette* that the National Rifle Association had phoned him between
votes, but that had "<u>nothing</u> to do with" his
change of mind.

The NRA had already given Smith $5,000 the year
before. This year, political action committees led
by the NRA "*are flocking to Smith,*" according to
the *Kenosha Daily News*.

As you know, I am running for congress in the 25th
District against Smith and the <u>gun-loving</u> Gingrich
Contract for Disaster he represents.

He and his NRA allies are *scared*. They should be.

In the state legislature, I <u>led the fight for sane
gun laws</u>. I introduced bills to ban assault weapons and to keep weapons confiscated by the police
from returning to the streets.

The NRA knows that despite the pro-gun atmosphere
of the current state legislature, I got a bill
passed that denied gun permits to those under re-
straining orders for domestic abuse or stalking.

I've beaten the gun nuts in Wisconsin. They know
I'll beat them in congress, too.

John predicted he would spend about *$1 million* in his race to defeat me.

I don't have PACs "flocking" to me like John does. That's why I need the help of <u>friends like you</u> to ensure that our voices, the voices of sanity, will be heard in the next congress' debates on gun control.

If you believe as I do that we need to keep guns out of the hands of the lowlifes who shoot neighbors walking home from work and unloading groceries, then you must *help me* in my campaign by making a contribution today of $500, $300, or $200.

We can <u>win</u>! We can take the guns and the cop-killer bullets out of the bad guys' arsenal.

Or, we can watch as John Smith, <u>at the bidding of his NRA backers</u>, continues killing the gun-control legislation we desperately need to take our streets and neighborhoods back from the *gun-toting scum* prowling out there right now.

I know those streets. I worked my way through college delivering mail. I want the next generation of kids working at jobs like the one I had <u>not to be in danger every time they walk outside.</u>

If John Smith goes back to congress, not only will there *not* be more gun controls, there will be *fewer* gun controls. John favors repealing the current assault weapons ban and repealing the Brady Law, which requires a five-day waiting period to buy a gun.

Guaranteed, John, Newt, and their NRA-owned allies will make <u>putting more guns in the hands of criminals</u> their number one priority.

Every day, John's treasury of NRA and PAC money grows. But you can fight these outsiders by making a contribution to my campaign of $500, $300, or $200. Please write your check to **Baxter for Congress** and mail it in the enclosed envelope <u>today</u>!

We have more to lose than an election. We might just lose *a cop or a kid*, too.

Sincerely,

Bill Baxter

P.S. Did you know <u>gun-related deaths went up 23%</u> between 1981 and 1992 while the population grew by only 4%? The NRA and other Washington D.C.-based PACs that own John Smith don't want you to.

<u>Don't let organizations made up of people who don't even live here determine who will represent our community</u>! Add your voice to mine in the fight against gun violence by writing a check to **Baxter for Congress** <u>right now</u> for $500, $300, or $200.

BIBLIOGRAPHY

BOOKS

Boswell, Thomas. *Why Time Begins On Opening Day.* New York: Penguin, 1984.

The Community Media Workshop. *Getting On The Air & Into Print (6th edition).* Chicago: Columbia College, June 1996.

The Forbes Scrapbook of Thoughts on the Business of Life, Vols. I, II, and III. New York: Forbes Inc., 1950, 1984, 1989.

The New Encyclopaedia Britannica, Chicago, Encyclopaedia Britannica, 1991.

Ross, Robert S. *American National Government.* Chicago: Rand McNally, 1972.

Simpson, Dick. *Winning Elections.* New York: HarperCollins, 1996.

Sorauf, Frank J. *Party Politics in America.* Boston: Little, Brown, 1976.

Weiler, Michael, and W. Barnett Pearce, eds. *Reagan and Public Discourse in America.* Tuscaloosa, Alabama: The University of Alabama Press, 1992.

Volunteer Handbook 1995-1996, Urbana: University of Illinois Alumni Assn, 1995.

Women in Communications Inc., Chicago Chapter. *22nd Annual Career Conference Handbook.* Chicago, 1986.

ARTICLES/PERIODICALS

American Psychologist, American Psychological Assn., Washington, DC:
"Specialty Guidelines for the Delivery of Services by Industrial/Organizational Psychologists," 36(6), 1981.

Campaigns & Elections, Campaigns & Elections Publishing, Washington, DC:
Allen, Cathy. "Women on the Run," Oct./Nov. 1995.
Clinton, Wally. "Telephone Campaigning," Oct./Nov. 1995.
Hazelwood, Dan N. "Targeting Persuasion Mail," Sept. 1995.
Johnson, Duff. "Political Information Management," Oct./Nov 1996.
Persinos, John F. "Gotcha!", Aug. 1994
Persinos, John F., and Tom Russell. "Life of the Parties," Dec./Jan. 1996.
Persinos, John F. "Pushing the Envelope," June 1994.
Simpson, Burney. "Rainbow Machine," June 1996,.
Sonis, Larry. "Understanding Direct Democracy," Dec./Jan. 1995.
Tron, Barrie. "Staging Media Events," Dec./Jan. 1996.
"Campaign Screw Up 103," June 1994.
"Inside Politics, " Sept. 1996.
"Mad About You," Oct./Nov. 1994.
"Off the Record," July 1994.
"Off the Record," Aug. 1994.
"Off the Record," Dec./Jan. 1995.

"Off the Record," Aug. 1995.
"Off the Record," Sept. 1995.
"Off the Record," Aug. 1996.
Dec./Jan. 1996.

Communication World, International Association of Business Communicators, San Francisco:
Gerstner, John. "Cyber-skeptic Cliff Stoll," June/July 1996.
Williams, Joe. "On Becoming a Strategic Partner with Management," March 1996.

Chicago Reader, Chicago:
Custer, Charley. "The Education of Richard Murray, Candidate," March 4, 1983.
Lehigh, Scot. "New Collar," Dec. 6, 1985.
Miller, Bryan. "The Art of the Campaign." July 12, 1991.
Peck, Grant. "Gary Politics in Black and White: The Mayor's Race--Guess Who's Coming to City Hall," Nov. 17, 1995.
Shepherd, Chuck. "News of the Weird," July 5, 1996.

Chicago Sun-Times, Chicago Sun-Times Inc., Chicago:
Kirk, Jim. "Ad Spending Picks Up Pace at 11th Hour," March 18, 1996.
Oclander, Jorge. "In Mell's World, It's Politics as Usual," March 23, 1996.
Steward, Janet Kidd. "Campaigns Ice the Cake for Industry," March 18, 1996.

Communications Concepts Management Report on Media Relations, Communications Concepts Inc., Springfield, Virginia:
No. 8, May 1995.

Crain's Chicago Business, Crain Communications Inc., Chicago:
Hornung, Mark. "A Few Rules for Racial Appeals," Jan. 16, 1989.

DePaul University Magazine, DePaul University, Chicago:
"There's No Business Like Show Business—Unless You're Running for Office," Spring 1996.

Extra! Update, Fairness and Accuracy In Reporting, New York.:
"Language: A Key Mechanism of Control," Feb. 1995.

Foreign Affairs, Council on Foreign Relations Inc., New York:
Buruma, Ian. "Taiwan's New Nationalists," July/Aug., 1996.

Liberal Opinion Week, Cedar Valley Times Inc., Vinton, Iowa:
Baker, Russell. "Ado About Dole," May 27, 1996.
Germond, Jack, and Witcover, Jules. "Exit Gramm," Feb. 26, 1996.
Simon, Roger. "Media Frenzy Turns Political 'Ad' Into News," June 17, 1996.
Solomon, Norman. "Polls Give Numbers, But Truth Is More Elusive," May 20, 1996.

Loyola Magazine, Loyola University Chicago, Chicago:
Baumhart, Raymond, S.J. "It's Not Easy Being a Manager and a Christian," fall 1990.

National Review, National Review Inc., New York:
"For the Record," Nov. 11, 1996.

Near West Gazette, Near West Gazette Inc., Chicago:
"Runoff Averted in 42nd Ward but Charges Continue to Fly," April 1, 1995.

NFC Notable$, Nonprofit Financial Center, Chicago:
Stillwell, Scott, and Roling, Dick. "NPOs Guard Tax Exempt Status," Summer 1996.

The NonProfit Times, Davis Information Group Inc., Cedar Knolls, New Jersey:
Grandy, Fred. "Honorable Professionals," Aug. 1996.
Pope, Tom. "Voter Registration," Aug. 1996.
Robinson, Andy. "Grassroots Fundraising, " Aug. 1996.

Prism, International Association of Business Communicators/Chicago Chapter:
Sept. 1995.

Quill, Society for Professional Journalists, Huntington, Indiana:
Winternitz, Felix. "990 & Nonprofits," April 1995.

The Political Speaker:
"Most Amazing Winners of '94," Feb. 1995.

U.S. News & World Report, Washington, DC:
Barone, Michael. "The New America," July 10, 1995.
Cooper, Matthew, with Gloria Borger and Michael Barone. "Dirty Tricks? Cheap Shots? Says Who?," July 6, 1992.
"How to influence press coverage," Feb. 19, 1996.
"Speak up! You can be heard!," Feb. 19, 1996.
"Washington Whispers," March 11, 1996.

Utne Reader, LENS Publishing Co. Inc., Minneapolis, Minnesota:
March/April 1996.

Writing Concepts, Communications Concepts Inc., Springfield, Virginia:
"Do Negative Messages Work in Politics?", March 1996.
"Negative Messages Prove 'Tricky and Risky' for Business," March 1996.
"Use Special Techniques When Writing Online Materials," May 1996.
"Rules to Break and to Keep in Writing Direct Mail," June 1996.

WORKSHOPS

Leadership 2000 Conference, Democratic Leadership for the 21st Century, Chicago, Oct. 16, 1993:
McPartlin, Brian, advisor to President Bill Clinton, workshop.
Campaign training workshop.

Jesuit Midwest Advancement Conference, Loyola University Chicago, Chicago, June 18-20, 1990:
Norman S. Fink, senior counsel, John Grenzebach & Associates, "The Capital Campaign in Year 2000."

Management Directions '89, Public Relations Society of America, Chicago, Feb. 28, 1989:
DeBofsky, Greta, corporate vice president, public relations, Quintessence Incorporated, and Lou Williams, president, L.C. Williams & Associates Inc., "Time Management."

Seminar for Chief Publications Officers, Council for Advancement and Support of Education, Chicago, March 17-19, 1993:
Chic Thompson, head, Creative Management Group, "Using Creativity as the Key to Competence in Changing Times."

Jesuit Advancement Administrators National Conference, Loyola University of New Orleans, New Orleans, Louisiana, June 29, 1993:
Williams, Lou, president, L.C. Williams & Associates Inc., "Analyzing and Tracking Issues."

OTHER

"The 50 Things Not to Do in a Political Campaign," *The Best of Campaigns & Elections,* 1996 (pamphlet).

Handicapping Language. Springfield, Illinois: Illinois Department of Rehabilitation Services, 1990 (pamphlet).

INDEX*

* Index to headings/subheadings

ABOUT THE AUTHOR

William S. Bike is vice president of ANB Communications, a public relations, writing, direct mail, and political consulting firm in Chicago, Illinois.

Previously, he worked for two years in communications and publications for the University of Chicago Graduate School of Business; for ten years in public relations and publications for Loyola University Chicago; and, since 1995, in fundraising for the University of Illinois at Chicago. He and the staffs he has directed have won more than 40 local, national, and international publication awards, and Bike himself has won two Peter Lisagor Awards, the highest honors conferred by the Chicago Headline Club, the local arm of the Society for Professional Journalists.

Bike also has worked for several newspapers and magazines, including the *Near West Gazette* in Chicago, which he has served as associate and political editor since 1983, and the *Oak Park News* and the *Berwyn-Cicero News*, two suburban Chicagoland publications which he, at age 24, served as editor-in-chief.

A 1979 political science graduate of DePaul University, he served since 1997 as communications chair for Democratic Leadership for the Twenty-First Century, a political organization dedicated to empowering and educating the next generation of progressive Democratic political activists and leaders.

His first book, *Streets of the Near West Side*, was published by ACTA Publications, Chicago, in 1966.

Mr. Bike can be reached at:

ANB Communications
3632 N. Central Park Avenue
Chicago, IL 60618-4107
Phone (773) 866-0024
Fax (773) 866-0025